Bandaging
the Blitz

Bandaging the Blitz

1938-42

PHYLL MACDONALD-ROSS
with I. D. ROBERTS

sphere

SPHERE

First published in Great Britain in 2015 by Sphere

A CIP catalogue record for this book
is available from the British Library.

ISBN 978-0-7515-5991-0

Typeset in Granjon by M Rules
Printed and bound in Great Britain by
Clays Ltd, St Ives PLC

Papers used by Sphere are from well-managed forests
and other responsible sources.

MIX
Paper from
responsible sources
FSC® C104740

Sphere
An imprint of
Little, Brown Book Group
Carmelite House
50 Victoria Embankment
London EC4Y 0DZ

An Hachette UK Company
www.hachette.co.uk

www.littlebrown.co.uk

For my beloved husband, Alistair

For our family

Foreword

When my grandmother, Phyllis Macdonald-Ross, finally retired from nursing back in 1995, my grandfather badgered her to finish off the book she'd started in the late 1960s about her journey to become a nurse. She had no ambition to publish, nor any thoughts of doing so; it was just a body of work to pass on to the Queen's Nursing Institute, and perhaps for her family to enjoy in later years. Phyll would be the first to admit that she's no writer, but she spent the next decade or so doggedly typing out her experiences of those early days of nursing, of her drive to succeed, of her dreams of caring, of her passion to tend the sick and needy, because, as she says in her original introduction, 'The book may be the means of some young man or woman deciding upon nursing as their career.' Completed, she put it away in a drawer and subsequently forgot about it.

Then in 2010, a television production company got in touch and asked if she would talk about her war experiences for a documentary they were making for Channel 4 to mark the seventieth anniversary of the Blitz. Sitting down to watch the finished programme, *Blitz Street*, I was stunned not only to hear what Nan had to say, but at just what she had witnessed and lived through during those nine long months of the Blitz that began on 7 September 1940.

Typical of their generation, my grandparents had never really talked of their war, of what they did, what they saw, or indeed what everyday life was like for them. So I asked Nan more about it and, although she still didn't say much, she did surprise me by digging out her memoirs.

As I began to read through the roughly typed pages, I was more and more amazed. I had no idea. Was this young woman I was reading about, the one standing with her fellow trainee nurses listening to Prime Minister Chamberlain announcing that Britain was at war with Germany, or rushing about Casualty dealing with the horrific consequences of the first night the Germans dropped their bombs on London, really my grandmother? And was the young, handsome man who asked her to marry him before being sent off to war really my grandfather? They couldn't have been. They were just boring old Nan and Pop, who liked watching *Crossroads* and *Nationwide*, going to church a lot, reciting poetry, playing the piano, as well as all things Scotland. I couldn't believe the life they had led as early twentysomethings.

And the more I read, the more I came to realise just what a remarkable woman my nan is, and how her story is all the more remarkable for what she had to live through during the war of 1939–45. She, like the rest of the men and women of Britain, treated each day as another gift and just got on with things, enjoying life while she still had it. They called it the 'Blitz spirit'. Perhaps it has been lost now, but the memory of that spirit lives on in the words and deeds of those who survived and those who died.

I was enthralled, and genuinely moved too, by the things Nan had to endure during the four years of her training in the East

End of London. But more amazing than that were the details of my grandparents' blossoming relationship, of how they met, fell in love and married, all against a frightening background of continual air raids. I was totally captivated. And that was when I knew I had to get her story out to a wider audience.

Nan wasn't convinced. These events had occurred nearly seventy-five years previously, and, inevitably after such a long period, her memory for precise dates wasn't always accurate. However, her recall for names, places and key events is as vivid today as it was when she was swotting for her hospital final in 1941.

'Why would anyone want to know about me, dear?' she said, but in the end I convinced her that people would, and she trusted me to take her memoirs away to get them ready for press.

I hope no generation has to experience the fear of waking to air-raid sirens ever again, of hearing the dreaded whistling of the bombs as they fall closer and closer, of feeling the world explode around them, of seeing their homes and communities turned to rubble and dust, of finding their neighbours, friends, even families gone for ever. But we must never forget what happened and what people endured. And how people like my grandparents kept calm and carried on, learning a new profession, going to work, finding the will to play, to sing, to dance, to make love, to marry, to defy the tyrant Hitler and put two fingers up to death.

So now, in my grandmother's ninety-fifth year, a year that also happens to mark the seventy-fifth anniversary of the Blitz, I am delighted to present her story. I hope I have done it justice; I hope that I have done the memory of her friends and family and colleagues, as well as that of her beloved late husband Alistair, justice, too.

I. D. Roberts
Somerset, February 2015

For a book of this kind there must be a reason. And it is this: I feel there is need of a work that will enlighten those who are thinking of entering the nursing profession as a calling. It has many heartaches, quite a lot of kicks, but for those who feel they want to give something back in life, it has the uplift and the intense joy of something accomplished.

The book may be the means of some young man or woman deciding upon nursing as their career. Should this be so, I for one would feel the task of writing this more than justified.

If I were asked at this moment in time, would I choose the same career again, I would not hesitate in saying, 'Yes. A thousand times yes.' It is not a well-paid task, but the joy of doing a worthwhile job such as nursing produces an inward happiness that all the wealth in the world could not buy. If you enter in the right spirit you will not be disappointed; not only that, others will live and give thanks because of you having passed their way.

Phyll Macdonald-Ross
Cheltenham, February 2015

Prologue

London, April 1941

There is a familiar rat-tat-double-tat on my bedroom door, and I turn to see Mac's chirpy round face peering in.

'You off now, Phyll?' Her big brown eyes ran up and down my uniform as I clasped my cloak around my neck.

'I'm just going to pop down to Sydenham to see my parents,' I said, turning back to the mirror and pushing my hair into shape.

'Do they know you're coming?'

Mac was ever eager to accompany me, especially to visit my parents. There was always a possibility of some of Mother's home-made cake on offer.

'No,' I said, 'I just want to see them before we transfer to Claybury. We may not get the chance to travel through the city for some time, you know.'

'Oh, rot, Phyll,' Mac scoffed, closing the door and slumping her heavy frame down on my bed.

'Ever the optimist,' I chuckled, adjusting my cap.

We'd been told that as a respite from the relentless air raids a selection of the medical staff were being posted out of London to the peaceful countryside of Essex. And I can't tell you how the buzz of excitement was running up and down the corridors of Hackney Hospital. Yes, we all felt slightly guilty at the thought of abandoning our friends and neighbours in the little community around Homerton High Street, but so many of us were exhausted, some even to the point of hysteria, living day to day with the dreaded anticipation of the air-raid siren and then enduring the wait for that chilling whistle of falling bombs. And all of this while still having to go about our duties, dealing with an endless parade of the sick and injured.

'How do they like Sydenham?' Mac said. 'Bit of a change from the seagulls and sand of Dovercourt, I'll bet.'

'I'll say. Father misses the sea so much. And as for Mother ...' I trailed off.

Poor Mother. She'd suffered so much with her nerves of late. Dovercourt, sleepy little Dovercourt Bay on the Essex coast, had taken such a pounding, what with the Germans targeting nearby Harwich, that my mother was at her wits' end. Father managed to secure a transfer with his Customs job and they'd found digs with one of my aunts in the suburbs of London. But how Mother missed her home.

I checked the fob watch that was pinned to my breast. 'Gosh, Mac, I'd best run if I'm to catch my train.'

'Well,' Mac said, puffing her cheeks as she pulled herself up off the bed, 'Eddie and I are off to the pictures. There's a late show of *The Philadelphia Story*.'

'What, again?' I said, holding the door open and letting Mac out ahead of me. 'That's the fourth time this week.'

Mac turned at the threshold and gave me a wink. 'He's a dish, that Cary Grant,' she beamed. 'Besides,' she added, 'I haven't managed to see it past the second reel. There's always a bloody air raid.'

'Olive MacKenzie,' I hissed, looking to my left and right, 'language!'

'Oh, balls,' Mac grinned.

Evening was rapidly approaching as I turned out of the gate lodge and picked my way along the debris-strewn High Street, glancing back over my shoulder every few paces to see if a bus was coming. There was so much destruction all around now, nothing but broken bits of people's homes, some little more than half a wall with the frame of a window still intact. Bomb craters full of foul water sat where once buildings had stood, and the ground was littered with rubble and timber, parts of furniture, buckled prams, even children's toys. I just couldn't imagine how long it would take to clear up.

I could never get used to it, although I was finding it increasingly hard to picture how the street had looked two years earlier, when I had first arrived here. That was when the world was still at peace, with no idea that war was waiting like a lurking thief just around the corner. Were we to live like this for ever? I thought. Yet the hospital still stood proud, remarkably undamaged, like a beacon of hope to the East End.

It wasn't long before I spotted the familiar red of my bus, its headlights just two slits in their blackout cowls, weaving its way towards the temporary stop up ahead. I climbed to the top deck and sat down in my favourite seat, the bench at the very back, next to the stairwell.

My mind drifted, and I stared blankly out into the dusk. Twilight was already lengthening the shadows.

'London Bridge,' the conductor shouted, jolting me out of my daydream. I glanced at my watch. It was just six o'clock and I knew that there was a train to Forest Hill at seven minutes past.

I skipped down the stairs and off of the bus, and dashed towards the station entrance.

'Hold up, miss,' a policeman said, blocking my way. 'Where are you going?'

'I'm catching the train to Forest Hill.'

'Sorry, love,' he said. 'The line's been bombed.'

'Oh.'

'You'll have to catch a bus at the Elephant,' he added.

For a brief moment I stood there nonplussed. What elephant?

'Only two stops on the Underground,' the policeman smiled.

'Yes. Thank you. I'll do that.'

At the Elephant and Castle I joined a long queue of coughing and sneezing workers waiting for the no. 12 to Forest Hill Station. I was just thinking about how nice it would be to see my parents after such a long time, and on my birthday, too, when the atmosphere was cut by the sudden wail of the air-raid siren. I looked up to the skies. It was a clear night, and already the search-lights were criss-crossing in readiness for the bombers. But there was still no sight or sound of the enemy aeroplanes.

A car toot-tooted by and an ARP warden blew his whistle shrilly, stepping off the pavement, shouting after it.

'Oi! You bleedin' idiot. Get off the road!'

But the car sped on. I was standing watching as it shot up the street, when a hand touched my shoulder.

'Run along, miss,' the warden said to me, 'into the shelter.'

I turned and followed the rest of the people from the bus queue back towards the Underground station. The crowds, though hurrying, weren't panicking. This was such a regular occurrence these days that people had grown accustomed to – some, like that motorist, even blasé about – air raids.

People streamed into the entrance from all directions, some just in the clothes they stood in, others, more prepared for a long stay, clutching blankets and food parcels in their arms. The whine of the sirens continued as I shuffled into the station, through the ticket area and down the packed escalators to the platforms.

Already the passageway and platforms were crammed with people, as well as the tracks down the tunnels themselves. They were mostly civilians, but there were a few khaki uniforms dotted about and I even spotted a sailor worming his way through the throng, a bulky kitbag strung over his shoulder. It was stuffy down there and smelled like mouldy bread.

I picked my way along the platform, carefully stepping over outstretched limbs, catching the eye of a few people, giving them a soft smile in return. I realised that my uniform gave people a small amount of comfort, knowing there was at least one nurse amongst them in the shelter.

As I sat on the cold, hard floor, clutching my overnight bag to my breast, I wondered how long the raid would last and cursed myself for deciding to make this impromptu visit to my parents in the first place. But that was a silly thought: it was too late now. I sighed and leaned my head back against the tiled wall, preparing myself for a long wait.

Suddenly the faint drone of the sirens stopped, and an eerie silence fell over the platform. Now was the moment I hated the most, the dreaded pause of nothingness when everyone held their breath, praying, eyes scanning the ceiling, hoping it was just a false alarm. But it never was these days.

And then it starts. The muffled thumps of the ack-ack fire are followed by the rumble and the shake of the floor beneath you as the bombs hit home.

This time was no different, although it was the first time I'd been caught in an Underground station. The platform beneath me shuddered and I could hear the train tracks rattle. Dust fell in thick clouds from high above my head, followed by muffled thumps that just went on and on. I looked up to the ceiling. Would it hold? The lights flickered on and off and someone screamed from the opposite end of the platform. I shivered, pulled my cloak about me, covering my legs, and stared down at my shoes, already scuffed and dusty.

Although we Londoners – I counted myself as one of them now – were used to the daily onslaught of Hitler's Luftwaffe, it did not stop us from being afraid. Only the occasional cough, sneeze or child's wailing, or the haunting sob of an inconsolable woman, broke the deathly quiet.

My skin tightened and my stomach turned. But I knew I wasn't alone, and gradually our collective fear turned to something else, a kind of strength. We were in this together, and we would get through it together.

Then I noticed something wrong.

Above the sobs of the woman I could hear a different kind of moaning, a moan I knew only too well, a moan of pain. I pulled myself to my feet and began to pick my way down the platform. The moans were getting louder and a number of people were craning their necks to see where the noise was coming from.

'Is there a doctor?' one voice shouted from the gloom.

''Ere, what's goin' on? Is someone 'urt?' another said.

'Look, 'ere's a nurse,' a man said, getting to his feet to let me pass.

'God bless you, ducks,' an old woman said, looming out of the shadows, clutching a foul-smelling bundle of clothes to her chest. 'She's down the end 'ere,' and she grabbed hold of my sleeve. Her bony hand gripped me like a vice as she hurried me along.

At the very end of the platform, just before the dark tunnel began, an advert for Guinness stretching far above her head, a young woman, little more than a girl really, lay propped against the wall. Her face was dripping with sweat and her eyes were wide with fear. But when she focused on my square cap and realised who I was, what I was, a wave of relief seemed to wash over her. Then she winced, screwed her eyes shut, and gave another cry.

I crouched down and noted the pool of water around her feet, quickly realising that it wasn't fear or even an injury that troubled her. I pulled back the coat that the young woman had wrapped herself in and saw that she was heavily pregnant. Not only that, her waters had broken. This girl was about to give birth.

The old woman with the bundle of clothes was standing over my shoulder, and she gave a sharp intake of breath when she saw the state of the girl.

'Would you be so kind and see if you can find some water, alcohol, anything? And a peg,' I asked her.

'A peg?'

'For the cord.'

She nodded and scuttled off, asking each and every person she passed for the items I'd requested. I watched her make her way back along the platform and as my eyes took in all the faces staring back at me, I kept hoping for a doctor to appear coming back the other way, a medical bag clutched in his hand.

The girl cried out louder and gripped my hand. There was nothing for it: I was going to have to summon all the skills I'd learned over the past three years and deliver this baby myself. I gently prised her hand away and stood up.

I considered getting some of the men to help me carry her out, but I dismissed the notion. It was so cramped and crowded that it would be impossible to get her through the people without causing her considerable pain. Besides, where would I take her? The bombing raid was in full swing and the closer we went to the surface, the more risk we'd be at. No, this platform would have to do.

I removed my cloak, rolled up my sleeves and set about getting the girl into position. Right next to us was a family, a plump woman in her thirties with three grubby young children and an older man whom I took to be their grandfather. I asked them to turn their backs to give the young girl some privacy.

'Course, dearie. 'Ere, give us your cloak and we'll 'old it up like a screen. 'Ow's about that?' the woman said. 'Come on, Dad, you can 'elp.'

'That would be most kind,' I said, amazed at how calm my voice was.

'Can I 'elp, love?' A tall soldier, cigarette smouldering between his lips, emerged from the nearby shadows.

'You can put that out,' I said, waving a cloud of tobacco from the expectant mother's direction. 'But you can keep the crowds back, thanks.'

'Sorry. Will do,' he said, crushing out his cigarette and moving to stand next to the plump woman holding up my cloak.

''Ere, 'ere, mind the way!' I glanced up to see the old woman with the bundle push through. She had an extra blanket in her arms and a bottle of gin, bless her.

'One o' the ticket inspectors gave me this,' she said with a toothless grin, handing me the pint bottle of gin. ''E's boiling up a kettle, too, and'll be down as quick as 'e can. And 'ere, yer peg.'

'Thank you so much,' I smiled. 'Here, this is bigger.' I handed the blanket to the plump woman and her father.

They dropped my cloak and took up the blanket in its place.

I opened the bottle of gin and passed it back to the old woman. 'Would you be so kind?'

'Eh?' she said as I stepped to the platform edge. Then her face lit up in understanding, and she began to pour the gin over my hands.

I wrung my hands together in the pure liquid as it fell on to the tracks, hoping they'd be sterile enough.

'Coo, what a waste,' I heard the old man say.

'Dad!'

I smiled to myself and turned back to the girl. She was panting and shallow-breathing, doing her best to remain calm.

'Ready?' I said, with a reassuring smile.

The girl nodded nervously and tried to return the smile through her pain. As the ceiling above us rumbled and shook, I knelt down beside her and set to work.

At five o'clock in the morning, the all-clear finally sounded, and with it the wails of a newborn baby, his first cries echoing up and down the platform. There was a ripple of applause and everywhere I looked smiling faces shone back at me. The people who had been crowding the platforms began to drift back to the surface in the hope that they still had homes to go to. The plump woman with the three children handed me back the blanket with a gentle pat and a 'Well done, dearies' to me and the girl.

The tall soldier gave us both a wink and a salute and set off back to his barracks. Not only had he helped to give myself and the mother some privacy during the birth, but he had loaned me his bayonet when I had suddenly realised, after clamping the baby's umbilical cord with the peg, that I had nothing to cut it with.

The girl was weak but radiant as I handed her her son, wrapped in my cloak.

'What's yer name, miss?' she asked, pulling her eyes away from her child's face with difficulty.

'Phyllis,' I said, rolling down my sleeves. 'But my friends call me Phyll.'

'As in Philip?'

I nodded and smiled again, looking back down at her baby. He looked healthy enough.

'I likes it. 'Ello, Phil,' she said to the child.

'Where's your husband?' I asked.

'Over there somewhere,' she nodded.

I glanced behind me, and she chuckled.

'No, miss. I mean "over there", in France. 'E was at Dunkirk, but never came back.'

Her eyes took on a distant glaze, and I busied myself with washing up. The platform inspector had been true to his word, providing hot water, a towel, a bowl and a cake of Pears soap. I wasn't sure what to say to the new mother about her husband. So many women had been left wondering if they would ever see their menfolk again. And here was a newborn who might never even meet his father.

'Well done, ducks,' the old woman with the bundle said to me with a friendly pat on my cheek. 'I can't stay. Got to get 'ome and see if me Charlie's all right.'

'Charlie?'

'Blackbird, ducks,' she chuckled. 'Found 'im after the last raid. Poor mite. Busted wing and frightened to death, 'e was.' She leaned down over the young mother. 'You got a strong un there, ducks. Mind you looks after yerselves.'

I watched as she shuffled away down the platform, passing the ticket inspector on her way. He was carrying three steaming mugs of tea.

''Ere, love, bet you could use one o' these?' he said, handing me a scalding tin mug. He placed another down next to the girl, cooing briefly at the baby.

'Thank you,' I said.

He straightened up again. 'I sent for an ambulance,' he said. 'Shouldn't be long now.'

We stood looking down at the mother and her newborn son, and as I sipped at the strong, metallic-tasting tea, I thought how amazing it was that even in our darkest hours, new lives still come into this world. It was one of the most beautiful moments of my fledgling career.

PART ONE

1938

Daily Express
Friday, September 30, 1938

The Daily Express declares that Britain will
not be involved in a European war
this year, or next year either

PEACE!

AGREEMENT SIGNED
AT 12.30a.m. TODAY

Daily Express

WORLD'S LARGEST DAILY SALE

No. 11,970   Friday, September 30, 1938   One Penny

The Daily Express declares that Britain will not be involved in a European war this year, or next year either

| Ultimatum withdrawn at Munich |

PEACE!

| Cession less than Hitler plan |

AGREEMENT SIGNED AT 12.30 a.m. TODAY

German troops may go in tomorrow: Then occupation gradually: No plebiscites

DUCE DRAWS FRONTIER

IT IS PEACE

AT 12.30 A.M. TODAY HITLER, MUSSOLINI, CHAMBERLAIN AND DALADIER SIGNED AT MUNICH A FOUR POWER AGREEMENT WHICH SOLVES THE CZECHO-SLOVAK PROBLEM.

When Mr. Chamberlain returned to his hotel at 1.35 a.m., after a series of conferences which started before noon yesterday and continued almost without interruption, he said: "Everything is fixed up now." He is returning to London to-day.

Tomorrow morning, October 1, the date named in Hitler's famous memorandum, German troops will cross the Czech frontier. But instead of steel helmets they will wear forage caps, and they will march in quietly to begin a progressive occupation of Sudetenland.

An international commission will define the new frontier; an international force, including British, French and Italian troops, will police the areas to be surrendered to Germany.

By October 31 the new frontier should be finally fixed and all cause for friction removed.

SUBMITTED TO PRAGUE

That is the plan; the only doubt was that the Czecho-Slovak Government might not be able to accept the plan in time. In this case London diplomats hope that he would be willing to extend the time limit until Sunday.

Writing at 2 a.m., the Daily Express Political Correspondent says:—

"Proposals have been submitted to the Czecho-Slovak Government on these lines:—

"Cession of the most densely populated Sudeten German areas within ten days;

"Substitution of negotiation for plebiscite as a preliminary to cession of other areas. Parties to the negotiations to be France, Italy, Germany and Czecho-Slovakia. Time limit will be set for the conclusion of the negotiations.

"Germany will guarantee integrity of new Czecho-Slovak state.

AREA NOT SO LARGE

Meanwhile there is no question of Germany ordering a general mobilisation, as threatened earlier in the week.

Mussolini is described as being particularly elated as he ordered his special train to return to Rome at midnight. A German spokesman said that a revised line of demarcation between

Germans and Czechs in Hitler's map of Czecho-Slovakia was drawn by Mussolini himself.

The area to be surrendered is not quite so large as was demanded by Hitler at Godesberg.

Nazi Storm Troopers formed a cordon in the lobby of Mr. Chamberlain's Munich hotel last night. There were shouts of "Heil Chamberlain" and "Hoch Chamberlain" from the Germans when the Premier returned from the conference for dinner.

Field-Marshal Goering, in the uniform of his rank, raised a big laugh in the lobby when he strolled over to the French Premier and slapped him on the back, saying:—

"Well, Herr Daladier, you had better stay here for the October Festival."

The "Oktoberfest" is Germany's great annual beer festival, which began four days ago and is still in progress.

This is the Peace Plan

By GUY EDEN.

THIS, I understand, was the peace plan taken to Munich for discussion between Mr. Neville Chamberlain, Herr Hitler, Signor Mussolini, and M. Daladier, the French Premier:—

1. Handing over to Germany after tomorrow of "token" areas of the Sudetenland;

2. Appointment of an international commission to draw the new border-line between Germany and Czecho-Slovakia, and to see that the transfer of populations—Czechs to Czech territory and Germans to German—is carried out fairly and quickly;

3. Demobilisation of the "abnormal" civil armies on each side of the frontier, and the appointment of an international force of British, French, Italian, Belgian and Dutch troops to take over control of the areas scheduled to be ceded to Germany;

4. On stated dates, the Germans to occupy the areas under the control of the international force, the Czech troops having previously withdrawn from the areas.

One series of districts, it is suggested, should be given up on October 15, the second on October 21;

5. Partial settlement, on October 31, of the new frontier.

THE PRIME MINISTER MEETS MUSSOLINI AT MUNICH
Picture wired last night; see also Back Page.

Weather: cooler
(see page 11)

HE MAY BE SIR NEVILLE

Daily Express Staff Reporter

MR. NEVILLE CHAMBERLAIN is likely to be the most amazing man in the British Empire.

Mr. Chamberlain's half-brother, Sir Austen Chamberlain, was at work in bringing about the Locarno Treaty.

Mr. Chamberlain may share with his "Dic." Although Mr. Chamberlain would probably prefer to remain plain Mr. Chamberlain, as his predecessor wished to do, it has been ruled that the honour should go to him.

The Order of Merit would not be conferred on a Prime Minister while in office, and was the last bestowed Premier.

Premier's wife mobbed

CROWDS of women, rejoicing at the news of peace, besieged the gates the beil of Mrs. Chamberlain this morning when she arrived at the bell St. Michael's Church, Chester-square, W., where the Archbishop of Canterbury had addressed a beautiful prayer.

The big crowd that waited outside the church would not give several messages by the Mrs. Chamberlain.

So she stepped into her car again surged round, cheering enthusiastically.

Mrs. Chamberlain, almost overcome by emotion, repeated: "Thank you, oh, thank you." As she drove away she smiled and waved her hand.

Very many people have attended Thanksgiving services at the churches as their brought the best results of the exciting papers announcing the peace.

People went to the Opera and Private Theatre when the announcement was made, and the green announced.

At a Croydon theatre three thousand people cheering heard the first minutes when the manager came to announce the success of the conference.

MAP (showing areas involved) PAGE 8

(to PAGE TWO, COL. ONE)

I

I do not know where the compulsion to become a nurse came from. Perhaps it was those childhood history lessons about Florence Nightingale that I loved so dearly, but ever since I can remember I have indulged a passion for caring.

It started when I was very young, sat alone in my room practising nursing on my dolly and my toy bear. That was always a favourite game of mine and one which later developed into practising on my friends, for I had no brothers or sisters to try out my skills with. I used to usher my friends into the pantry, where I would bandage their arms and legs, or force a saucepan on to their heads and then bandage that as well. This all came to an abrupt end when my mother burst in one day and scolded me for using her best napkins as bandages.

However, the desire remained, and encouragement came from my father. He was chopping wood one autumn day in the back yard and got an enormous splinter. I recall him cursing, using words I didn't know or understand, as he tried to pull the thin needle of wood out while my mother fussed about him. And then he stopped, looked at me, and sat down there on the tree stump he used as a chopping-block.

'No, Violet,' he said to my mother, 'let Phyll do it.'

My chest swelled with pride as I ran inside to fetch what we quaintly called the first-aid box, little more than a rusty biscuit tin containing some bandages, plasters, iodine, scissors and a pair of tweezers. I knelt down in front of my father and delicately teased the bloodstained splinter out of his hand with the tweezers. I cleaned the wound, for the splinter had pierced the flesh between his thumb and forefinger, and wrapped a bandage, a proper one this time, around his hand.

'As good as new,' Father said with a warm smile and a wink as he flexed his hand.

After that, if Father ever cut or grazed himself, he would come to me. Even Mother let me see to her occasional nicks from a careless slice with a kitchen knife now and again.

Then, during the summer of 1938, I was walking down the street, alone with my thoughts, trying to decide what to do with my life now that school had come to an end, when a neighbour took a tumble and fell hard against her garden wall.

At that time my parents and I had only been living in our newly constructed semi-detached house for little more than six months. It was in Portland Avenue, a wide tree-lined road not far from the terraces of Fernlea Road where I had grown up. The people of Portland Avenue were relatively new to us but they were friendly and, Dovercourt being a small seaside community, one knew most people by sight at least.

Mrs Clarkson was one of these new neighbours, a cheery soul, a widow in her late fifties, who always had a smile on her face and a warm hello on her lips. And the morning she fell was to change the direction of my life for ever.

I rushed over to her side and helped her to her feet.

'Are you all right, Mrs Clarkson? Do you feel faint?'

She shook her head. 'No, dear. Look.' She thrust her double chin at the low step that led from her garden path down to the pavement. One of the bricks was loose. 'Nothing sinister,' she added. 'Just rather a shock . . . Phyllis? It is Phyllis, isn't it?'

'That's right,' I smiled, keeping hold of her arm. 'Phyllis Elsworth. I live at the other end of the Avenue.'

'Of course you do, dearie,' she smiled. 'Alfred and Violet's daughter. Oh, my, look at me.' She held up her arm; her elbow was cut and bleeding.

'It doesn't look too deep, Mrs Clarkson,' I said. 'Do you have some ointment in the house? I'll clean it up for you.'

Although Mrs Clarkson wasn't badly hurt, she was a little shaken, so I put my arm in hers and helped her back up the garden path and into her house.

She led me through to her kitchen and I sat her down at the table and set about cleaning up her cut.

'It'll be a little sore for a while. But go and see the doctor if it stiffens up,' I said as I washed my hands in the Belfast sink.

'You're a natural, dearie,' Mrs Clarkson said, as she bent and straightened her arm. 'I don't think the doctor could have done a better job.'

I felt myself blushing at her compliment.

'How old are you now?' she asked as she moved over to the stove and set a kettle to boil. 'You will stay for a cup of tea, won't you?'

'Thank you, yes,' I said. 'And I'm eighteen now.'

Mrs Clarkson opened up a cupboard and I quickly stepped over to help, taking down two cups and two saucers.

'Now, tell me dear,' Mrs Clarkson said, as she placed a slice of lemon in her cup, 'have you thought about what you're going to do now that your schooling is over?'

I felt myself blushing again. How silly, I thought, to be embarrassed about such a simple question. But I was embarrassed, because I just didn't know what I was to do. Mrs Clarkson, bless her, could obviously see that I was rather flummoxed.

'What about nursing?' she said.

My heart leapt at the thought, but I knew it was an impossible dream.

'I'd love to,' I said, 'but I don't think my parents could afford it.'

Mrs Clarkson leaned back in her chair again. 'Have you asked them?'

I shook my head. 'No, Mrs Clarkson. I can't. It's not fair to.'

'Well, my dear, I think you would be quite surprised if you did,' she said. 'Ask them.'

Over the next few days, I thought long and hard about what Mrs Clarkson had said. I spent hours walking alone along Marine Parade, overlooking the lower promenade and the beach with its wooden groynes pointing out to sea like the fingers of a skeletal hand. Summer was in full swing and the sand was crowded with holidaymakers, the air electric with the laughter of children splashing in the water and the cries of seagulls gliding overhead, as enticed as I was by the smell of freshly fried scampi and chips billowing up from the little café down by the shore. I would always resist, but on occasion I would treat myself to an ice-cream.

Then one evening, while we were sat around the dinner table with the evening sun streaming in through the open window and the wireless humming a gentle melody in the background, I suddenly blurted it out:

'I want to be a nurse.'

A deathly silence fell over the table and all I could hear above my pulse pounding in my ears was the ominous scrape of cutlery on plates. I caught a glance between my parents and repeated what I said, but calmer this time.

'Mother, Father, I've made a decision about my future. I would like to be a nurse. But I'll need your blessing,' I paused. 'And I'll need your help.'

Mother put down her knife and fork and gave me one of her hard stares over the top of her long, straight nose.

'I was hoping, Phyllis,' she said, 'that you might consider taking up a teaching post. Or perhaps a secretarial position. Your father says that the customs office is al—'

'I don't want to stay in Dovercourt for the rest of my life!' I burst out, a touch petulantly.

'Don't be selfish, young lady,' Mother said, her eyes black with anger.

'I'm not being selfish, Mother. You are. It's my life. And this is what I want to do with it. Nursing.' I felt my face go hot. I had never spoken to my mother so harshly before, but the passion and the desire to choose my own future were pouring out of me now.

'Do you know how much it will cost to put you through training? Do you?' Mother said, the colour rising in her cheeks. 'Your father can ask the office man—'

'Mother,' I interrupted again, 'I don't want to work in an office, and I don't want to teach. I want to nurse. It's what I'm good at. I love caring and nursing and I think it would be the perfect vocation for me. One that would make you both proud.'

Mother blinked back at me in silence and turned to Father. She raised one of her severe eyebrows.

Father gave a soft smile in return. That was the way he calmed things, and it always worked. He was devilishly handsome and Mother adored him. He turned in his seat and fixed me with his pale-grey eyes.

'Is that what you truly want to do, Phyll?' he said.

He always called me Phyll, something Mother detested, but he knew how much I hated my own name. Father was always on my side and I felt a flutter of hope.

I nodded eagerly. 'Yes, Father,' I said. 'I have truly thought long and hard over my decision these past few wee—'

'Ha!' Mother exclaimed, but she remained tight-lipped when Father shot her a pleading glance to let me finish.

'I have always loved nursing, you both know that. You both know how much I adore helping others. You both—'

Father held up his hand to stop my tirade. I glanced at Mother. Even though she could be strict and set in her ways, she had a heart of gold and wouldn't wish me unhappy. Of course she would rather I stayed local, perhaps married one of Father's younger colleagues, even a dockhand, but not if I was to spend my days moping about. She wanted the best for me, both my parents did, and I knew they would do anything to help me fulfil my dream if they could.

'We've already discussed it, Phyll,' Father said, taking out his tobacco and papers and the little machine he used to roll himself cigarettes.

'Alfred,' my Mother exclaimed. 'How many times? Not at the dinner table.'

'Sorry, dear,' Father said with a sly wink at me. 'I was only making it inside. I wasn't planning on smoking it here.'

'I should think not,' Mother fumed. 'My lovely new curtains. I'd never get the smell of smoke out.'

'Seriously, Phyll,' Father said as he began the laborious process of constructing himself a cigarette, 'if you truly want to be a nurse then your mother and I are agreed to put you through training.'

How foolish did I feel about my little outburst? They had already decided to help me. But then I realised that perhaps they wanted me to react in such a way, to see how passionate I felt about the idea.

'Oh, Father,' I said, jumping from my seat and throwing my arms around his neck. I kissed his cheek and turned to embrace Mother. But she had already set about clearing the table.

However, I couldn't not thank her equally and I hugged her all the same.

'Thank you, Mother, thank you.'

'That's quite all right, Phyllis,' she said, standing still with her hands full of dirty dishes as I clung to her, 'but we've got the letter of application to get right first, and then, if you are the kind of girl they are looking for, the interview.'

I let go and looked her in the eye as she turned to face me. 'Yes, Mother, I realise.'

'There's a lot of hard work before we've even started,' she said.

'Yes, Mother,' I said. 'I won't let you down.'

'Of course you won't,' Father said, scraping back his chair as he got to his feet.

'Alfred!' Mother snapped.

'Come along, Phyll, keep me company while I smoke this.'

I glanced at Mother, who gave a nod to excuse me from helping with the dishes. I followed Father out into the garden.

'And mind you don't throw your stub on the rose bed again,' Mother called after us.

'I never throw my stubs away,' Father whispered to me. 'An old habit from the Middle East during the war. Waste not, want not.' He tapped his nose. 'You'd be amazed how few stubs it takes to make up an extra cigarette.'

He sat down on the back step and nodded for me to join him. Then he struck a match against the outside wall of the kitchen and began to smoke away in silent contemplation.

It was a warm evening. The sun had set and there was a sprinkling of stars dusted across the inky black sky. The moths were out, whirring and dancing in the artificial light streaming out from the kitchen window. Behind us, through the back door, we could hear Mother working away at the dishes, singing softly to herself. Father had a slight smile on his face as he listened. I suddenly felt like I was intruding and turned to go and help Mother. But he put a hand out to stop me.

'Just relax, Phyll. Your mother is fine.'

'Are you sure, Father? It's a big commitment.'

'What?' he said, turning his gaze upon me with a slight raise of his eyebrow. 'Doing the washing-up alone?'

'No, silly,' I said, slapping his arm playfully. 'Financially, I mean. Putting me through nursing.'

Father grinned back at me through a cloud of tobacco. 'Not half as much of a commitment as you'll have to make.'

'I know, Father.'

'Of course you do, Phyll. I trust you. I understand you.'

'And what about Mother? Really?' I said, lowering my voice as I glanced over my shoulder to check she couldn't overhear us. 'I know she's not happy about my choice of career, not really.'

'She'll come round,' was all Father said before he fell into silence again.

We sat there on the back step for a while, just staring out into the night.

'That Mrs Clarkson sang your praises for helping her, Phyll.'

'Oh, you met her, did you?'

'Of course. She couldn't stop telling me and your mother how kind you were and what a wonderful nurse you'd make.'

'She was very kind,' I said feeling my face go hot with embarrassment.

'She's also very forward,' Father chuckled.

'Whatever do you mean?'

'Well,' Father shrugged, 'didn't take long for her to get around to asking me to fix her garden step.'

I sniggered.

'Don't you laugh. I was due to play darts at the King's Arms. Missed my spot by the time I got away.'

'Oh, Father, you're kinder than I'll ever be.'

'Nonsense. Still, it got your mother and me talking. About this nursing lark. And that can only be a good thing, right?'

'Right,' I said, putting my arm through his and resting my head on his shoulder.

Father gave a sigh and pulled my arm away, taking my hand in his.

'Look, Phyll, we both love you very much. And you must trust me when I say that it will all be all right. We want the best for you, me and your mother, always have, always will. But we want you to make something of your life too. And if a nurse is what you want to be, then a nurse you shall be. Yes?'

I had tears of happiness in my eyes, but I kept my composure and nodded my head vigorously.

'Good. That's settled then. First thing tomorrow you're to go down and see Dr Blake and discuss what you have to do to go about getting an interview. Now, be a love and put the kettle on.'

I gave Father a peck on the cheek, jumped up and went back inside to make tea for everyone, unable to wipe the beaming smile from my face.

The next few weeks were a whirlwind of meetings, discussions and endless forms. Mother was with me every step of the way, as Father was busy at the Customs House down at the docks. Dr Blake and his nurse were both very kind to give up their time to advise me, but I hardly recall a word of what they said, I was so excited. The letter of application took me nearly two days to write, I was so worried about saying the wrong thing. And then

I had to wait. I was so nervous that I thought I was going to be sick every time I tried to eat anything.

In the end I popped along the Avenue to see Mrs Clarkson. Bless her, she was such a brick about it, plying me with tea and cake and moral support, that I soon forgot my nerves.

After taking my usual solitary stroll along Marine Parade, breathing in the salty sea air and gazing dreamily at the holidaymakers frolicking on the beach, I returned home to find a letter propped up on the mantelpiece. I was being called for an interview in eight days' time, at the East Suffolk and Ipswich Hospital. Mother would accompany me and together we would look around the nurses' home, near to the main hospital buildings, where I hoped I would be staying in the near future.

I wore my smart grey suit dress in checked wool, with a matching felt slouch hat and a light tweed coat. My hair was freshly curled and cut just below the ear, pinned close to my head, and I felt grown-up and sophisticated. Mother was wearing her favourite afternoon dress and her ever-reliable brown cloche hat with its deep crown and no brim.

I sat in silence during the journey, nervously tapping my toe as my mind went over and over the kind of questions I might be asked. It was only a short walk from the station to the hospital, and my legs felt like jelly as we approached the formidable ivy-covered, three-storey building.

The interview, held in a large echoing room rather like a school assembly hall, was daunting. I sat on a hard wooden chair facing a table behind which were three people, a senior consultant with matinée-idol looks and slicked-back silver hair, a junior doctor with thick-lensed spectacles, and a sour-faced, bosomy matron. But my confidence was high and I breezed through their questions.

'How did it go, Phyllis dear?' Mother asked me as I stepped out of the interview room with a slightly giddy feeling.

'I ... I don't know, Mother,' I said rather distractedly as we made our way out into the blazing sunshine of the late-summer afternoon. 'I answered all they asked.'

Mother patted my arm. 'Well, that's all you can do. Did they say when they would let you know?'

I nodded my head. I remembered that bit. 'Within two weeks. They have a lot of girls to see.' Suddenly I didn't feel so confident.

True to the interview panel's word, ten days later a letter postmarked IPSWICH tumbled through the door. I waited remarkably patiently for Father to come home from work that evening, and then all three of us gathered round in the parlour as I held the letter of acceptance or rejection in my trembling hand.

'Go on, Phyll, open it,' Father said with a reassuring smile.

Even Mother was on tenterhooks.

I was all fingers and thumbs as I tried to pick the seal open, so I just tore off the end of the envelope and pulled out a worryingly thin single sheet of paper.

In just a few lines of black type my future was decided. I glanced up at my parents with tears of joy in my eyes: I'd been accepted as a trainee nurse and was to begin my studies in November.

I glanced back down at the letter and my face fell. Not through disappointment, just surprise.

'Whatever is it, Phyll?' Father said, taking the letter. He read it with Mother looking over his shoulder.

A footnote explained that I wasn't going to be training in Ipswich; I was being sent to Hackney Hospital. For the next four years of my life I was going to be living and studying in London.

2

Summer ends and the holidaymakers leave Dovercourt. The evenings grow darker, a cold wind blows in off the North Sea and the leaves begin to fall from the trees. November comes round quickly, and on the eve of my departure, Mother sits with me in my room, helping me to mark my clothes. Barely a word passes between us as I pack for the day when I shall be leaving home for the first time.

When Father eventually returned from work, I had already helped Mother prepare the evening meal: my choice, bangers and mash with onion gravy, followed by spotted dick and custard. We ate in relative silence, just a music programme for company on the wireless. I helped to clear away the dishes, then Father handed me my coat.

'Come on, Phyll, let's go for a walk.'

'Don't be too late,' Mother said. 'Phyllis and I have an early start tomorrow.'

'Are you sure you won't join us?' Father asked.

'No. Phyllis and I will have plenty of time together on the long journey.'

'All right,' he said, helping me on with my coat, 'if you're sure.'

He grabbed his hat and overcoat and passed me his tobacco pouch and papers. 'Roll one for me, Phyll.'

He opened the front door and we stepped out into the cold night air. It already smelled of bonfires, and the smoke of burning wood and coal puffing away from so many chimneys.

'Marine Parade?' I asked.

'Not tonight, Phyll. I thought I'd buy you a drink at the King's Arms.' He gave me a sheepish grin.

'What about Mother?' I said, knowing that she wouldn't approve of me drinking. It wasn't Christmas and it certainly wasn't my birthday.

Father pulled me down the garden path and out of the front gate. We turned away from the wind whipping up the Avenue from the seafront, and walked briskly towards Main Road, him with one hand holding his hat securely on his head and the other thrust through my arm as I made a pig's ear of rolling him a cigarette.

'I invited her,' he said, 'and she turned me down.'

'Father!' I exclaimed, though I could barely keep the amusement from my voice. I passed him the cigarette and he paused and cupped his hand to protect his match from the wind. He took a few puffs and straightened up again. We carried on walking through the High Street.

'I want to celebrate my daughter's success. And I can't think of a better way than at the King's, can you? Here.' He passed me the cigarette.

I hesitated, but he just nodded, and I put the cigarette to my lips.

'You're grown-up now, Phyll. Eighteen years old. Besides, I know you smoke.'

'Only on occasion,' I protested.

Father grinned back at me. 'On occasion. And this is an

occasion, is it not?' He jerked his head in the direction of the pub, standing invitingly on the corner, its red paintwork and lights shining out like a Christmas bauble. 'They've got a piano,' he added.

'I haven't played for a while, Father.'

'Come on,' he said, 'play some tunes for your old man.'

'I don't think Mother would be best pleased if she knew I was playing the piano in a public house.'

'Well, I won't tell her if you don't.'

I had to laugh at that, and I linked my arm in his and let him take me into the saloon bar. A fug of beer, tobacco and the scent of men hit me squarely in the face as we pushed our way through the revellers towards the bar. The landlord, a tall, thick-set man with a bulbous nose, sparkling eyes and mutton-chop whiskers, was standing there polishing a pint glass with a white rag. He looked up as we approached, slinging the rag over his shoulder.

'Evening, Alf,' the landlord said. 'Who's this pretty little thing on your arm then? Your Violet know you're out with another girl?'

'Hello, Bob,' Father said. 'This is Phyll, my lovely daughter. She's off to the Smoke to become a nurse and I'm buying her a farewell drink.'

'Well, then,' the landlord said, shaking me by the hand, 'what will be your pleasure, miss?'

I didn't hesitate. 'A pink gin, please.'

I awoke the next morning with the sun streaming in through a gap in the curtains on to my face, and with the sound of last night's piano-playing ringing in my ears. I stretched and smiled, and suddenly remembered. Today was the day, 3 November, the day I was to leave the protection of my parents and go and live alone in the capital. Gosh, I thought, was this what I really wanted? What had I gone and done?

A sudden hard rap on my door gave me a start.

'Phyllis?'

I sighed. *Actually, I don't think I will miss this*, I decided.

I lifted myself up, threw the blankets aside and swung my legs out of bed. I shivered at the biting cold. I could actually see my breath clouding in front of my face. I swung my legs back into bed and pulled the covers tightly round me again, up to my neck. 'Come in,' I squeaked.

'I've brought you a cup of tea,' Mother said as she opened the door. She paused and tutted, glaring down at me. 'You really should be up and dressed by now, Phyllis.'

She marched in, deposited the cup of tea on my bedside table and wrenched the curtains wide. A pale autumnal sunlight filled the room.

'You're going to have to improve on this habit of yours, young lady,' she said, standing over me, hands on her hips, 'of struggling to get up in the mornings. Especially in the winter. What will you do if you're on duty at six a.m.?'

'Use my alarm clock?'

'Don't you be cheeky with me.'

'Sorry, Mother,' I said rather sheepishly, and reached out from under my blankets for the steaming cup of tea.

'All I'm saying is that it's not a good start for a prospective nurse,' Mother added.

I put my lips tentatively to the rim of the hot teacup and sipped. Mother was right. I would have to change, and change fast, I knew that. I found it so hard to get up in the mornings, especially when it was still dark outside. Winters were just so bothersome.

Mother reached out and took my cup and saucer from me.

'You run along to the bathroom. Father and I will wait and have breakfast with you. You can have the rest of this tea downstairs.' And with that she left, leaving the door wide open.

I shivered at the draught coming up the stairs. I was sorely tempted to throw the covers over my head and bury myself in my bed – I didn't relish the dash across the landing to the freezing bathroom – but I resisted the temptation. This was a new start.

Fifteen minutes later, wearing a slim, checked everyday dress with puffed sleeves and lace collar with a duck-egg woollen cardigan, I sat down between Mother and Father at the breakfast table to boiled eggs, toast and more tea. Mother had made an effort for her trip and looked nice in her blue day frock with a four-piece skirt and wrist-length sleeves. We ate in silence, each lost in their own thoughts, each dreading this final meal together (for quite a while at least) coming to an end. When I had finished my last mouthful of egg, Father reached under his chair and came back up holding a small brown packet.

'A little going-away present,' he said with a smile, though I could see the sadness in his eyes. Oh, how I was going to miss him.

I tore open the wrapper to find a book inside. It was called *Etiquette in Society, in Business, in Politics and at Home* by Emily Post, and offered thousands of tips on correspondence, wedding-planning, party-giving and conduct in every public or private setting. I couldn't help but laugh. Just where did Father think I was going? But I threw my arms around him.

'Thank you, Father.'

'Come along, Phyllis,' Mother said, 'we don't want to miss our train.'

My luggage had been sent on a week beforehand, so I only had a weekend case to carry. Father slapped on his hat, pulled on his navy-blue double-breasted woollen coat, and took charge of my suitcase, as all three of us stepped out of the house into a crisp, frosty morning. Mother had on her cloche hat, and was wrapped up in her rather frumpy deep-red Harris tweed coat, while I, always conscious of making an impression, especially as I was travelling to London, wore my lightweight black wool coat, cream-stitched leather gloves and a wide-brimmed hat at a jaunty angle. A few familiar faces were out and about already and there were plenty of shouts of 'Good luck, Phyll!' and 'Enjoy the Big Smoke,' as well as a surprising amount of 'Send my love to Chamberlain.'

'This town needs a new joke writer,' Mother quipped as we turned on to the High Street.

We crossed over into Kingsway, and as we reached the end of the street, with a biting wind off the River Stour whipping at my coat, I spotted two more familiar faces standing at the entrance to the station. My heart sank. It was two of my aunts, Lily and Rose, and although they meant well, their words of advice always seemed to be tinged with doom and gloom.

'Bloody hell,' Father muttered, 'what do those two clowns want?'

'Alfred!' Mother snapped. 'How many times do I have to say it? Don't talk about my sisters in that way.'

'Phyllis! Phyllis!' said Aunt Lil. She was the youngest of my mother's six sisters, but she was also the most gossipy and the most fussy. 'Are you sure you want to go through with this?' she said, pulling her black coat about her. 'It's not too late to change your mind.'

I caught Father's face as he rolled his eyes. I stifled a snigger and gave both my aunts a peck on the cheek. 'No, Lil,' I said, 'I'm sure.'

'You'll be miles away from home,' Aunt Rose added with a shake of her head, a crocodile tear in her eye. She was a woman of large frame, shall we say, and her round cheeks were a good advertisement of her name. 'You're sure you won't feel homesick, Phyll love?'

'Now, you two,' Mother snapped. Lil and Rose stopped their clucking and just blinked back at me in silence, their heads shaking and their eyes full of tears.

I wasn't going to let these two caring but overbearing women spoil my last few moments with Father. He was not going to be coming to London with me as he had to work. I loved Mother dearly, but, oh, how I wished it were he who would be accompanying me on the train.

Father pulled me aside, touched his palm to my cheek softly, pressed a ten-shilling note into my hand, and hugged me tight.

'You take good care of yourself in London, Phyll,' he whispered in my ear. 'Don't do anything I wouldn't do.' He pulled away and it almost broke my heart looking at his handsome, lined face. He looked so sad.

'You'll be late for work, Alfred,' Mother said.

'For the train,' Father said, handing her his newspaper.

'Thank you, dear,' Mother said, offering her cheek to Father. 'Come along, Phyllis, the train's coming in and we'd better get along the platform.'

I gave both my aunts a hug and followed Mother. There was a toot and a whistle as the 8.55 to London approached in a cloud of steam and choking smoke. It had only come one stop from Harwich Town, but already it was busy.

Mother and I walked along the platform, looking for our carriage. I glanced to my left and spotted Father and Aunts Lil and Rose still waiting on the other side of the fence. 'She won't last six months, Alf,' I heard Lil say above the sound of the engine.

'Yes, don't you worry, Alf dear,' Rose chipped in. 'Phyll'll be back sooner than you think, mark my words.'

I missed what Father said in response as it was drowned out by the stationmaster's sharp blast on his whistle, but those two comments grated.

I'll show you, I thought as I climbed up into the Third-Class carriage and slammed the door shut behind me. I helped Mother lift my case up to the rope luggage net above our heads and then sat down heavily beside the window. As the smoke from the engine cleared, I caught sight of Father's face, still standing there, peering over the fence, his hand held up in a farewell gesture, the Victoria Hotel looming behind his shoulder. The train shunted forward and then began to pull away. I kept him in sight until he faded into the distance, then wiped a tear from my eye, sniffed and turned to see Mother staring back at me from the seat opposite. She had a warm smile on her lips.

'You just ignore your aunties, Phyllis,' she said. 'I can't say I'm happy about you leaving home so young, but, like your father, I fully support you.' She paused, as if unsure whether to say what was on her mind, then leaned forward slightly and rested her hand on my knee. 'And I for one think you will make a marvellous nurse.'

'Thank you, Mother,' I choked, genuinely touched by such rare praise.

'Now,' she said, leaning back in her seat, 'pull yourself together, dear; we've a long journey ahead and you must look your best.' And just as quickly as the softness had entered her face, it hardened again. She opened Father's *Daily Mirror* and began to read.

Mother was a hard woman at times, but I knew she loved me and I now knew for certain that she supported me. I was glad she was here. I sat for a while in silence, listening to the clickety-clack of the train's wheels bumping along the joints in the tracks, the movement gently swaying me calm again. I watched the flat, floodplain scenery of the estuary pass by as we headed towards Manningtree, pondering just what lay in store for me at the end of the line. What would London be like? What would the hospital be like? And, more importantly, what would my fellow trainee nurses be like? Would I make friends?

'The buffet car is now open.' The steward, smart in his white jacket, passed through the train making his announcement.

'Can we, Mother?' I said, thinking perhaps a coffee and a sticky bun would lift my spirits.

'Very well, dear,' she said. 'I think we deserve a little treat.'

By the time we returned to our seats, the view outside the window was starkly different. The outskirts of London had suddenly sprung up around us and I was taken aback by how dirty everything appeared. Grime and black soot caked everything: walls, windows; even the odd string of washing hung out to take advantage of the late-autumn sun looked more grey than white. There were factories and warehouses and countless chimney stacks all coughing a seemingly endless fug of smoke up into the watery blue sky. How could people live in such an atmosphere? I thought. I had taken for granted the bracing sea air and the ocean waves that I had grown up around, and the reality of the Big Smoke was a shock.

I had only a vague recollection of the last time I had been to London. Father had taken me to see the Changing of the Guard, but the memory had long since faded. How old had I been, seven, eight? I couldn't quite recall, but now I was eighteen, and all ready to embark on a new and exciting life.

'Final stop. Liverpool Street. All change. All change.'

3

Mother and I step down from the train to an orchestra of sounds and sights. My ears ring with doors opening and slamming shut, with footsteps clumping and click-clacking by as passengers hurry along, with whistles and shouts and jets of steam. We are swept along the crowded platform towards the barriers, where we flash our tickets to the guards, and finally emerge into the chaos of the concourse.

I had never seen anything like it! Even the beach at Dovercourt in the height of summer couldn't compare to this. It was a delirious bedlam of colours, sounds, smells, accents and creeds. Gentlemen in pinstripe suits and bowler hats, umbrellas in hand; ladies in smart overcoats with soft fur collars, matching hats and bright red lipstick; servicemen smart in their uniforms, with bulky kitbags slung over their shoulders; station porters, their brass buttons dazzling like jewels, pushing barrows laden with trunks and boxes; newspaper vendors screaming out the headlines. There were two Chinese men talking in a staccato fashion, while nearby an African man and an Indian in a turban stood studying the timetable pinned to the wall. Everywhere I looked there was a multitude of nationalities. My head was in a spin, but I was enthralled. I felt like Alice must have done when she first fell down the rabbit hole. And the smells! The air was tinged with smoke, of both tobacco and coal, and there was something else, too, underneath . . . Roasted chestnuts! Yes, I could hear the cry:

'Two penny a bag! Get yer chestnuts!'

Kicking through a group of pigeons picking at the floor, my gaze followed their startled flight upwards. High above us was a vast cathedral-like roof of glass and iron like those I'd seen on a botanical garden greenhouse. Other pigeons were nestling way up in the rafters. Then my eye fell on the huge station clock. It was a little after eleven and I wasn't due to report to the hospital until two.

Finally we emerged into the city itself; though the streets were crowded, the noise wasn't so contained. The sunny morning had now turned into a typical November day, dark, damp and dreary. There was a sheen of cold moisture on every surface and the air smelled musty, like damp clothes drying around a kitchen stove. Traffic was crawling along the main thoroughfare and I was elated at the sight of my first red London bus.

'Mother, look,' I said pointing.

The bus nearest us was the no. 22 and its destination Clapton Park, calling at Liverpool St, Shoreditch, Dalston Junction, Hackney Central and Homerton. I watched fascinated as people hopped on and off the open back of the bus.

'Yes, dear, I see it.' Mother had opened up the letter with our instructions of how to get to the hospital. 'That's the bus we need to catch all right. But not for a good while yet. Your father gave me a few shillings so we could buy lunch. How about we find a nice little restaurant and get a decent meal in you? Heaven knows the kind of food you'll be given in the nurses' home.'

We found a pleasant little place just off the main road. We sat in the window so that I could watch the black cabs and the red buses jostling for space with the coal trucks and delivery vans. I positively wolfed down my ham, egg and chips, conscious that Mother might be right and it might well be my last decent meal until I returned home for a holiday.

'Phyllis,' Mother hissed over the gingham tablecloth, 'it's not becoming of a young lady to eat so fast.'

I blushed and sat up straight and proceeded to finish my meal at a dignified pace. I really must start reading that book on etiquette Father had given me.

By the time we left the restaurant, the weather had brightened up a little and a pale, watery sun was doing its best to burn through the mist.

There wasn't long to wait before a no.22 rounded the corner and pulled up. The conductor, a burly man with a red complexion and wearing his hat at a jaunty angle, stepped off the open platform at the back to help me with my suitcase.

'Where are you off to, ducks?' he said with a smile.

Before I had a chance to answer Mother butted in with a disapproving stare.

'Hackney Hospital, if you please.'

'Can we sit up top, Mother?' I asked, *for what better place to see London from the top deck of a bus,* I thought.

'You can leave yer case 'ere,' the conductor said, rolling out two paper tickets for us. 'I'll keep an eye on 'em.'

I hurried upstairs and, although the bus was busy, two seats were free at the very front.

Mother barely had time to sit down before the bell dinged twice and the bus juddered off.

As I stared wide-eyed out of the window, wiping off the cold condensation every five minutes or so, I began to feel rather disappointed. This wasn't quite the London I was expecting, hoping, to see. Where were St Paul's, Buckingham Palace, Piccadilly

Circus? But then I realised that those were in the opposite direction. The East End was a different city altogether, all urban rawness. However, it was still fascinating and felt a million miles from sleepy Dovercourt Bay. It wasn't the rows and rows of houses, or the traffic-choked streets, that grabbed my attention; it was the people. So many different colours and creeds. It might have been a group of representatives of the League of Nations.

'Isn't it exciting?' I said, gripping Mother's hand.

''Ackney Central,' the conductor shouted, and I felt a chill pass over my body. Ours was the next stop: soon Mother and I would have to say goodbye, and as quickly as the excitement had filled my every fibre, I felt my spirits drop.

''Omerton 'Igh Street next stop,' the conductor called. ''Ackney 'Ospital for those that need it.'

Gosh, I thought, sitting bolt-upright, *this is it!*

'Steady, Phyllis,' Mother said, pulling her hand from mine.

'Oh, sorry,' I said, realising I had been squeezing her harder and harder in my anxiety.

'Come along,' she said, getting to her feet.

I followed her down the steps as the bus pulled over to the kerb.

''Ere you go, ducks,' the conductor said with a smile, handing me my suitcase. ''Ospital's right across the road.'

My stomach was doing somersaults and I felt a wave of giddiness pass over me. There across the street was the imposing brick edifice of the hospital. My ears were ringing with the traffic and the cockney cries, and I felt like I was drowning.

'Phyllis? Phyllis?'

My mother's concerned voice brought me back to my senses. I gave her a brave smile and took her hand in mine.

'I'm all right, Mother,' I said, 'I just can't quite believe I'm actually here.'

She smiled back and together we crossed the busy road and walked up to the gate lodge, a long, newly built (judging by how clean the brickwork appeared), two-storey building with iron railings either side of the arched entrance. This led through to a courtyard and the main hospital complex.

I looked up at the black letters stating HACKNEY HOSPITAL as we passed under the arch, and paused at a door marked PORTER.

A window slid open and a military gentleman with a walrus moustache, dressed in a peaked cap and a dark jacket, gave a brief, stiff nod.

'Good-day to you, miss, ma'am,' the porter said, tipping his hat. 'May I help you?'

'Yes. Hello,' I said, rather nervously. 'My name is Miss Elsworth. I'm here to report as a new trainee nurse.'

The porter gave a quick smile.

'Well, you've come to the right place, miss. Just walk across the courtyard and turn left, where you'll see the sign "A1" on the wall. The nurses' home will be in front of you. Go through the main door to reception. There'll be someone there expecting you.'

'Thank you very much,' I said.

'A pleasure, miss. And the name's Joe.'

'Thank you, Joe.'

Mother and I turned and walked arm-in-arm into the big, open courtyard.

'He called me miss,' I said rather girlishly.

'And me ma'am,' Mother said. 'A real gentleman. Joe, did he say?'

But I didn't really register what she said as I pulled up, transfixed by all the hospital staff hurrying to and fro. There was a nurse whose uniform sported three blue chevrons on the sleeve, rather like those of a police sergeant, and I wondered if I'd ever have those on my uniform. There were handsome doctors striding along, their white coats billowing behind them, some with stethoscopes around their necks. A group of young nurses passed by and started to giggle as they glanced our way. I felt myself redden and quickly let go of Mother's arm, suddenly embarrassed.

I spotted A1 on what I thought at first was a luxury hotel, with its well-kept lawns and flowerbeds leading up to the double-door entrance. It was a modern, seven-storey brick building. Could this really be just the nurses' home? Perhaps I'd misheard the porter. I held the door open for Mother and we made our way into the entrance hall and stopped on the polished linoleum floor, looking about for someone to report to.

Footsteps approached. I turned to see a young nurse with sharp eyes and a warm demeanour smiling curiously back at us.

'Can I help you?' she said, her voice tinged with an accent I couldn't quite place. Not Liverpool, but something not far off.

'Yes,' I nodded. 'I'm to report here. I'm a new trainee nurse—'

'Oh, well,' the nurse interrupted me, 'then you'll need Gladys, the maid. If you just wait in there' – she nodded her head towards a door marked PRIVATE VISITORS ROOM – 'I'll go fetch her.'

The visitors' room smelled overwhelmingly of polish and was simply furnished, with hard-backed chairs and a coffee table with a couple of magazines.

Mother sat herself down. 'I wonder if we'll be offered tea and biscuits,' she mused, picking up a copy of *Life* magazine.

The door opened and I turned to see a round face, pink with exertion, pop into the room.

'Are you the new nurse, ducks?' she puffed.

'Yes,' I replied.

'Well, follow me and I'll take you to the sister.' Mother and I followed the plump, pink-check-attired Gladys through the foyer and down a short corridor. She knocked twice on a door that bore a brass nameplate stating HOME SISTER, opened it and stepped aside to let us enter.

The room took me rather by surprise, being an almost exact replica of the Headmaster's study at my school. There was a large oak desk with a chair, a bookcase on one side and a metal filing cabinet on the other. The only difference was the lack of pictures on the walls, the full-size medical skeleton in the corner, which rather startled Mother initially, and the woman rising from the chair behind the desk.

She was immaculate, perhaps of a similar age to Mother, maybe a little older. She was wearing a dark-blue dress and a pristine white apron. Her head was crowned with a starched cap from which protruded small curls of grey hair. She looked at me with eyes of steel, as if making her mind up in that brief moment whether she would like me or not. She opened her tight, thin-lipped mouth.

'Good-afternoon,' she said, her voice as stiff and starchy as the cap on her head. 'You are Phyllis Elsworth, I presume, one of our new intake of student nurses.' It wasn't a question. 'Can you explain why you are late?'

'L . . . late?' I stammered.

'Yes, Nurse. By two days. You were expected on the first. Today is the third, is it not?'

'I don't understand, Sister. My letter clearly says the—'

'Show me!' Home Sister thrust out her hand.

Shakily I pulled out my letter of acceptance and passed it to her. I glanced nervously at Mother, but she was glaring back at the home sister. *Oh dear*, I thought, *I hope she isn't going to say anything.*

Home Sister looked up from the letter and gave a snort of derision.

'Yes. It appears there's been an error,' she said. 'Never mind. You're here now.' She passed the letter back.

I felt dreadfully embarrassed, as if it was all my fault. What a start. The Home Sister could obviously see that I was mortified and gave me a quick, albeit rather insincere, smile.

'Don't let it trouble you, Nurse Elsworth. You will catch up in no time.'

Catch up? Already? I hadn't even had the chance to prove that I could get out of bed in the morning!

'And this,' Home Sister continued rather sniffily, 'will be your mother. I will leave you for a few moments, Nurse, to say good-bye. Then would you kindly make your way to the dining hall for tea. Gladys will escort you. I will see you later.'

With that she walked briskly past us, the bunch of keys attached to her belt jangling noisily, and out of the office, with Gladys on her tail.

'Well,' Mother said, looking back at the closed door, 'what a dreadfully abrupt woman!'

But my feelings were totally different. Yes, Home Sister seemed frightful, yes she seemed strict, yes she was blunt, but she had called me 'Nurse', and with that one word, that one title, my feelings of nervousness vanished. All I felt now was an eager, no, desperate, impatience to begin my training.

It took me a moment to realise that Mother had been talking to me while fussing with my coat. ' . . . write home, regularly please, and just be careful where you go and with whom.'

'Yes, Mother,' I said half-heartedly. 'I'll be careful.'

She looked long and hard into my face as we stood opposite each other. There were tears in her eyes, but I felt strangely unemotional for once. I just wanted her to leave as quickly as possible.

We embraced and I felt her hand pat my back, then we pulled

apart and I walked her to the door. Gladys was waiting for me outside.

The strangest feeling of elation mixed with genuine fear suddenly engulfed me. This was it. For the first time in eighteen years I was truly on my own.

'Ready, Nurse?' Gladys said.

I picked up my suitcase. 'Ready.'

4

The dining hall is a tremendous size, well furnished and with a long serving hatch at the far end, behind which I can see and hear the kitchen staff busy with preparations. The food looks good and the smells emanating from the ovens set my stomach grumbling.

Gladys directed me over to a table in the far corner where all the girls were dressed in the beginner nurse's uniform, a rather frumpy affair of a blue checked dress almost completely covered by a white apron. This was topped with a butterfly hat worn at a most unattractive but, I soon learned, regulation angle. I was the only one in 'civvies', and I felt most uncomfortable. But that didn't last long, for no sooner had Gladys excused herself than a stout and jovial girl stood up and thrust out her chubby hand.

'Welcome to the flock of white-coats,' she said with a beaming smile, her voice rich with a Welsh lilt. 'My name's Olive MacKenzie, but everyone calls me Mac.'

I put down my suitcase and took her hand. 'Pleased to meet you. I'm Phyllis, Phyllis Elsworth. But my friends call me Phyll.'

Mac gave a chuckle. 'My, what manners. We'll have to call you Etiquette Elsworth, hey, girls?' She turned and gave a wink to the rest of the table, who broke out laughing.

I felt my face redden. *How rude*, I thought. But before I could say anything in response, Mac grabbed hold of my arm and pulled me down into the empty seat beside her.

'Don't look so miffed,' she said, 'I'm only jesting, Phyll. Say, have you met the Dragon yet?'

There was another ripple of sniggering.

'The Dragon?' I said, removing my gloves.

'One of the senior ward sisters,' Mac said. 'Dragon Dinsdale, we call her.'

'No, I've only met the home sister. She seemed a little ...' I hesitated, trying to be diplomatic, 'stern.'

'What, Miss Lee?' Mac exclaimed. 'She's a pussycat compared to the Dragon.'

'But the sisters will all mean for us to do well.'

'Ho, ho!' Mac said, pouring me a cup of tea from the pot that rested in front of her. 'You'll learn. I've only been here two days and I've had a few run-ins already. But never mind, drink up, we only get half-an-hour's break. Then it's back to the schoolroom.'

'Shouldn't I get a uniform first?' I said.

Mac frowned back at me. 'Whatever for? You're not going to be a nurse, not now you're late. You've missed too much already.'

My face must have been a picture of hurt and disappointment, but Mac burst out laughing. 'My, my, you are easy to rib!' she said.

I slapped her playfully on the arm and couldn't help but smile. Mac was a real card, and I knew that we would be bosom buddies.

As it turned out, I hadn't missed much at all. My fellow trainees had spent the morning getting fitted with their uniforms and having a guided tour of the nurses' home as well as a breakdown of the rules and regulations of the hospital.

And, much to my relief, there were half a dozen other girls who had also been victims of the 'administrative error'. Home

Sister was waiting in the corridor, clipboard in hand, and separated us from those now in uniform.

'Uh, oh,' Mac hissed, 'in trouble already.'

'That will be enough, Nurse MacKenzie,' Home Sister barked. 'Run along.'

Mac gave me a sly wink and scuttled off with the others.

'Don't look so worried, girls,' Home Sister said. 'The . . . error has affected enough of you that I have decided to give you a brief introduction to how things will be for you here at Hackney. After which you will be shown to your rooms.'

There was an audible sigh of relief from us girls.

'Right,' Home Sister said, 'follow me, quick sharp.' She turned on her heel and marched off, with all seven of us relieved newcomers trotting along behind, trying to keep up.

We were escorted to a lecture room that was disappointingly similar to the classrooms I had been educated in as a child. It was large, with a high ceiling. Three rows of desks faced a large table on a raised platform, behind which was a blackboard. Above this protruded the top of a pull-down screen, I presumed for educational slide shows. To one side of the teacher's desk was an easel for displaying diagrams. There was one such diagram already there, a cross-section of the human torso showing all of the vital organs in vivid pinks, reds and yellows.

'Take a desk, girls,' Home Sister said.

An excited buzz of conversation started up, quickly silenced by a rap of wood on wood. We turned to face Home Sister, who was glaring back at us, wooden pointer in hand. We stood stiffly, as if to attention.

Home Sister eyed us all one by one then gave a nod of satisfaction.

'Sit down, girls,' she said. 'Now,' she continued, 'my name is Miss Lee and not Sister. I am only responsible for your welfare, to see that you keep your rooms tidy and that you obey the rules, which, I might point out, are for your own benefit.' She paused, as if daring one of us to make a comment, but was met only by a deathly hush. Again she gave a nod of satisfaction.

'You must be in by 10 p.m., lights out at ten-thirty sharp. You are allowed one late pass a week, which you must apply for. There is a kitchen on each floor, with a gas stove and kettle which you are at liberty to use while off duty, but please tidy up after use. If at any time you are ill, report to me at my office. If you are too ill to do so, ask one of your friends to report for you. Clear?'

'Yes, Miss Lee,' we all said as one.

'Very well,' Miss Lee continued. 'After unpacking, please put your cases in the storeroom, the key of which is kept in my office. Supper is at seven, breakfast at seven-thirty. PTS – that's Primary Training School for those of you who don't know – starts at eight a.m., when you will meet the sister tutor. At 9 a.m. you few will report to the sewing room to collect your uniforms. That is all for now. I hope you will be comfortable and happy here at Hackney. If you have any problems, my door is always open. Any questions? No? Good.

'Spend the rest of the afternoon getting unpacked and familiar with your surroundings, and then come down to the dining hall for seven.

'I will now show you to your rooms and issue you with your keys: one for your room, one for your wardrobe and one for your safe box.'

With a great scraping of chairs against the linoleum floor, we stood and followed Miss Lee into the corridor. She led us, her keys jangling, to the living quarters, where she said there were eighty rooms to each floor. She halted on the ground floor outside Room 14 and left Nurse Jackson there. On the first floor she stopped outside Room 27.

'Elsworth, this is you.' She handed me my keys and offered me her clipboard and pen. I signed my name.

'Thank you, Miss L—'

But she had already marched on. I watched as she led the other girls further down the corridor then turned, my hand resting on the handle as my eyes read and reread the nameplate attached to the door: NURSE ELSWORTH. I smiled proudly to myself, turned the key in the lock, and stepped inside.

The room was smaller than my own back in Dovercourt, but it was cosy and pleasant. There was a divan bed, with a bright yellow coverlet, against one wall, matched by yellow curtains hung at the window. It gave an atmosphere of perpetual sunshine. Opposite the bed was a built-in wardrobe, a bookshelf and a cupboard. There was a lamp on the dressing-table and a single electric bulb in a yellow lightshade hanging from the ceiling. The dressing-table itself was cleverly designed to convert into a desk, and in the far corner was a washbasin with hot and cold taps. The room was heated by a wrought-iron radiator attached to the wall under the window. How compact everything was, I thought, as I took off my hat and gloves and undid my coat. I was pleased to see that my trunk had arrived safely and was stuffed under the desk. I dropped my suitcase and handbag, flung off my coat and flopped on to the bed. I stretched out like a cat and gave a satisfied laugh. How special it all felt. As I lay there listening to the muffled sounds of movement coming from the other rooms and passing snatches of conversation from outside my window, I wondered what tomorrow would bring. I was vaguely aware of music coming from somewhere nearby, and I began to hum along.

All of a sudden my room was dark, with just a pale light coming in through the window from the streetlamps in the courtyard. I sat up and reached for the switch. Wincing at the sudden glare of light, I glanced at my watch. It was 6.45 p.m. I must have fallen asleep.

There was a knock at the door.

'Come in,' I yawned, getting to my feet and pulling the curtains closed.

The door opened and I turned to see a pretty face topped with a halo of baby-blonde hair peer around the edge.

'Sorry to bother you,' she said, accent clipped and well educated, 'but what time is supper?'

'Hello,' I said. 'It's at seven.' I glanced at my watch again. 'It's nearly that now. Shall we go down together?'

'Oh, that's frightfully good of you,' she said, stepping inside. 'I'm Edwina, Edwina Thompson. I'm next door.'

We shook hands. 'Phyll,' I said.

'Good-oh. Call me Eddie – not so stuffy.'

'Edwina's a nice name,' I said.

Eddie crinkled up her little nose. It was as petite as she was, and just as pretty.

'Only Ma'ma calls me that.'

'Only my mother calls me Phyllis.'

We both giggled, and I followed her out, locking my door. We linked arms and made our way towards the stairs. A door opened at the end of the corridor and who should step out but Mac. She beamed with delight.

'Well, fancy that. We're almost neighbours!' she said.

'Mac, this is Eddie. Eddie, Mac,' I said. Eddie gave a mock-curtsy and Mac bowed.

'Well,' Mac said, 'Phyll, Eddie and Mac. We'll have to book ourselves into the music hall with names like that. Come along, let me buy you "boys" dinner.'

I wasn't impressed by the food, Irish stew. The meat, when I could find any, was gristly at best.

Mac leaned forward and lowered her voice. 'Never fear, girls. My room, nine o'clock. Bring whatever goodies you have.' She winked.

Eddie giggled in girlish delight. 'Good-oh,' she hissed, 'a midnight feast.'

'We can't,' I said, glancing over my shoulder to see if we were being listened to. 'What if we're caught?'

'Oh, stop your worrying, Phyll,' Mac said. 'We just have to be cautious. Call it a . . . medical challenge. The first of many.'

After attempting to eat some of the dreadfully thin rice pudding that was served up as dessert, Mac gave us a tour of the nurses' home proper. As well as communal kitchens on each floor there was a large lounge on the ground floor, with comfortable furniture, an upright piano and a bookcase full of medical reference books, as well as a large table in the centre with various magazines and periodicals stacked neatly on top.

Lowering her voice, Mac said, 'The lounge is on the opposite side of the building to Home Sister's office, with the dining room and kitchens in between.' She winked meaningfully.

Eddie smiled wickedly.

We split up to get ready. I pattered down the corridor to the communal bathroom, where I enjoyed a long hot soak. Back in my room, I put on my nightclothes and was just filling my hot-water bottle from the tap when Eddie knocked and came in.

'Ready, Phyll?' she giggled.

I turned and I think my mouth must have dropped.

'Whatever's the matter?' she said. 'Is my dignity showing?' She twisted her lovely figure to the side and looked down at herself over her shoulder.

'No, Eddie, it's just . . . you look absolutely ravishing!'

She was wearing a blue kimono that hugged her figure perfectly. Her hair was piled up on top of her head, held in place with a chopstick. Under her arm was a brown-paper packet, suspiciously bottle-shaped.

'Oh, silly you,' she smiled, shrugging off my compliment. 'It's just my little Japanese number. Are you ready?'

'Just a moment,' I said, putting the stopper in my hot water bottle and slipping it under the covers. I picked up a tin that contained a home-made cake given to me by Mother as a hunger reserve, and trotted down the corridor after Eddie to Mac's pad.

It had just gone nine and the corridor was bustling with nurses coming off or just going on duty. I felt rather intimidated brushing by them, looking at their proper uniforms, their square caps and their capes. They looked so sophisticated; I couldn't imagine ever looking that way. I was relieved to get to Mac's door. There was no mistaking the right one, as we could already hear laughter and music coming from the other side.

The room had the same layout as my own, but it looked like a wreck. There were items of clothing hanging here, there and everywhere, books piled in a haphazard way, a few dirty plates and a stack of records propped up under the window. It was as if Mac had been living there a few months, not just a few days.

'We get ours tomorrow,' I said to Eddie.

'Our what?' she scowled.

'Uniforms, silly,' I said, and nodded at two second-year nurses reclining on the bed, smoking and chatting, still dressed in their uniforms.

The rest of the girls were in their night attire, some skimpy, some frumpy, all sat around the floor chatting and drinking from teacups, only I don't think they were full of tea. There was a fug of tobacco smoke in the air, and on the desk an HMV portable wind-up gramophone was blasting out the swing number 'Tiger Rag' which Mac, who was slumped on her linen basket, kept speeding up by winding the handle too fast.

'Here, Phyll,' Eddie said, thrusting a teacup into my hand and sloshing gin into it, 'have a drinkie.'

'Are you tight?' I said, with a frown.

'Oh, don't be so square!' Eddie grinned. She put the bottle down and perched on the edge of the bed, letting her kimono fall open to expose her long, shapely legs. She stretched them out, admiring them.

'What do you think?'

'A few years on the wards and you won't want to show them off,' one of the second-year nurses said.

'Whatever do you mean?' Eddie said. 'These are dancer's legs!'

'Ha! They'll be full of varicose veins after being on your feet for twelve-hour shifts,' the older nurse added.

'So where are you from, Phyll?' Mac asked, offering me a cigarette.

'I'm from Dovercourt Bay. It's a seaside resort on the Essex coast. Near Harwich.'

'What else do you do, Phyll?' Mac asked. 'By the sea.'

'What do you mean?' I said.

Mac shrugged. 'Do you play tennis? Like to dance? Swim, I bet. Are you a lifeguard?'

I chewed my lip, suddenly unsure of myself. Then a light went on in my frazzled brain and I remembered seeing the upright piano in the lounge. *What a fool*, I thought.

'The piano. I play the piano,' I said.

'Never!' Eddie gasped. 'Oh, Phyll, that's simply marvellous. You'll have to play for us.'

'We put on shows,' one of the older nurses piped up. 'Here at the hospital. Usually at Christmas time. They're always looking for musical types. For concerts and that.'

'But that's ideal! I can sing,' Mac said. 'Eddie can' – she looked at her friend's legs momentarily – 'strip—'

'Hey!' Eddie smirked.

'—and you can play,' Mac continued, grinning at me. 'What a team!'

I gave a non-committal shrug. Playing for my friends and my parents back home was one thing, but playing at a concert, well … The doubt must have shown on my face because Mac started prodding my arm.

'Go on. What harm would it do?'

'None, I suppose,' I said with an unsure smile. 'But we'll have to be asked.'

The older nurse leaned in. 'I'm Sally by the way, Sally Sharp. I'm on the committee. I'll put your names forward, if you like.'

'Rather,' Eddie said, hiccupping.

Mac clapped her chubby hands together. 'Well, that's settled. Let's have a little toast. Eddie,' she said, thrusting out her teacup, 'fill them up.'

The door suddenly burst open and one of the other new girls, Sammy, stuck her head in.

''Ere, you gals,' she gasped in her thick Durham accent, 'Lee's on the prowl.'

'Oh bugger,' Mac cursed, whipping the arm off the gramophone with an ear-grating screech. 'Party's over, girls.'

Everybody scrambled to their feet, falling over one another in the confined space. It was like a Marx Brothers sketch, I thought, as a couple of the girls collapsed in a heap of legs and silk and cotton.

'Chop, chop,' Mac hissed, opening up her window and making a vain attempt at wafting away the smoke.

We all piled out of Mac's room and hastily made our way back to our own bedrooms. I unlocked my door and gave a wry smile to Eddie as she fumbled with her key.

'Goodnight neighbour!' I said.

'Goodnight neighbour,' she replied.

'Keep the noise down won't you,' I added.

Eddie giggled and all but fell into her room, slamming the door shut behind her.

I glanced up the corridor, which was now a lot quieter than a moment earlier, and just as I heard the jangle of keys and I saw the form of Miss Lee appear at the far end, I let myself into my room and closed and locked the door behind me.

I stood with my back leaning against the door, letting my racing heart calm down. *If Father could see me now*, I thought, and put my hand to my mouth, stifling a laugh. These girls! Mac, what a rebel she was, and Eddie ... she was just a good-time girl. But I knew that I'd found two good friends. They were like a new family.

5

Somewhere I can hear ringing.

'Half-past six, Nurse.'

I groaned and reached out for my alarm clock.

There came a knock at my door.

'Half-past six, Nurse.'

'Thank you,' I croaked, fumbling for the light switch.

The voice from outside moved on and I listened as it repeated the message further down the corridor. I rubbed my eyes. It was still dark. *This is inhuman*, I thought, and sluggishly pulled myself out of bed.

I washed and, quickly putting on my day dress, went and knocked on Eddie's door. It was flung open.

'Hello, Phyll, sleep well?' She seemed insufferably bright-eyed and bushy-tailed. 'I wonder how Mac's head is this morning? She's a card, that one.'

'I thought you'd be the one with the sore head,' I said. 'You didn't half put away the gin.'

'Oh, don't worry about me,' Eddie smiled. 'I've got hollow legs, like Daddy.'

The dining room was much quieter than it had been yesterday, all the student nurses still half asleep and blinking into their breakfast plates. I found I was famished and was pleased to see sausages, toast and tea being served up.

'Look, here's Mac!' Eddie said.

I turned to see Mac bounding over to us. Her hair was sticking up at angles and she was struggling with her cap.

'Have I missed breakfast?' She checked her fob watch.

'Nearly,' I said.

'Cor, that was a close thing last night,' she said. 'I thought Miss Lee would have caught us for sure.'

'Didn't she smell the tobacco?' I said.

Mac shook her head. 'If she did, she didn't say. She just walked right past my room anyhow.'

'Really?' Eddie said.

Mac nodded. 'I gave her my best snores.' And she started snorting and grunting in demonstration.

After breakfast we returned to our rooms to prepare for the day ahead. I nipped off to the bathroom and on my return found Eddie and Mac lounging on my bed, flicking through a fashion magazine.

'Come on, let's go down to the PTS room, have a look round before Sister Tutor gets there.'

I checked my watch. It was a little before eight o'clock.

'Whatever for?' I said.

'I want you to meet Jim.'

'Jim?'

Mac nodded. She had a twinkle in her eye. 'Devilishly handsome. You'll adore him.'

'Why not?' I said, my curiosity aroused.

The Primary Training School was an interesting place. One half was schoolroom, with desks facing a blackboard similar to the one we were in with Miss Lee yesterday. However, here there were also glass cases full of specimen jars and baffling instruments lining one wall. The other half was made up like a hospital ward.

'That's for practical work and demonstrations,' Mac said.

This part contained two hospital beds, both with dummy patients and all the necessary linen for learning the art of proper bed-making. Around the room were tables and shelves containing various dummy heads and limbs. The room had large windows, but these were frosted, no doubt to stop wandering eyes and minds from being distracted by the goings-on outside.

'What's all this? It's like a wax museum,' Eddie asked, prodding a false arm.

'Oh, for demonstrating bandaging,' Mac said.

'So where's this Jim?' I asked as nonchalantly as I could.

Mac jerked her chin to a blue-painted door in the corner. 'He's usually in there.'

I knocked politely on the door. 'Jim?'

There was no reply, so I pulled the door open and nearly jumped out of my skin. A skeleton stared back at me, all bones and grinning teeth.

Mac and Eddie fell about laughing as I cursed. Then I laughed too. 'You rotters,' I said, catching my breath.

I stepped closer and took the skeleton's hand in mine. 'Pleased to meet you, Mr Jim. I'm Nurse Elsworth. But you can call me Phyll.'

A sudden commotion of voices made the three of us scuttle out of the demonstration room. The rest of the students had arrived and Mac, Eddie and I took our places at the desks. After a moment, a tall, slim woman, dressed in a similar uniform to Miss Lee's, entered, stepped up to the platform and waited as we stood before her. She smiled warmly.

'Sit down, girls. I'm Sister Tutor, Miss Watson. It's hospital tradition that you call me "Miss" and not "Sister". Got that?

Good. Now, your basic training proper will start after elevenses, as those of you whom I can see in day dresses have still to collect their uniforms.' Her eyes fell on me briefly and I felt my face redden. Oh, how I wished it wouldn't, but I knew Miss Watson was attaching no blame.

'. . . basic cleaning practice,' Miss Watson was saying. 'So later today we'll begin your three-month course proper, which will involve a series of lectures on hospital etiquette, bed-making, blanket baths, enemas' – there were a few childish smirks here, but Miss Watson just ignored them – 'vital signs, TPR. Can anyone tell me what TPR stands for?' She cast her grey eyes over the room. 'No? It's "temperature, pulse and respiration". Then there are the various medicines you'll need to familiarise your-selves with, then ward-cleaning, equipment care and, of course, food preparation. You won't have a real live patient to work on just yet, so we will be practising on one another, as well as on our two dummies, Fred and Ginger over there.' She paused, nodding towards the two hospital beds. 'And I can see some of you have met Jim.'

I spun around, realising I'd left the cupboard door open and hoping Miss Watson couldn't read the guilty look upon my face.

'He is of vital help,' Miss Watson continued, 'in letting you girls get to know the working and layout of the human skeleton.'

There was a hum of excited conversation, which stopped as Miss Watson raised her hand.

'Now, I realise that there is a lot to take in,' she continued, 'but take it in you must. I expect you to make notes at each and every lesson and after each lecture you are to write up these notes, ready to be handed in to me the next day. No excuses. All this goes towards your final marks.'

Again there was a buzz of excited conversation, which once more Miss Watson silenced with a raised hand.

'Now,' she said, glancing at the wall clock above the main door, 'we have a little over half an hour. So open your desks and take out your notepads, and we'll have a little run-through of hospital etiquette.'

'Golly, that etiquette stuff was excruciatingly dull,' Eddie hissed thirty minutes later as we tottered down the corridor on our way to the sewing room. Mac and those others already with their uniforms stayed behind to dust and clean the practice room.

'Anyone would think Sisters, Matrons and Doctors were royalty.'

'Well,' I said, 'they are, of sorts.'

'Rot, Phyll,' Eddie said, pulling me along. 'This way.'

We hurried down a set of stairs that led to a long corridor lined with overhead pipes. On we marched, passing endless other corridors leading off in all directions. The basement of the hospital seemed to be a colony of its own. We passed the kitchen two or three times, which, at 9 a.m., gave out exciting odours that positively set my stomach rumbling. On we went, passing the Dispensary, where a group of porters were stacking up the ward dispensary baskets.

'Oi oi,' one of the men called, followed by a few cat-calls from his comrades.

'Cheeky,' Eddie giggled as we hurried on. We saw the Pathology Lab, and the Physiotherapy and X-Ray Departments. I was ready to give up when one of the other girls piped up: 'Over there!' A sign pointing the way to the sewing room lifted our spirits.

Four women were sat at sewing machines, bright lamps burning at their elbows. A line of high windows above let in daylight, and on the other side of the room, in front of a full-length mirror, stood a formidable-looking ward sister. She had dark hair tied in a rather severe bun, her eyebrows were bushy and her face was long and plain. She was well built, rather like those girls who were good at hockey. She was having a dress fitted by someone I took to be the senior seamstress, a big woman in her late fifties, who looked up and blinked blankly at me. My eyes went from hers up to the stern hard stare of the ward sister.

'I'm ever so sorry. We're the student intake here for our uniforms,' I said rather meekly.

The sister harrumped and returned her attention to her reflection. 'The latecomers, Mrs Amos,' she said dismissively.

'I see.' Mrs Amos frowned back at me and the others. 'Well, just you wait there. I'll be with you in a jiffy.' She turned back to pinning the hem of the ward sister's dress.

'How's that for length now, Sister Dinsdale?' she said.

I took a sharp breath. Sister Dinsdale, the Dragon, as Mac had called her.

'Is that ... ?' Eddie hissed in my ear.

I nodded. 'Yes.'

'Hush, you girls!' Sister Dinsdale snapped, glaring back at us via the mirror. 'I think that will be all right, Mrs Amos,' she said.

'Good,' Mrs Amos nodded. 'I will have it ready for you tomorrow morning.'

'Excellent,' Sister Dinsdale said, and stepped behind a screen to undress.

Mrs Amos pulled herself stiffly to her feet and walked towards us.

'Over to the hatch, girls,' she said, and directed us to the far side of the room. There was a serving hatch there, beyond which I could see a storeroom of sorts, lined with shelves of uniforms, hatboxes and the like, as well as coats and dresses in protective garment covers. Mrs Amos disappeared through a door to the side and reappeared at the hatchway.

We formed an orderly queue, giving our names one by one. After ticking each name off a list, Mrs Amos would turn and collect up the various items of our uniform: white apron, cap, blue and white dress, detachable collars and sleeves and a woollen cloak.

As we left the sewing room I hesitated, looking left and right. The door behind me opened again and out stepped Sister Dinsdale in her full uniform. She looked down her nose at me.

'What are you still doing here?'

I swallowed. 'Excuse me, Sister, can you direct us back to the PTS?'

She stared back at me with a fierce glow in her eye. 'Do I look like a policeman to you, Nurse?'

'No, Sister. We just got rather lost on our way here. And we don't want to be late back.'

She fixed me with a hard glare for a moment. I shifted uneasily on my feet and felt my face redden.

'I think it's best you go back to your quarters in the nurses' home and change into your uniforms first. Don't you?' Sister Dinsdale said.

'Yes, Sister,' I squeaked.

'You do know the way to the PTS from there, I trust?'

'Yes, Sister,' we nodded.

'Very well,' she said, 'then I shall direct you back to the nurses' home. Turn about and head towards the kitchens. Take the first left and follow the corridor all the way to the very end where you will come to a staircase. Up two flights and you are back at the home.'

'Thank you, Sister,' we said in unison and turned about.

It took all of our will-power not to break into a run as we headed in the direction she'd told us.

We made it back without getting lost this time and dispersed to our rooms to change. The maid had already been in to vacuum and make up the bed. We had to keep our rooms tidy, but a maid still came in each day. It was a lovely touch of hotel luxury, I thought. If only we could get tea served in our rooms, too.

I quickly stripped off my dress, and started to rummage through the pile that Mrs Amos had given me. How ghastly it all was. I already had on my black stockings and flat black shoes – we had to supply those ourselves – but the regulation student nurse uniform was provided. And how I wished it wasn't. The dress was rather drab and a dreadfully unflattering shape, striped blue and white with a detachable and very stiff white collar, and oversleeves. Over this I pulled on the starched white apron, and to top it all I put on the starched cotton cap. I regarded myself in the wardrobe mirror.

'Well,' I told my reflection, 'not very fetching, but you do look like a nurse.'

Eddie came barging in, her bottom lip protruding like a petulant schoolgirl's.

'Don't we look ghastly?' she said ruefully. 'We can't walk around like this, surely?'

I had to stifle a laugh. Eddie was so glamorous, even in her nightclothes, but she looked thoroughly frumpy now.

'Look at the way we have to wear these caps,' she moaned, pulling at her hair. 'Right down over our heads! The other nurses don't do it, and their dresses look as if they've been fitted.'

That I had to agree with as I stood shoulder to shoulder with Eddie looking at our reflections in the mirror.

'We look like bundles of stew tied up with string.'

'That's such a silly saying,' Eddie said. She twisted this way and that studying her figure. 'But I have to agree.'

'I like the cloak.' They were navy blue wool lined with red.

'They're all right, I suppose,' Eddie conceded.

'Come on, we'll be late,' I said, checking my new fob watch hanging from my chest. No longer would I be wearing my wrist-watch. Jewellery and accessories were forbidden, as was make-up.

Eddie and I rushed back towards the PTS. Just as we were rounding the corner that led to the schoolroom, I bumped heavily into a ward sister.

'Good grief, Nurse, mind ho—' She stopped short. 'Oh, you again!'

My heart sank. It was Sister Dinsdale.

'You are the most clumsy person. It won't do in a nurse, you know?' she said, glaring down her nose at me. 'You will have to learn to go about more quietly, won't you, Nurse?'

'Yes, Sister,' I replied, sensing Eddie trying not to start giggling at my shoulder.

'What is your name?' Sister Dinsdale asked.

'Elsworth, Sister,' I replied.

Sister Dinsdale narrowed her eyes, glanced once at Eddie, then continued on her way.

Eddie and I stood frozen to the spot, listening as Sister Dinsdale made her way down the stairwell.

'Crikey, she's frightful, Phyll,' Eddie said.

'Yes, and now she knows my name.'

6

The first few weeks of PTS race by in a blur. I am introduced to new routines and bond even further with Mac and Eddie as we settle down to learn about anatomy, physiology, hygiene and the general theory of nursing.

Hospital etiquette was given a high priority. We had to address patients with their titles and surnames, never by first names. And the same went with one another: while on duty we were to use surnames only. But Mac found it ever so difficult when calling me Nurse Elsworth, and Eddie, Nurse Thompson, without breaking into a huge grin. This, of course, had the effect of making us smile in return and then that would inevitably lead to fits of giggles.

'You must remember, girls,' Miss Watson said, 'that you are to treat the patients as if they were guests in your own home.'

'I'd hope if a guest came to my home that they'd have the decency to use the toilet and not a bedpan,' Mac whispered in my ear. It took all my will-power to keep a straight face for ten minutes or so after that.

Worse still, certain parts of the body proved more of a challenge to bandage than others, and Mac and I would often get ourselves in a right tangle. Luckily, Miss Watson had a sense of humour. The work was hard but rewarding, and with 'Matron's exam' to be taken at the end of the first month, we made sure our clowning was studious too: the results of that exam determined how many of us were to continue with our training.

In fact, I was so wrapped up in my new life at the hospital that I only realised in early December that I hadn't written home even once. I didn't want to worry Mother and Father, so I sat down at my desk and told them about my new friends, how much study I'd been doing and how I was quietly confident, even though a tad apprehensive, about the upcoming exam. I pulled on my cloak and made my way outside. I walked through the gate lodge, waving the letter at Joe to show I was only going to the postbox at the end of the street. He raised his tea mug in return and gave a smile through the window of his little office.

It was a cold, frosty morning out, the pavement felt slippery underfoot, and I wondered if we'd get snow soon. Just as I came back to the gate lodge, I stopped. A newspaper vendor had a stand there, with a billboard. The words caught my eye: PLAN FOR VOLUNTARY NATIONAL REGISTER.

'Paper, miss?' the vendor said.

I fumbled in my pocket and gave him a penny for a copy of Father's paper, the *Daily Mirror*. 'Thank you,' I said and hurried back into the hospital grounds, scanning the paper. I made it to the dining room rather breathless. My friends and colleagues were gathered round our usual table, deep in conversation.

'We were just talking about having a party,' Mac said. Then her expression changed. 'What is it?'

I passed her the paper, folded open to the story, and she quickly scanned the second-page headline: VOLUNTEER CAMPAIGN FOR DEFENCE OF CIVIL LIFE.

'A National Register for War Service has been opened,' I said, glancing across the table and meeting Eddie's eyes. She looked positively startled.

'War?' she gasped.

'That German chap, Hitler, I'll bet,' piped up Dorothy Winter-worth, a slim redhead from Liverpool and one of our fellow first-year students.

'Tosh, Winters,' Mac spluttered. 'It's a load of hot air, you'll see.' She threw the paper aside.

'I don't know, Mac,' I said, picking it up again. 'It says, "But should war come the whole manpower, and woman power, of the nation would be enrolled under compulsory powers."'

Twenty million copies of a handbook were to be distributed to every household, detailing the requirements for these volunteers. I suddenly felt a little woozy, a kernel of fear hardening in my stomach. Father had fought in the Great War and even though it was over before I was born, I knew how recent it had really been.

Mac pulled the paper away from me again. 'Look, girls, it's all politics and men. You know what they can be like. And we have more important things to concentrate on.'

There was a worried hush around the table now, eyes turned to Mac.

'Matron's exam is only a few days away,' she said, 'and quite apart from that we will have to organise a party to celebrate our passing!'

The girls broke into a buzz of excited agreement.

'If we pass,' I caution.

'There you go again, Phyll,' Mac said. 'Worry, worry, worry. Trust me, we'll pass, hands down. Now, what music shall I get in?'

And bless Mac, for it turned out she was right. However, at first I felt I'd failed. The oral and practical were a breeze, they were what I loved, what I excelled at, just getting on with it. Theory was ... well, theory. I found the written work particularly challenging. So it was with real trepidation that I joined Eddie, Mac and the others waiting for the posting of our results on the noticeboard outside the lecture room.

There was already a crush of girls gathered there, all jostling to find their name and discover their fate. I bit my lip and grabbed hold of Mac's hand as I scanned the board for my name.

ELSWORTH, P.: 60 PER CENT. PASS.

There were squeals of delight as the girls jumped up and down and embraced one another. But I kept staring at the board, at my name, at that number: 60 per cent. *That's little more than half*, I thought blackly.

Mac gave me a slap on the back. 'I told you, Phyll. Didn't I?'

I nodded, but with little enthusiasm. 'But I've only just made it,' I said, knowing that this was just the beginning, and a fairly easy exam at that.

'Don't be down-hearted, Phyll,' Mac said. 'You haven't done so bad. In any case, you've made it. The main thing is passing the exam, not the number of marks.'

I couldn't really argue with that: 50 per cent was the required figure. Everyone had passed. Everyone was going to carry on.

'You both did well,' I said, seeing that Mac and Eddie's scores were in the low seventies. 'Congratulations,' I whimpered.

'Now stop that,' Eddie said. 'You did well enough. Better on the practical side by a long chalk.'

Mac nodded in agreement. 'Yes. You just need to swot up on your theory, that's all. You'll get there.'

I forced a smile. They were both being good friends, but I felt so deflated.

Eddie took me by the arm and turned me to face her.

'Now look, Phyll. I guarantee you will make the better

practical nurse out of the three of us. So chin up and let's go see what Sister Tutor has to say.'

I sniffed and nodded and told myself to stop being so dramatic. I had passed and Mac was right, that was what mattered.

We filed into the lecture room buzzing with excitement, but soon fell silent with one look at Miss Watson's face.

'Stand behind your desks, girls, chop chop,' she barked. 'Now, girls, I shall not keep you long. You have seen the results, I trust? And although you have all passed, not one of you has done so with merit.'

By now you could hear a pin drop in that room, such was the atmosphere of trepidation.

'So, girls, I suggest that you all put a lot more effort into your written papers, especially when it comes to the PTS exams.' She paused, passing her gaze over each and every one of us. 'Starting next Thursday, you will be on duty on the wards for one day per week, rotating every three months.'

She then criticised each of us in turn on a particular failing, and by the time we were dismissed, the elation of having passed was gone. 'Now, the rest of the weekend is yours. Report back here at eight a.m. sharp on Monday. Dismissed.'

'Thank you, Miss Watson,' we said in unison before filing out.

'So what's the plan of action, girls?' Sammy said as she trotted up alongside us.

'A little music and a dance perhaps, in the lounge.'

'What about . . . you know, a drinkie?'

'Home Sister will be on the prowl. Too risky,' I said.

'Not if we save it for later. Say in my room from nine,' Sammy suggested.

'Splendid!' Eddie said. 'I'm off to see my aunt in Chingford, but I'll be back in plenty of time. I'll see if I can pilfer a bottle of sherry, too.'

'We'll be in the lounge from seven for a sing-song and a dance,' Sammy said to Eddie before turning to me. 'You'll play for us, won't you, Phyll?'

'Of course,' I said. 'How much do we need to give for, you know, the "party spirit"?'

'Two shillings, I'd say,' Sammy said.

'Then it's just the task of smuggling it in,' Mac said.

'Oh, leave that to me,' Eddie volunteered with a sly smile.

'Fancy doing a bit of Christmas shopping with me, Phyll, see the lights?' Mac said. 'Up the West End.'

'Good idea. It'll be nice to get out of this uniform too.'

After I'd washed out my stockings for Monday, I changed into mufti and went along to collect Mac. It was so nice to be out and away from the hospital, despite the weather. The spirit of the festive season was plain to see on the shoppers' faces, especially the children, their eyes wide with wonder at all the fairy-tale novelties displayed in the shop windows: dolls, train sets, spinning tops, footballs and tennis rackets, rocking-horses and toy cars, soldiers and cowboys and Indians.

Friday had been our first pay day. Our salary in that first year was only thirty-eight shillings per month, and it didn't go far. Mother and Father were extremely generous, sending me a small allowance each month which helped, particularly with buying textbooks. Now Christmas was approaching, I so wanted to get them something nice.

I had to use a lot of will-power to stop myself buying what I'd love to, and followed Mac to the bargain basement of John Lewis and Co.'s. Here I purchased enough china to set a breakfast tray. If we left a tray outside our rooms on a Friday and a Saturday night, having placed an order the previous morning in the kitchens, then the maids would bring us breakfast in bed. What a treat that was on a weekend.

I pondered at length what to get Mother and Father, worried about the weight and postage cost. With Mac growing impatient at my dithering, I eventually grabbed some good-quality tobacco for Father and a piece of brass for Mother, to add to her collection. By now it had gone 1 p.m. and we were famished. We emerged back on Oxford Street laden with packages, rather flushed from the warmth inside. How the cold air bit at my lungs, but it was exhilarating.

'How about the Corner House on Coventry Street for lunch?' Mac suggested. 'We deserve a treat.'

I adored the Lyons Corner House, its rich Art Deco style and mellow lighting, all the tables neatly laid out with menus and cutlery, waitresses smart in their black dresses with white aprons, collars and cuffs and their sweet little caps with the Lyons monogram in the centre. I loved how the pillars that ran down both sides of the vast restaurant were uplit, as were the wall lights. But most of all I loved how music drifted gently from a small orchestra in the far corner. It was such a pleasant way to spend the afternoon.

By the time we got back to the nurses' home, quite a few of the girls were already in the lounge, chatting away gaily about what they'd been up to. Eddie wasn't back from her aunt's yet and there was no sign of Sammy either. I sat down with Mac and began to write out some Christmas cards.

The fire popped and burned cheerfully in the grate, and the radio sang out some seasonal tunes. Winters was skimming through the *Daily Express*, and the headline BRITAIN DECLARES WAR made me start. But when I read it properly, it actually said BRITAIN DECLARES TRADE WAR. Still, as I stared at those ominous black and white words, I wondered just how serious the talk of civil defence was. Oh, how I wished I could talk to Father. He'd be able to explain what all the fuss was about.

Just then a cheer went up and I turned to see Sammy and Eddie coming in clutching various parcels in their arms, a few of which were clinking provocatively. It wasn't long before the carpet was rolled back and I made my way over to the piano.

'How was your aunt?' I asked Eddie.

'Stupendously dull.'

'Oh, I'm sorry,' I said, and started to run my hands up and down the keys.

'Don't be,' Eddie grinned. 'I pilfered a bottle of sherry, as promised.'

'Bravo,' I smiled.

'It's a shame we can't have any men,' Eddie said, watching as a couple of the girls started dancing together.

'Who needs men when we have these?' Mac beamed, snatching up two vases from the mantel. She passed one to Eddie and they started to waltz around the room with them balanced on their heads. The others gathered round and started to clap and cheer, almost willing the vases to crash to the floor. I played faster and faster, and then brought the tune to an abrupt end. There was a round of applause and Mac and Eddie took their bows.

'Wind it down, Phyll,' Sammy whispered to me, and she and Eddie disappeared off with their bundles of clinking shopping.

I played two more tunes, then we left the others to the radio and hurried to our rooms to change into our nightwear. I grabbed my toothmug and a donation of some biscuits and cheese, then hurried along the corridor. Winters was at the far end, sat on a chair with a book in her lap.

'What are you doing out here?' I asked.

'I've drawn the short straw. First to be dog.'

'Dog?'

'Guard dog, silly. I'm on watch.' She tapped her nose. 'Ruff! Ruff! Keeping an eye out for Home Sister.'

I made my way up to the third floor and knocked on Sammy's door. Just like Mac's had been, Sammy's room was a mess, with girls slumped in any available space, squeezed on the bed, crowded on the floor, perched on the windowsill. The air was thick with tobacco smoke, perfume and girlish laughter, and there was music blaring out from a portable radio on the floor. I stepped gingerly through, passing Eddie, lost in her own world, dancing away to a Tommy Dorsey number with Moody Malone, a little dark-haired girl from Belfast. I weaved my way over to the window, where Sammy was perched on the sill, deep in conversation with Mac.

'Phyll, help yourself to punch!' she shouted.

'Punch?' I said, looking around. 'Where?'

'The sink.' Mac pointed.

Sure enough, Sammy had put the plug in the handbasin and tipped whatever drinks she'd got hold of in, adding some slices of orange for good measure.

I dunked my toothmug in and had a sip.

'Crikey!' I coughed. It was strong stuff, but I had to concede that it tasted really rather good.

I picked my way back to the window and accepted Sammy's offer of a cigarette.

'Isn't this just grand?' Eddie shouted. 'Here's to us,' she added and raised her toothmug.

'To us,' we all shout in unison.

I lifted my mug to my lips and hesitated. There, folded on the windowsill, was Winters' newspaper from earlier, with the ominous headline that I'd misread. Only now it was folded over in such a way that all I could see were the words 'declares war'. A chill ran through me.

7

With December comes the next stage of our nursing training: we are to be assigned ward duty. Thursday morning
can't come around soon enough and Mac, Eddie and I practically
run to the PTS room for 8 a.m. My stomach is in knots as I
wonder just where I'll be reporting.

The door opened and Sister Tutor strode in. 'Good morning,
girls.'

We all pushed our chairs back and rose to our feet. 'Good
morning, Miss Watson.'

'Sit down, please,' she said with a smile and a nod. 'No doubt
you have been looking forward to working on the wards, so let
us hope you will make yourselves useful to your particular Sister
and her staff.'

There was a murmur of excited conversation, quickly silenced
by a raised hand from Miss Watson.

'Remember,' she continued, 'you will be at everyone's beck and
call. The dirtiest jobs will be thrust upon you and at the end of the
day you will be very tired, with aching feet and, at times, an
aching heart. But do not get despondent: this happens to us all at
the beginning.'

She picked up a clipboard from her desk and began to read out our names in alphabetical oder. I held my breath as she approached the Es.

'Nurse Elsworth ...'

I stood up. 'Miss?'

'A9 for you. Men's Surgical.'

'Thank you, Miss Watson,' I replied and sat back down again. I could barely keep the smile from my face. This was going to be a huge bonus to my learning. I couldn't wait to get there.

Winters was going to A8, Men's Medical, which was opposite my ward, while Sammy had B4, Women's Medical, Eddie B2, Women's Out-Patients, and Mac D5, the Children's Ward.

Outside it was cold, fresh and still dark, with a light flurry of snow falling.

'Damn it all,' Eddie cursed. 'I can't believe I'm going to have to be in the women's ward with a bunch of moaning old hags. Would you swap with me, Phyll?'

I shook my head as we made our way towards the hospital blocks. 'Sorry, Eddie, I don't think that would be allowed.'

'Well, I for one can't wait,' Mac said with a laugh, 'I love children.'

'Yes, they assigned the right clown there,' Sammy said.

Winters and I entered A block. By now my heart was beating so fast I thought it would explode. Finally we were standing outside Wards 8 and 9.

'Good luck,' I said to Winters.

'You too,' she said. 'It'll be nice to see a familiar face through the ward door.'

I gave her a final nod and turned to A9. The doors were closed, but through the windows I could see the Sister's figure bent over the desk in the centre of the room, hurriedly engaged in writing. I could also see a Senior Nurse at the far end of the ward tending to one of the patients.

The ward was very long, with about ten beds running along each wall. It was bright with large floor-to-ceiling windows that ran down both sides, about one for every other bed, and there was a triple ceiling-high window at the far end making the room bright and airy. Near to the main entrance I could see two more doors off to the left, and on the other side yet another door. Behind me, in between Wards 8 and 9, were the Male and Female bathrooms.

I swallowed hard and tentatively pushed the door open.

The first thing that hit me was the smell, an overpowering aroma of disinfectant and, not sweat as such, but . . . men.

To my left was the ward kitchen, and I could see the back of a maid standing at the sink washing up. She was singing along happily to herself, a rather off-key version of 'Tea for Two'.

'Excuse me,' I said rather meekly.

'Hello, who are you?' The maid was drying her hands, frowning back at me.

'Nurse Elsworth. I'm from PTS,' I said. 'I've been assigned to this ward. A9?'

'That's right,' she said. 'I'm Ethel. Hang your cloak in the linen cupboard next to the bathroom.'

I did as she said and came back in.

'What's Ward Sister like?' I asked.

Ethel gave a non-committal shrug. 'Not bad really. Her bark is worse than her bite. But she's got one of her bad days today, so you just want to watch—'

'You there!' an oddly familiar voice called out.

I turned to see the ward sister staring back at me from the desk. 'What are you doing here?' she said.

'Excuse me,' I said to Ethel, then marched briskly over to the sister, my heart in my mouth.

As I got closer I realised with a cold chill that the ward sister was none other than the Dragon herself, Sister Dinsdale.

'On duty, Sister,' I croaked, my voice all but a whisper.

Sister Dinsdale stared back at me for a minute. Then she raised her eyebrows. 'Oh, it's you again. Nurse Elsworth, isn't it?'

I nodded.

'Well, let's hope you won't be so clumsy on my ward.'

'Yes, Sister.'

'Very well then, Nurse Elsworth. Go to the sluice and collect a tray for dusting one side of the ward.' She paused and turned, raising her voice: 'Nurse O'Reilly?'

The nurse I'd seen earlier working at the far end of the ward walked briskly over to us. 'Yes, Sister?'

'Nurse O'Reilly,' Sister Dinsdale said, 'show this little white-coat the sluice and take her with you to dust the ward.'

'Yes, Sister,' Nurse O'Reilly said. She turned her green eyes on me. 'Come along.'

I followed her, thinking how pretty and sophisticated she looked in her proper uniform dress. She had three blue chevrons on her arm, indicating she was a third-year nurse.

'Don't look so scared,' she said as we entered the sluice, where the aroma of disinfectant immediately assaulted my nostrils. 'I know just how you're feeling; I had to go through it, too. Once today is over you won't feel so bad, all right?' Her soft Irish lilt was as gentle as her smile.

I nodded, 'Thank you, Nurse O'Reilly.'

'I'm Maggie,' she whispered, holding out her hand.

I smiled. 'Phyll.'

'Good,' she said. 'Now, hurry and get that tray set up and let's get started. There's a lot to do in the mornings.'

I quickly gathered up the relevant cleaning products from the shelves, then with quiet diligence I went from bed to bed, smiling nervously at any patient that caught my eye, damp-dusting and removing bits and pieces from the lockers, just as we had been taught in PTS. It wasn't thrilling, basically doing little more than a cleaner would, but I enjoyed just doing something. As I passed each bed I wondered what each man's case history was.

At the last bed but one, a middle-aged man was lying there, dreadfully pale, his eyes and cheeks so sunken and dark that he looked skeletal. But his face lit up as he focused on me.

'Hello, lassie,' he said. 'Come to work yourself to death?'

I smiled back and he nodded.

'God bless you,' he whispered. Then he closed his eyes again.

I stood and stared down at him for a moment.

'Where's my little white-coat?'

How I wished she wouldn't call me that. I turned to face Sister Dinsdale as she strode towards me, her shoes clacking ominously across the floor.

'Yes, Sister,' I gulped.

'Nurse, you will be off duty this afternoon,' she said. 'Go to second dinner at one-fifteen, then return to the ward at four-thirty p.m.'

'Yes, Sister,' I replied, resisting the overwhelming urge to curtsy.

'When you have finished dusting, go for your tea break.'

'Yes, Sister,' I replied. 'Thank you, Sister.'

As Sister Dinsdale turned on her heels, a man in the bed opposite raised his hand.

'Nurse, could I have a bottle, please?'

For a brief moment I stared blankly back at him. What was he talking about? He couldn't drink, not in bed, not on the ward. Sister would— Oh! My mind suddenly clicked, and I felt my face flush. A bottle. Not that sort of bottle; *that* sort of bottle! I glanced down the line of beds, searching for Nurse O'Reilly. She was at the far end.

'A moment, sir,' I said to the patient, and hurried over to Nurse O'Reilly.

'That man,' I said, 'he needs a ...' I didn't quite know how to put it. It was silly, but I felt so embarrassed.

Nurse O'Reilly's face broke into a huge smile. 'In the sluice,' she said. 'Lined up on the shelves. And don't forget the cover.'

After my morning break I returned to the ward to find Sister Dinsdale had been replaced by a staff nurse. Her name was Ellis and she was the polar opposite to Dinsdale, kind, gracious, helpful and good-humoured. It made the rest of the day fly by, and I found myself getting into my stride and actually enjoying my duties, however grim or tedious. Staff Nurse Ellis actually took the time to take me with her on her round, giving me each patient's name and diagnosis. I felt so much more at ease after that.

I watched Staff set up a dressings trolley, and while I moved the screens to give the patient some privacy, I watched keenly as she dealt with various bandages, clips, swabs and dressings of all kinds. She seemed to take everything in her stride, and with such sharp efficiency, too. Could I be like her one day? But whatever happened in the future, right then and there in those first few hours I learned so much.

The last patient we came to was the gravely ill man who had spoken to me earlier.

'This gentleman,' Staff said in hushed tones, 'is Mr Swartzbard. He has a perforated appendix, and peritonitis has set in following an appendectomy.'

I nodded then watched as she checked over Mr Swartzbard's dressings. They were dry and the patient himself was more or less unconscious most of the time she worked on him. She pushed the dressings trolley away and took me to one side.

'Mr Swartzbard is dying, Nurse,' Staff said softly. 'There's nothing that can be done for him, other than to make him comfortable.'

'Oh,' I said, not sure how to take this news. I had never known death before.

'Now, you keep an eye on him. See if you can tempt him with some warm milk. Can you do that?'

I nodded meekly, went behind the screen and sat for a moment looking down at Mr Swartzbard. I picked up his wrist and felt his pulse. It was very weak and rapid, and his breath rattled in his chest. Every now and then he appeared to stop breathing and I sat bolt-upright, holding my breath. Then he would start again. It was the most traumatising experience, just watching him and waiting for the inevitable. By the time 1.15 came around I was glad to be relieved, just to let my poor nerves have a break.

'Did he drink anything?' Nurse O'Reilly asked.

'I tried him with some warm milk, but he's not interested.'

'All right, off you trot,' she said. 'See you back at four-thirty. Cheer up,' she smiled: 'you've done well.'

I gave her a weak smile, but I felt so awfully unhappy. Poor Mr Swartzbard.

Despite everything I'd seen that morning, I was still ravenous once I entered the dining room, and I made quick work of the steak-and-kidney pudding that was on offer. It was good to see Mac, Eddie, Sammy and the others, and the hall was abuzz with our excited chatter, everyone with her own horror story about duties and ward sisters. Mac, though, just could not get over the fact that I have been lumbered with Sister Dinsdale.

'That's ghastly,' Eddie said, 'poor you.'

I returned to my room, but I was too excited to sleep so I sat down to write out a few Christmas cards and a letter home.

It had been nearly two months since I left Dovercourt, and

heaven knew when I'd have the time to return for a visit. I'd already had to break the news that I would be on duty over the Christmas period, and I could only imagine how that had gone down, especially with Mother.

Returning to the ward, I found Sister Dinsdale back on duty, but the place had a slightly more relaxed atmosphere. Nurse O'Reilly set me the task of getting those patients who were fit enough to help with making Christmas decorations for the ward. It was not the kind of thing I had expected a nurse to do.

Supper came and went, where I helped the orderly with his round. Then I returned to sit with Mr Swartzbard, filling a pillowcase with cotton-wool swabs to keep me occupied. Now and again he would stop breathing and it would seem that I too would stop with him. But he kept holding on.

Eight-thirty couldn't come fast enough. But at twenty minutes past, Nurse O'Reilly came and fetched me.

'Prayer time,' she said.

Baffled, I followed her over to the medicine cupboard.

Every evening Sister Dinsdale conducted prayers for 'her nurses', the day staff going off duty and the night staff coming on. Sister had us all kneeling as she said a brief, dignified thank you to the Lord, then wished us all good-night.

Nurse O'Reilly, Staff Nurse Ellis and I collected our cloaks and walked briskly back to the nurses' home, our feet crunching on the thin layer of snow that had settled on the forecourt once the sun had gone down.

'Have you enjoyed your first day, Elsworth?' Staff Nurse Ellis said.

'It's been wonderful, Staff,' I said. 'Thank you both for being so kind.'

'Our pleasure,' Staff smiled.

'Tell me,' I said. 'Mr Swartzbard . . . Is he really going to die?'

'He'll not last the night, I'll wager,' Maggie said. 'Empty bed in the morning. But it will soon be filled again.'

I fell into stunned silence. *What a callous remark*, I thought.

'Don't be shocked, Phyll,' Maggie said. 'You'll have to come to terms with death, become hardened to it. We have to.'

'It's true,' Staff said. 'Otherwise this job would be impossible.'

They were right, I knew that. But it was still a shock to my naïve young ears.

8

Maggie was right, of course. During my break the next day, I pop up to the ward to ask about Mr Swartzbard. He died in the night. And already there is another patient in his bed.

The news makes me feel sad, but I couldn't wait for next Thursday to arrive so I could get back to the ward.

I quickly came to understand that a ward ran like clockwork. The day would start at 7.30, with the night staff helping the patients wash and clean their teeth before they ended their shift at 8 a.m. The day staff's routine would start with breakfast, then blanket baths, bed-changing and attending to pressure points to fight against bedsores. Then it would be the administering of medicines and the changing of dressings. Bedpan and toilet rounds took place before each meal, although one thing I soon learned was that, no matter how Sister wanted things to run, the human body wasn't a machine and each person had their own ... how should I say it? ... routine.

During the afternoon visiting hour, the nurses had to remain on the ward in case any relatives needed support. Tears were quite a common occurrence, and at times I felt more like a Samaritan than a nurse. When we weren't needed by patients or visitors, there was always some little job or task to do.

On top of ward duty, Christmas was rapidly approaching. At

the nurses' home the mail had been arriving fast, parcels, letters and cards in their hundreds. The day mine arrived, two porters had to carry it to my room for me. It was a huge tea chest and when I opened it up, I found it to be a Christmas hamper from Mother and Father. They'd thought of everything, bless them, and packed it with all kinds of seasonal treats including a rich fruitcake and a bottle of wine. Oh, how I was going to miss them on Christmas morning.

The PTS was closed for three days over Christmas itself and for this period we were to work on our assigned wards. I reported to Men's Surgical as usual, only to find Sister Dinsdale to be in a much more jovial mood and the rigidity of ward etiquette slightly relaxed. There were sprigs of mistletoe over some of the beds and naturally there were endless offers of a Christmas kiss. It amazed me how the sight of a nurse in uniform perked the men up so. And now there seemed to be three times the usual amount of wandering hands and nips of my bottom. I wished I'd swapped wards with Eddie when she'd asked earlier in the month; she was much better at that kind of thing than I was.

I did my best to carry on and brush it off with good humour, and I soon learned a thing or two from Maggie. She had eyes in the back of her head and was lightning-quick to react to any saucy behaviour, threatening the perpetrator with a sponge bath. But as it was Christmas Eve, even she was a little more forgiving, and there was a real buzz of excitement amongst the men. It was as if they were little kids. Heaven only knew what Mac would be putting up with in the Children's Ward.

Nurse Anderson, one of the second-year nurses, a well-spoken, efficient and friendly woman from Hampshire, called me over with a request. 'Would you mind taking Mr Mason his breakfast tray?' she said. 'I plumb forgot, and Sister has asked me to clean out the steriliser.'

I felt myself go all aflutter. Mr Mason was a professional footballer who had fractured a femur during a match. He was devilishly handsome and had a winning smile of perfect teeth. He was the heartthrob of the ward, and I knew Maggie had taken rather a shine to him.

'Must I?' I whispered, suddenly all shy.

'Don't be silly. Here.' Nurse Anderson shoved the tray into my hands.

I made my way over to Mr Mason's bed, feeling as if everybody was watching me. But I told myself to grow up. This was part of my job, and Mr Mason was just another of my patients. As I approached, he seemed to be dozing. *Poor man*, I thought, *how rotten to be here for Christmas*.

'Good-morning, Mr Mason,' I said. 'Here's your breakfast. And a Merry Christmas.'

As I put his tray down, he sprang forward suddenly, grappled me in a bear hug and planted a huge kiss on my lips.

'And a Merry Christmas to you, Nurse!' he said.

I pulled away, feeling my face redden. I was about to slap him when laughter and clapping broke out behind me. I looked round to see not only the other patients, but Maggie, Nurse Anderson and even Sister Dinsdale laughing and clapping with the rest.

'Oh, you rotters!' I said, spotting the huge sprig of mistletoe above Mr Mason's bedhead. I grinned, straightened my uniform and walked away to cat-calls and more laughter.

'Just a little Christmas initiation, Nurse Elsworth,' Maggie sniggered.

'Come along, Nurses,' Sister Dinsdale said, and she led us to the ward kitchen. 'I have a little festive treat in store.'

Sherry and mince pies were laid out, and we all toasted one another with 'Merry Christmas'.

The telephone rang in the office and Maggie went to answer it. Moments later she rushed back in.

'Duty calls, girls,' she said. 'Road accident.'

'Right,' Sister Dinsdale said, 'Nurse Elsworth, you help Nurse O'Reilly prepare a bed. Nurse Anderson, with me.'

I went to the sluice and filled a number of hot-water bottles to warm the bed while Maggie prepared the patient's case papers, then I fetched bed blocks. While all this commotion was going on, the ward around us went deathly quiet.

Within minutes we heard the lift gates clang open in the hall outside, and then the ward doors sprang open. Sister Dinsdale led the way, followed by two male nurses pushing a trolley. Nurse Anderson brought up the rear. I held the screens aside, then helped the two male nurses lift the patient on to the bed. He was painfully young and looked very bashed about. *How awful*, I thought, *and on Christmas Eve, too*.

'All right, Nurse Elsworth,' Sister Dinsdale said, 'you start serving teas to the other patients. Nurse Anderson will assist Nurse O'Reilly with getting the patient comfortable.'

'Yes, Sister,' I said, barely able to drag my gaze away from the young man's battered face.

Eventually Maggie emerged from behind the screens and I was able to get her alone in the sluice room.

'How is the new patient?' I whispered. 'Is he very ill? Does he have any relatives?'

Maggie smiled gently. 'He has two broken ribs, a broken leg and a fractured skull. He hasn't regained consciousness yet, but he's not going to die.'

I was so relieved to hear that. 'Could I take a look at his case papers sometime, do you think?'

'You can take a look any time you like,' she said, 'when the ward's quiet.'

'Sister wouldn't mind?'

'Not at all. The opposite, in fact,' Maggie said. 'She'd be pleased to see you taking an interest.'

That evening the nurses assembled in the dining room in preparation for carol-singing. Word had got round about my piano skills, so I had the pleasure of playing the small harmonium that was pushed from ward to ward. We carried lanterns with red paper wrapped over the glass, and turned our cloaks inside-out so the red lining was showing: we looked like rather glamorous Santa assistants, much to the joy of the patients, particularly the men. Eddie broke a few rules by wearing some bright red lipstick, but I don't think any of the ward sisters minded, or even saw, for that matter, since she spent most of her time having to reapply it due to the sheer amount of mistletoe that was thrust over her head whenever we met a male patient. But Eddie, of course, didn't mind in the least: 'It's good medicine for them.'

Seeing the patients lying or sitting in their beds, politely listening to us, some even joining in, I was reminded that I wasn't the only one who couldn't be with their family at Christmas. Mac grinned over to me at one point, and suddenly I couldn't think of a better way to be spending the festive season than helping these patients forget their troubles, if only for the length of a few carols.

We were exhausted by the time we made it back to the lounge, but were rewarded with mince pies and hot coffee with just a wee tot of rum in, courtesy of Mac. The air of the lounge was soon filled with laughter and cries of 'Happy Christmas!' Even Miss Lee had a smile on her face and a friendly nod if you caught her eye.

'I wonder how the Dragon will be over Christmas?' Mac whispered.

'Who, Dolly Dinsdale?' I said nonchalantly. 'Oh, she's all right really.'

'Pah,' Mac said, 'you've changed your tune about her.'

I guessed I had. Seeing how she ran her ward, how she worked, I could understand why hers was regarded as one of the best wards in the whole hospital, why it ran so smoothly. She used a rod of iron, yes, but I could appreciate her strictness; it had a purpose.

'Here,' Mac said, thrusting a wrapped bundle at me and Eddie. 'Merry Christmas.'

Eddie and I too had gifts for one another.

'A penny for them, Phyll,' Eddie said. 'You keep drifting away.'

'Oh, sorry. I was just thinking about my parents.'

'Me too,' Eddie said. 'What did you get them in the end?'

'The usual, tobacco and brass,' I shrugged. 'Oh, but I did get them a photograph.'

'When? What photograph?'

'It was Maggie O'Reilly's idea,' I said. 'She's the Senior Nurse in my ward and suggested I get one of those studio portraits taken.'

'What get-up were you in? Cleopatra? Salome?' Mac joked.

I playfully thumped her arm. 'As a nurse.'

'Not in this ghastly uniform?' Eddie spat, pulling at her white coat.

'Eddie,' Mac said, 'how is *your* uniform ghastly? It hardly resembles ours, does it? Look at how you've adjusted it to be flattering to your figure.'

'Well, I had to do something, didn't I?' Eddie said. 'Couldn't go out and about in that frumpy thing we were issued with, could I? Anyhow, Phyll, you were saying . . .'

'I borrowed a uniform from one of Maggie's friends. So the shot is of me as a first-year nurse. With a single chevron and everything.'

PART TWO

1939

Evening Standard
London Friday, September 1, 1939

GERMANS INVADE
AND BOMB POLAND

BRITAIN MOBILISES

Warsaw, Cracow, Nine Other Towns
Bombed: Danzig is "Annexed"

FRANCE DECLARES "STATE OF SIEGE"

Evening Standard

No. 35,808   LONDON, FRIDAY, SEPTEMBER 1, 1939   ONE PENNY

GERMANS INVADE AND BOMB POLAND BRITAIN MOBILISES

Warsaw, Cracow, Nine Other Towns Bombed: Danzig is "Annexed"

FRANCE DECLARES "STATE OF SIEGE"

GERMANY INVADED POLAND TO-DAY. COMPLETE MOBILISATION HAS BEEN ORDERED IN BRITAIN.

Orders in Council for the complete mobilisation of the Navy, Army and Air Force were signed by the King at a Privy Council today. The King also approved other Orders in Council dealing with the emergency.

Warsaw has been bombed. Other German aircraft raided Kursk, Gdynia, Thorn, Bialystock, Grodno, Dilikin and Bydgoszsz. A few hours later, Cracow, Kalowice and Czenstowice were bombed.

THE EVENING STANDARD LEARNS THAT THE POLISH AMBASSADOR SAW LORD HALIFAX TODAY. HE INFORMED THE FOREIGN SECRETARY OF THE GERMAN ATTACK UPON POLAND, WHICH HE SAID CONSTITUTED A CASE OF DIRECT AGGRESSION, AND HE INVOKED THE ANGLO-POLISH TREATY.

French aid has also been invoked.

The French Cabinet met for an hour and 35 minutes. They decided to call Parliament immediately, to order general mobilisation of Army, Navy and Air Force beginning tomorrow, and to proclaim a "state of siege."

The Germans attacked without having delivered any ultimatum.

Attack On Both Sides

They are striking at the "Corridor" both from the East and the West—from the East at the town of Dzialdowo, on the East Prussian frontier, and from the West at Chojnice, about 60 miles from Danzig.

Dzialdowo is about 90 miles northwest of Warsaw.

(Continued on PAGE FOUR)

Air Raid Warning System In Force

LOCAL authorities have been instructed to put their air raid warning systems into full operation.

From now on, the sounding of factory hooters and hooters is prohibited except by giving air raid warnings.

'BRITAIN WILL FULFIL HER OBLIGATIONS'

Parliament Meeting Tonight

THE BRITISH CABINET MET TODAY IMMEDIATELY AFTER ONE HOUR AND FIFTY MINUTES.

AFTER HOURS OF PARLIAMENT WILL BE MEETING AT SIX O'CLOCK TONIGHT. BEFORE THE PREMIER PROCEEDS TO MAKE A FULL STATEMENT TO THE COMMONS AND AFTER THE THE HOUSE IS BEING ASKED TO PASS EMERGENCY LEGISLATION AT ONCE, AND TO GIVE CREDITS. LORD HALIFAX IS MAKING A STATEMENT IN THE LORDS.

MEMBERS OF PARLIAMENT WILL BE IN POSSESSION OF THE CORRESPONDENCE BETWEEN GREAT BRITAIN AND GERMANY WHICH WILL BE PUBLISHED IN A WHITE PAPER.

IT was pointed out in official circles in London to-day that if the proclamation to the German people by Herr Hitler should mean, as it would seem to mean, that Germany has declared war on Poland, it can be stated on the highest authority that Great Britain and France are definitely determined to fulfil to the uttermost.

(Continued on PAGE FIVE)

9

With the new year we return to full-time PTS. Listening to and writing up all those lectures is hard, having had a taste of real nursing on the wards. Still, it has to be done and there is another exam looming, the first prelim, which will determine our passing out of PTS.

For weeks I'd been swotting up in readiness. I was determined to get my theory up to the standard of my practical. At times I'd been sorely tempted to go to the pictures with Mac and Eddie, but I mastered the urge. And when the day of the exam finally came, once I had settled down, listening to the sighs, soft curses and scratching of pens upon paper from the other girls, I actually enjoyed it. The questions were fair and varied and I felt I did pretty well. So when the results were pinned up on the notice-board I was delighted to see that I had passed with merit. No one failed, which meant the intake of 1938 would all carry on with our training together.

On our last day in PTS we presented Miss Watson with a spray of flowers.

'Thank you, girls,' she said, slightly taken aback by our kindness. 'I'm proud of you all. Well done.' She smiled, placed the flowers on her desk and turned to address us once more. Her expression became serious.

'Don't think this means you can relax, though,' she said. 'Things will get harder. But I believe that you all have the ability to make first-class nurses.'

'Thank you, Miss Watson,' we chorused.

'Run along now, you have a long weekend ahead. Enjoy yourselves: you don't have to report back for duty until Monday evening.'

Golly, I thought as I slumped down on my bed, relieved that this latest stage in my training was finally over. *That's nearly three days off. I wonder ...*

I pulled out my copy of the *ABC Railway Guide* and flicked through the pages until I found the Dovercourt Bay timetable. I was off duty from 4.30 p.m. and didn't have to report back until 8.30 on Monday. If I left that evening, that would give me two whole days of freedom. It was the perfect opportunity to go and visit Mother and Father back home. I hadn't been back for nearly four months, and it was high time to correct that.

I hurried along to Mac's room and burst in without knocking. 'Are you doing anything this weekend?'

Mac shook her head, a slight frown of query on her forehead. 'Fancy a trip to the seaside?'

'Oh, do I!' Mac beamed. 'To meet your parents?'

I nodded.

'Hang on,' she said. 'Do they know?'

'No, but Mother loves surprises,' I said. 'And she'll love you.'

'Are you sure, Phyll? I don't want to be a bother.'

'Nonsense. Mother knows all about you and your fondness for cakes,' I smiled.

'Rotter!' Mac said, giving me a playful shove. 'What about Eddie?'

'She's off to Devon to see her parents. Unless you'd rather go with her. I hear Devon's beautiful.'

'No fear,' Mac said, 'Her folks will be too posh for me, I'll bet.'

'What are you saying?'

'You're more ... normal, Phyll,' Mac said.

I didn't know whether to be insulted or complimented, but I let it go. Mac meant well, she always did.

'Good,' I said. 'Get packed and then we'll go and see Miss Ward to ask if we can get a weekend pass.'

Mac's face fell. 'Oh yes, I'd forgotten. Bit late, aren't we?'

'Have faith, Mac dear,' I grinned, and skipped off to pack.

Ten minutes later Mac and I were standing outside the Assistant Matron's office. I knocked.

'Come in.'

Miss Ward lifted her head of tight curls and raised an eyebrow in query. 'Nurses? What is it you want at this hour?' she said, lifting her fob watch from her ample bosom. It was just after five-thirty by now.

'Could we have a weekend pass please, Miss Ward?' Mac blurted out.

'Who is "we"?' she asked sarcastically.

'Nurse Elsworth and me – Nurse MacKenzie,' Mac spluttered, her face turning red.

My heart was thumping in anticipation as Miss Ward glared back at us.

'Why do you need a pass so suddenly?'

'We've just finished PTS, Miss Ward,' I piped up, 'and, having from now until Monday evening free, I would very much like to visit my parents, whom I haven't seen since November.' I paused. 'And I've invited Mac – Nurse MacKenzie – to come along.'

Miss Ward leaned her heavy frame back in her chair, folding her chubby arms across her chest. 'The rules are, Nurse Elsworth, that passes must be applied for in person, to Matron, at nine a.m.'

'But, Miss W—' I started to say.

'But nothing, young lady,' Miss Ward snapped. 'Rules are there for a reason.'

'Yes, Miss Ward,' I said meekly. 'I'm sorry, I didn't know.'

'That's a poor excuse, Nurse Elsworth. You have been here long enough to have found out.'

She sat glaring back at us, and Mac and I stood there like naughty schoolgirls on detention. It was ridiculous and so unfair. Yes, I should have known, but I'd been so busy studying that I hadn't even thought about weekend passes before. Surely Miss Ward would understand this? But what was the point? It was clear the old bag had made up her mind. I felt like running out and slamming the door behind me. But I didn't; I just waited and hoped.

Miss Ward pointed her stubby finger at the door. 'Come back to me at seven o'clock. In the meantime, I'll see Matron. It will be up to her if she grants you the passes or not. Dismissed.'

'Thank you, Miss Ward,' I said.

'Thank you, Miss Ward,' Mac repeated, and we filed out.

'Well,' Mac hissed, 'what do you think?'

I shrugged. I didn't feel hopeful. I glanced at my watch.

'We've got just over an hour. Let's change out of our uniforms anyway, have some supper in the dining hall, and see. We'll never make the six-twenty now, but the last train leaves at eight-forty-five. Mind you,' I said, biting my lip, 'that doesn't get in until gone eleven. Mother will have a fit, us turning up at that hour.'

'What, her only daughter? After four months away?' Mac said. 'She'll be over the moon, I'll bet.'

Mac was ever the optimist, but I was more realistic. But we didn't even have the passes yet, so no sense worrying about what might never happen.

'Will we have time to buy a bucket and spade?' Mac joked as we trotted off back to the nurses' home together.

At 7 p.m. prompt we were back at the Assistant Matron's office. We were dressed and ready to go, but I'd suggested we remove our coats and hats and leave them with our luggage around the corner so as not to look too expectant. I knocked, waited, and eventually tried the handle. It was locked.

We slumped down on the two chairs outside the office and fell into silence. I checked and rechecked my wristwatch. Ten-past, twenty-past . . .

'Do you think the old bag was just ribbing us?' Mac said, a touch of annoyance in her voice. 'You know? About actually asking Matron?'

'Hush, Mac,' I hissed. 'Look.'

Further down the corridor I spotted Miss Ward bounding towards us. She sailed past, unlocked the office door and went through.

'Come on in, Nurses,' she called, as she squeezed herself into her chair. 'Well, you may not have your coats and hats on, but I'd say you look like you're about to go somewhere. Are you, Nurses?'

'Er . . .' I said, looking her straight in the eye. 'We hope so, Miss Ward.'

Her face broke into a broad smile and she pulled a pair of passes from her pocket.

'You were lucky this time, Nurses. But remember next time to use the correct procedure.'

'Yes, Miss Ward,' I said, 'Thank you ever so much.'

'Well, run along. I assume you have a train to catch.'

'Thank you, Miss Ward,' Mac said, and I practically yanked her out of the office. We had little over an hour to get to Liverpool Street now.

We hurried along the forecourt, slipping and sliding on the slushy ground, handed our passes in to the porter at the gate lodge and emerged on to the High Street, craning our necks to see if a bus was coming.

'Do you think they'll have a buffet car on the train, Phyll?' Mac said, stamping her feet against the cold, her breath puffing clouds into the icy air.

'We've only just had supper,' I said.

'No, silly, for a cocktail.'

'A cocktail? It's not the Orient Express, Mac, it's the boat train to Harwich Town. Probably be full of merchant seamen.'

'All right, rum then,' Mac said with a cheeky grin.

Liverpool Street Station was relatively quiet, and actually looked quite pleasant, with the lights from the refreshment rooms and bookstalls shining out across the concourse.

'The train standing on Platform Ten is the eight-forty-five for Harwich Town, via Colchester and Manningtree.'

The train was quite busy, but Mac and I found two corner seats in a Third-Class compartment.

I closed my eyes, relieved to be on the move, excited to be going home, glad to be away from the hospital for a bit. This was to be my first real break in nearly four months. It was hard to believe I'd been away from home so long. I couldn't wait to see Dovercourt, to look at the sea, to hear the waves washing on to the sand and the seagulls crying up above, to smell the brine on the air. How I missed it.

The journey passed slowly, but at last I could see the lights of Harwich in the distance. I opened the corridor window and stood with my face being whipped by the bracing salty air. Home!

I checked my wristwatch: 11.05 p.m. I just hoped Mother and Father would still be up.

'Dovercourt Bay, Dovercourt Bay. Next stop, Harwich Town.'

'Do you think there'll be a taxi, Phyll? I don't fancy lugging my case too far.'

There weren't too many passengers alighting, and Mac and I managed to get over the footbridge to the main station building first. We handed our tickets to the stationmaster and luckily there was a lone taxi parked outside.

In just a few minutes we'd arrived at my parents' front door on Portland Avenue.

'Are you sure about this, Phyll?' Mac whispered. 'Maybe we should go to a hotel? There's no lights on.'

'Yes. Now just relax,' I said, pushing the doorbell.

The front-bedroom light went on. I bent down and peered through the letterbox. The hall light came on and I saw Father coming down the stairs, fastening his dressing gown.

'Who is it? Who's there?' he called, a touch of irritation in his voice.

'It's me, Father. Phyll.'

'Bloody hell,' I heard him mutter as the bolt was thrown and the key turned in the lock. He pulled open the door and blinked back at me, a look of bewilderment on his face.

I practically knocked him over as I threw myself into his arms. 'Surprise!'

'But ... but ...' Father stammered, 'is everything all right?'

'Yes, Father. A last-minute weekend pass. I hope you don't mind? I brought a friend.' I pulled myself out of his arms. 'This is Olive MacKenzie. Mac to her friends.'

'Not at all, not at all,' he said. 'I ... Come in, come in. Mac, you say? Let me take your bags. Violet? Violet?' Father called as he bustled us in and closed the door on the cold night. 'Look who's here to see you!'

'At this hour? Who—' Mother stopped mid-sentence on her

way down the stairs. As soon as she laid eyes on me she welled up and put her hand to her mouth. Then she flew down and gave me a tremendous hug.

'Oh, Phyllis dear, how I've missed you.' Then she pulled herself together and her face took on its usual frown. 'You might have warned us, Phyllis. And bringing a friend, too.' She patted her netted hair. 'We're not even dressed. Most embarrassing.'

But I just had to laugh. 'This is Olive, Mother. Call her Mac.'

'Pleased to meet you, Olive,' Mother said. Hell would freeze over before she used a nickname. 'Alfred, put the kettle on while I make up a bed for Olive. Then you must tell us your news.'

She smiled, put her hand hesitantly to my cheek, then shot back up the stairs.

'Come through to the kitchen, girls. Nice and warm by the stove,' Father said.

It was well past one in the morning by the time Mac and I closed the door to my bedroom. I lay down, listened to Mother and Father's hushed conversation through the walls, and gave a soft sigh of contentment. It felt so good to be home.

'Mac?' I whispered.

But all I could hear in return was her heavy breathing. I smiled to myself, turned on my side, and was asleep before I knew it.

10

My parents take to Mac straight away, as I knew they would. All she has to do is praise Mother's baking and she can do no wrong. We have a hearty breakfast and the conversation flows as Mac and I tell Mother and Father about our typical day in the hospital, our PTS training, our work on the wards. We both, though, avoid talk of our other activities, namely pubs, midnight feasts and parties.

'Well, it certainly sounds as if you two have found your calling,' Mother said as she poured us a fresh cup of tea. Father nodded in agreement, but he seemed a little distant.

'How are you, Father?' I said. 'Anything wrong?'

'No, dear. Don't be daft,' he said with a smile. 'Just busy at work. Been very hectic at the docks of late. And getting midnight callers doesn't help with my beauty sleep, either,' he winked.

Not one to let things go, I accompanied Father on his early-morning stroll down to the prom. Mac was quite happy to stay and help Mother with the dishes.

'How are things in London?' Father asked, passing me his rolling machine. 'Here, you do the honours.'

'They're good. Busy. I don't get a lot of time to see the sights. But I'm happy.'

I'd forgotten how fiddly Father's contraption was. But after a while I managed to roll us both a passable cigarette.

He grunted his thanks and lit us both up, and we walked arm in arm, huddled against the biting wind that whipped in off the North Sea.

'I meant the atmosphere, Phyll.'

'The atmosphere? What the fog? Pea soup—'

'No, sweetheart. Politics. These war rumours . . .'

'Oh.'

To be honest, I'd taken Mac's word that it was all a lot of hot air.

'I've been so busy with my studies, Father,' I said. 'I haven't really noticed.'

He nodded. 'Well, that's something at least.'

'What is?'

'That you haven't noticed anything . . . unusual.'

'Why, Father? Have you?'

'Not as such, Phyll. It's all paper talk, but . . .' He trailed off again.

'Father?' I pressed.

'This Hitler chap. I don't like him. I don't like what I read about Nazi Germany.' Father shook his head.

'I don't understand. Hasn't he helped to rebuild their country? With jobs and the like?'

'That may be, Phyll, but the man's a warmonger. I can feel it. And we're just sitting back and letting him get away with murder.'

'Murder?'

'Well, three months ago Britain, the United States and Italy signed something called the Munich Agreement, letting Germany annex the Sudetenland. All to appease Mr bloody Hitler.' Father shook his head. 'It's the beginning of a slippery slope. I've seen it before, Phyll. War. I just don't want you to have to live through that, for your mother to live through it. Not again.'

'Surely it'll come to nothing, Father?'

'I hope so, Phyll. I hope so. But all I can say is, I'm glad you weren't born a boy.'

'But boys are nurses, too,' I said defensively.

'That's not what I meant, Phyll. Charlie and Ethel are so worried about George,' he added, almost as an afterthought.

'George? Why?' I said.

Charlie and Ethel Bugg were our neighbours in Fernlea Road, and I'd played with their son George since I was a little girl. He was the nearest thing I had to a brother. But I hadn't seen him much since he'd joined the RAF when I was in my last term at school.

'Well, he's a fully trained mechanic now,' Father said. 'An RAF Sergeant in the ground crew. But there's talk that he's to be posted abroad next month.'

'Posted? Really? I had no idea,' I said. 'You never mentioned it in your letters. I wonder how he feels about that?'

'Ask him yourself,' Father said, stamping out his cigarette. 'He's home on leave. Got back on Wednesday. He'd love to see you.'

George Bugg, the boy next door. He was a good friend, a surrogate brother ... and something a little more. I felt a strange tingling sensation at the thought of seeing him again, and in his uniform too. How funny that we'd both ended up in the services, so to speak. I couldn't wait to get back and tell Mac.

Father popped into the newsagent's and I waited outside, staring back down Marine Parade at the sights I'd known all my life. All of a sudden I was struck by a strange feeling. Sleepy

Dovercourt Bay, dear, dull out-of-season Dovercourt Bay, looked no different from when I had left, yet I felt totally changed: grown-up, somehow an outsider, more of a Londoner. It was a very disturbing feeling: not only did it make me incredibly sad, it also filled me with joy. *I'm no longer an Essex schoolgirl, I'm a London nurse.* Father stepped out of the shop with his *Daily Mirror* under his arm and a bag of sweets in his hand.

'Bonbon?'

I shook my head. 'Not so soon after breakfast, thanks, Father.'

'My, we have changed, haven't we?' he teased.

If only he knew what I'd just been thinking.

We returned home and sat around the fire, with Mac holding court, telling tales about her run-ins with the Dragon. I knew most of it to be white lies, but Mother and Father were highly amused. In the afternoon, Father was off to Ipswich as he already had tickets for the football, and Mother had promised to help out at the jumble sale in the church hall.

So, wrapped up against the cold, Mac and I headed down to the seafront. I showed Mac the imposing Minesweepers Memorial and the more elegant Queen Victoria's statue, and walked on past the Cliff Hotel, down the green slopes into Cliff Park and on to the promenade. The tide was in and the waves were crashing and tumbling in a mass of white horses. But to be out in the bracing, briny spray was a real tonic. I filled my lungs and sighed happily.

'Is Milford Haven like this?' I said.

'Here's not so ... fishy,' Mac said after a moment. But it was clear that she didn't really want to talk about her home in Wales. She never did.

We strolled on in silence, heading towards the Park Pavilion, when a voice to my left called out:

'Phyll? Is that you?'

I turned to see a young man in a blue-grey RAF uniform with three stripes on his arm. He removed his forage cap, brushed his hand through his thick, dark hair and beamed back at me.

'Phyll, it's me, George. George Bugg,' he said.

I put my hand to my mouth. 'Oh, George! I'm sorry, I didn't recognise you.'

He stepped forward and we gave each other a rather awkward hug.

'What are you doing here?' he said.

'A last-minute weekend pass. You?'

'I've had a short week. Got to report back on Monday, though.' He paused and smiled. 'It's been a long time, Phyll.'

'Yes, yes it has,' I said.

'So ... how are you? I hear you're in London now. A nurse?'

I nodded. 'That's right. Nearly six months now.'

Mac shifted on her feet and nudged me.

'Oh, sorry, how rude,' I said. 'George, this is my good friend Olive, a fellow trainee.'

'Call me Mac.'

'Pleased to meet you, Mac. So, what are you two up to?'

'I was just showing Mac the sights.'

'Ho ho!' George grinned. 'Lively Dovercourt Bay, off-season. How mean of you, Phyll. Even the donkey-man is at home. Or playing bowls.'

'Bowls?'

'Yes, there's an indoor bowling green in the pavilion during the winter now. I've just been watching Dad play. It's quite good, actually.'

'Perhaps we'll have a look,' I said, glancing at Mac. 'It's lovely to see you, George. I wish we had more time.'

'Me too,' he said, hesitating. 'Say, you girls fancy going dancing tonight? Eugene Magyar's performing. It's only sixpence. Saturday night is party night, after all.'

'Who's Eugene Magyar?' Mac said.

'Oh, he's a very popular performer,' I said. 'His orchestra plays that sort of roving-Hungarian-gipsy mixed with the usual Viennese or Russian. Wonderful to dance to.' I turned back to George. 'And he's here off-season?' I said.

'Pre-Easter try-outs, apparently,' George said. 'So, what do you say?'

'Come on, Phyll,' Mac said. 'It'll be great.'

'But what about Mother and Father?'

'Bring them,' George said. 'My folks are coming.'

'All right then,' I said.

'Great,' George said, heading off. 'See you at seven,' he called over his shoulder.

Mac and I stood watching him go, then turned towards the pavilion.

'I say, Phyll, he's rather dashing,' Mac said with a snigger, trying her best to imitate Eddie's posh accent.

'What? George?' I said. 'George is just ... George.' But I had to admit, he did look very handsome in his RAF uniform.

'Dibs on the first dance,' Mac said as we hurried along, the wind snatching at our coats.

As it happened, Father had already thought about going to the pavilion that night, so he didn't take any persuading at all. Mother made us all a delicious meal of liver and onions followed by spotted dick and custard.

Luckily, on Mac's advice, we'd packed evening dresses on the off-chance, mine a figure-hugging black number with rich embroidery, Mac's a full black and pink skirt with a velvet bodice. She was a big girl, but she knew how to dress well. Father looked smart in his three-piece suit, and Mother handsome in her dated but still elegant tiered lace dress.

The pavilion was lit up like a Christmas tree and the interior was beautifully decorated, with plants dotted around the edges, and lights and hanging baskets dangling from the metal rafters of the domed glass ceiling. It looked rather like a giant hothouse, I thought as I gazed up. Eugene and his orchestra were at the far end, and there was a refreshments bar just to the right of the cloakroom.

The music was well under way, a lively piece full of gipsy charm, and a number of couples were twirling around the dance floor already.

We pushed our way towards the bar, only to meet George, smart in a double-breasted suit, hair combed in a side parting, coming back the other way. He had three glasses of rum punch clutched in his hands.

'I spotted you coming in, so I took the liberty,' he smiled.

'Chin chin!' Mac said.

'Cheers!'

'Let's head over to the dance floor,' George said.

We picked our way through the candle-lit tables and found a free spot near the orchestra.

'Come on,' Mac said, grabbing George and dragging him on to the dance floor.

As I watched them moving in time to the music, I felt a tap on my shoulder.

'May I, miss?' It was Father.

'I'd be honoured,' I said, curtsying.

Father was a terrific dancer. He wheeled me about the floor like a professional. The piece finished to rapturous applause, and a breathless George and Mac came over to us.

'Care to exchange partners, sir?' George asked.

'Delighted,' Father said, handing me over.

I stood looking at George and he back at me. I smiled softly and he took my right hand in his left. I felt a tingling sensation run up and down my body, as if an electric current had passed between us.

'I like your dress, Phyll,' he said.

'I like your suit,' I said, my heart pounding in my chest.

What was this feeling? For George? Surely not. He was like a brother. I'd known him all my life, grown up with him, played with him. Was I . . . in love with him?

He put his right hand on the small of my back and began to lead me around the dance floor. We spun in time to the melody and couldn't take our eyes from one another. I felt so light, as if I was floating.

'I've missed you,' George smiled.

'Really?' I said.

'I think about you an awful lot, Phyll. I always have.'

I blushed and turned my face away, catching Mac staring back at me. She was grinning from ear to ear as Father twirled her about. She gave me a wink and I smiled back girlishly, feeling suddenly embarrassed.

'How about you, Phyll?'

'How about me what?'

'How do you feel about me?' George said.

'I . . . I don't know. I feel silly. I've known you all my life,'

'Silly?' George looked hurt.

'No, not silly,' I corrected myself, 'funny.'

'Funny? In what way?'

'About this. About us.'

'Us?'

I nodded. 'If you want to.'

Was I really saying what I thought I was, that I wanted to be with George? Yes, yes I thought I was.

The piece ended and we stood for a moment staring back at each other, eyes locked, searching one another's face, hands still clasped.

Everyone was applauding, and I pulled my gaze from George's over to the orchestra.

Eugene, elegant in his blowsy silk shirt and baggy trousers, his violin under his arm, was holding his bow aloft to stay the applause.

'Thank you, lady and gentlemans,' he said in a thick Eastern European accent. 'We have short break and return in twenty minute.'

'Phyll?'

George pulled me closer to him, glanced to his left and right, then quickly kissed me on the mouth. I hesitated, then parted my lips and give myself to the moment, my body tingling with excitement.

George pulled his mouth away and whispered in my ear, 'Write to me.'

I nodded eagerly. 'Yes, George. Oh, yes.'

'Come on, love-birds,' Mac said, grabbing my hand. 'Let's get to the bar before the crush.'

We slept in late and Sunday passed all too quickly. Soon, it was time to say goodbye once again. Father left for work first thing on Monday, but he popped his head round my bedroom door before he went. I threw off the covers and gave him a big hug.

'Hey, now,' he said, 'you stay in bed. It's cold.'

'I've had such a lovely weekend, Father,' I said sleepily. 'I can't believe it's over already.'

'What time's your train?'

'Half-past one.'

'Good. At least you can spend the morning with your mother. Here,' he said, and slipped some cash into my hand.

'Father, don't.'

'Hush,' he said. 'It's for your train fares. Your wages are meagre enough as it is. Now, give us a kiss and we'll say farewell.'

I stood at the window and watched him walk down the garden path and turn down the Avenue. He glanced back and waved.

'You all right, Phyll?' Mac said, yawning.

'Sorry, did I wake you?'

'No, I was just lying here thinking, *What's for breakfast?* when your dad came in.'

I turned away from the window and sat down heavily on the bed.

'Cheer up, Phyll. Easter holidays will be here soon. You'll get three weeks at home then.'

'I'm sorry,' I said, giving her a warm smile. 'I'm being selfish, aren't I?' At least I've seen my parents, which is more than you have.'

Mac shrugged. 'Hey, do you know what else I was thinking?'

'About lunch?' I teased.

'About your George.'

My George, I thought. How funny that sounded. But yes, I supposed he was now. I smiled coyly.

'What about him?'

'Well,' Mac said, sitting up with a deep frown. 'His surname is Bugg, isn't it?'

'Yes?'

Mac nodded and tapped her finger on her lips thoughtfully.

'Well,' she said. 'If you get married—'

'Mac! We've only had one kiss and agreed to write to one another.'

'Let me finish. If you get married and have children . . .'

'Yes?'

'Then they'll be little Buggers, won't they?' She blinked back at me, her face all serious.

I stared down at her in momentary confusion, and then we both fell about laughing.

I'm back on Men's Surgical, and I am in my element. The evenings are still ours, and Mac, Eddie and I spend as much time as we can at the pictures or the occasional music-hall show. We don't often go to the pub, but the male nurses like the Adam and Eve, which is directly opposite the gate lodge, so the temptation is always there. In my spare time I also make sure to write to Mother and Father, and increasingly to George. He's currently based at Biggin Hill, and even though that's not too far from south London, our leave days never match. However, our correspondence becomes ever more intimate, and I find myself increasingly impatient to be able to see him face to face again, to see if I really do feel *that* way about him.

However, both work and leisure paled into insignificance whenever I picked up a newspaper, turned on the wireless or visited a news theatre. My father's fears seemed to be coming true, and I began to feel frightened by events in the outside world.

In March, just a few weeks before I was due to return home for the Easter break, it was announced that Germany had occupied Czechoslovakia. Hitler was growing in influence and the black cloud of Fascism appeared to be spreading. The Spanish Civil War came to an end in April, with Franco, another Fascist, in power, whilst another brownshirt, Mussolini, had threatened to turn the Mediterranean into 'an Italian lake'. It felt as if Europe had been on a slippery slope towards war for almost a year, and now I feared that it was almost upon us. But most chilling for us in the East End was the Fascist who *wasn't* in power. Yet. But Oswald Mosley was right on our doorstep, marching down Homerton High Street to Nazi salutes and cheers. It was terrible to see that kind of feeling in our own country. Was that what Britain was to become, a land of bullies and bigots?

My trip home at Easter wasn't a particularly happy one. Whilst I was glad to see Mother and Father again, I did miss my friends back at the hospital. Worse still, I didn't get to see George at all. It seemed he'd been posted to France as part of some kind of exercise, but his parents were just as much in the dark as I was. Secrecy was creeping into a lot of officialdom of late.

And by mid-Summer, when I was back at Hackney, that seemed to be the attitude of the hospital authorities, too. Mind you, Sister Dinsdale would have no mention of war in her ward, from nurse or patient.

Then one day the Ministry of Works descended upon us. Their men created quite a stir – and a good deal of mess, too – as they filled sandbags and piled them up against walls, windows and doors.

'I don't like this, Mac,' I said as we stood watching some men fit blackout shutters to the windows in the dining hall.

'I know. Black curtains. They're so gloomy,' Mac said, with a straight face.

'Mac. This is serious,' I said. 'I'm frightened.'

Mac took my hand in hers. 'We'll be all right, Phyll. As long as we stick together.'

Eddie rushed up to us. 'Golly, have you heard?'

'What?'

'That Hitler chappie. He's called up four hundred thousand more men for the German Army. It can't be long now.'

There was a loud clap of hands to attract our attention, and we turned to see the home sister, Miss Lee, standing at the dining-room entrance.

'Girls,' she said. 'Would you all report to the lecture room in fifteen minutes.'

We crowded in to the lecture room and waited, trying to guess why we had been summoned. Then Miss Lee entered, closely fol-lowed by a stiff, rather short soldier dressed in khaki uniform and with a swagger stick tucked under his arm. His highly polished boots clipped noisily against the wooden floor and he halted and turned to face us in the jerky manner that he undoubtedly used when on parade. A buzz of excited speculation rose up, only to be silenced by a sharp clap of Miss Lee's hands.

'Now, Nurses, this is Sergeant-Major Gregory. He's here to give you a very important lesson. Sergeant-Major?' Miss Lee opened her hand and stepped to one side to give the Army man the floor.

The sergeant-major nodded stiffly and took a smart pace for-ward, the leather of his boots creaking audibly. He cleared his throat and hesitated. One of the girls stifled a giggle.

'My name is Sergeant-Major Gregory,' he barked, 'and I've been asked 'ere by the Ministry to teach you young ladies about incendiary bombs.'

There was a sudden whisper of conversation.

'Now,' he said, twitching his brush moustache, 'that is not to say any bombs will fall and ... er ... 'it the 'ospital—'

Again an exchange of whispers amongst the nurses.

'Please, ladies,' the sergeant-major said, holding up his hand once more. 'Er ... that is to say, Nurses. If you will kindly remain calm and listen ... '

But the buzz of excited conversation increased. Miss Lee jumped forward. 'Quiet!' she snapped. 'Now, listen to the sergeant. Your lives may depend on it.'

We all fell into a deathly silence.

Sergeant-Major Gregory nodded his thanks and again cleared his throat. 'Yes, thank you ... er, Miss Lee,' he said, stroking his bristle moustache with his left finger. 'It's "Sergeant-Major", not ... er ... Now, then ... incendiary bombs ...' He turned to the blackboard behind him, picked up a piece of chalk, and began to draw a diagram.

After half-an-hour of instruction, we were split into teams of four for air-raid drills on the stairwells, practising how to move from floor to floor should a bomb have gone off and if the place was full of smoke. We also needed to learn how to move patients or injured colleagues.

'The roof could come in on you, the floors could collapse beneath you,' Sergeant-Major Gregory said, 'so the stairwells are the strongest part of the structure. 'Owever, you need to be able to 'aul people downstairs without 'urting them or yourselves. And for this you 'ave everything you need in the wards, namely on the beds.'

Mac, Eddie, Sammy and I made up a group, and it wasn't long before we were in fits of laughter. Mac had volunteered to be unconscious and was strapped to a mattress, but she was such a big lass that the three of us were struggling to haul her down the stairs.

'What the bleedin' 'ell do you ladies think you are doing?' bellowed Sergeant-Major Gregory as he marched up to us. 'You'll break 'er neck if you try and lift 'er like that. It's not a fairground ride! You'll do 'er a damage dragging the mattress that way.'

'Language,' Eddie said, with a flutter of her eyelashes.

Sammy and I were giggling as we tried to drag Mac upright again.

'I beg your pardon?' Sergeant-Major Gregory spluttered.

But Eddie wasn't one to back down, not from a bossy man.

'Please, sir,' she said, 'we don't take kindly to rude words.'

The sergeant-major's face was bright red now and his moustache was twitching. He looked as if he was about to explode. Eddie took a step closer and began to fiddle with his collar, patting and straightening it. 'You're ever so handsome, Sergeant,' she cooed.

'Kindly stop that, miss.'

Mac, Sammy and I were trying our best not to break out into further laughter as we watched the exchange.

'It's "Sergeant-Major", miss,' Sergeant-Major Gregory blustered.

'It's "Nurse", Sergeant-Major.'

'Kindly stop that, Nurse,' he repeated, and gently but forcefully pulled Eddie's hands from his tunic.

'Are you married, Sergeant-Major?' Eddie teased.

'I ... er ... no ... miss. I ... Look, you must—'

'Nurse Thompson! What the devil are you up to?'

Eddie jumped away from the sergeant-major as Miss Lee came marching over.

'Nothing, Miss Lee.'

'This is not a game, girls,' Miss Lee said, glaring at us one by one. 'Just remember that.'

'Yes, Miss Lee,' Eddie said.

'Sorry, Miss Lee,' I said, helping Mac to her feet. Her cap was crumpled and her dress had ridden up her thighs.

'Straighten yourself up, MacKenzie,' Miss Lee snapped.

Mac pulled her dress back into shape and adjusted her cap, as we all stood still as if at attention.

'Good,' Miss Lee growled. 'Now, I don't want to hear any more laughter. Carry on.'

Sergeant-Major Gregory glared at each of us in turn, then, with a snort of derision, turned on his heels and marched away.

'Bye-bye, handsome,' Eddie said huskily.

And that was it, we doubled up again.

'Oh, Eddie...' I said between pained breaths, 'you are... wicked.'

She shrugged. 'Well, he is rather dashing, don't you think?'

'Eddie!' Sammy gasped. 'He's old enough to be your father.'

'I don't know... Perhaps a young uncle,' Eddie said.

It was hard to know when Eddie was being serious or not. She was such a flirt. But we pulled ourselves together, knowing that what Miss Lee and the sergeant-major had said was true, that this was deadly serious and, as with other aspects of our duties as nurses and carers, this drill could be the difference between life and death. So, we set about running through the exercises once more, this time with Sammy playing the injured party.

It was apparent that the whole country was preparing for war. Everywhere one looked there were sandbags, blackout curtains and more and more military personnel. Soon the general mood amongst us nurses turned black.

'Look,' said Mac one evening, 'I'm getting mightily fed up with this doom and gloom. We've been working hard, so I say let's hit the West End tonight for a bit of fun.'

'I don't know, Mac,' I said. 'I should study.'

'Rot, Phyll,' Mac said. 'You need a break more than anyone. Come on. Eddie, surely *you* agree?'

'Yes, Mac's right, Phyll,' Eddie agreed. 'It's high time we had some music in our ears and some gin in our veins.'

'Bravo!' Mac clapped.

I smiled sheepishly. I shouldn't, but Mac and Eddie were hard to resist. What harm could it do? After all, everyone needed some time off.

At Piccadilly Circus I suggested Lyons Corner House to start things off. We ordered sandwiches and iced lager and listened to the orchestra playing all the latest hits. Outside the window, dusk was falling and all the neon signs were lit up with a magical glow. We moved on through the hustle and bustle of people and traffic to find a dance hall, where Eddie ordered us pink gins and we sat and tapped our toes to the orchestra as it played some captivating swing numbers. There were plenty of handsome, uniformed men eager for company, and it wasn't long before we were approached by a couple of soldiers. We didn't even have to spend any of our own money – indeed, I don't think I was without a drink in my hand for more than five minutes all evening. Feeling a little guilty about dancing with someone else other than George, I declined many an offer, but enjoyed watching Mac and Eddie as they were spun around the dance floor.

I barely remember hitting the pillow when we returned to the nurses' home, I was so exhausted. Perhaps I had been overdoing it, I thought. Sleep came quickly, but when I awoke later on I had a terrific headache.

'Oh, why did I drink so much?' I groaned.

But something wasn't right. I'd had a few hangovers before, and I was always careful to drink plenty of water before I went to sleep, no matter how tipsy I got. But this was different. My vision was starry and blurred, my temperature was high and my balance was off. My heart was racing in my chest and I was covered in a film of sweat. I managed to summon the strength to swing my legs out of my bed and sat upright.

I swooned, putting my hand out to steady myself on the bedside cabinet. When I tried to stand, my legs gave way.

I don't know how long I was on the floor, but I woke again to a loud knocking. I frowned, then realised there was someone at my door.

'Phyll? Phyll?'

'Mac,' I croaked. 'Mac, help me.'

There was a thump and a crash as my door was forced, and before I knew it, Mac's face was peering down at me.

'Phyll? What is it?'

'I ... I don't know, Mac. I ...' I felt myself slipping out of consciousness again.

I was aware of a strange feeling of weightlessness, and then I could sense my bed beneath my back. I opened my eyes again to see the home sister walking through the door, with Mac close behind.

'Miss ... Lee ...' I stuttered, and tried to sit up.

'Just you lie still, Nurse Elsworth,' she said tenderly, sitting beside me on the bed.

She put a thermometer in my mouth and then took my wrist in her hand to feel my pulse. There was a slight frown on her brow.

'How long have you been like this, Nurse?'

'Only since ... I woke up,' I moaned. I felt like a thousand pneumatic drills were going off in my skull. 'I'm sorry to cause such a fuss,' I whispered.

'Nonsense,' Miss Lee said. 'Have you been sick?'

'No, Miss Lee,' I croaked. 'But I felt like it.'

'Right. We shall have to get you moved to the sick bay, Nurse. You have a worryingly high temperature.'

'What time is it?' I said.

'About three,' Mac said.

'In the afternoon?'

'No, Phyll. Morning. I was on my way to the loo when I heard a crash in your room.'

I slumped back down as Mac and Miss Lee left to fetch some porters. I must have passed out again, for I was only vaguely aware of the porters lifting me out of bed and up on to a trolley.

When I awoke again, I wasn't in the sick bay, but on a general ward. There was a screen round me for privacy, and a nurse I half recognised was standing over me.

'Back with us at last, Nurse Elsworth?'

'Where . . . ?'

'You're on Women's Surgical. Sick bay was full up,' the nurse said.

'Oh, dear . . . What a fuss,' I said. Then I remembered who she was: the nurse I'd worked with on my very first ward.

'It's Nurse O'Reilly, isn't it? Maggie?' I winced suddenly.

'Well remembered. Bad head?'

'Like a hundred Mosley marchers.'

She grinned. 'I've just the thing to banish those Black Shirt bullies.'

She handed me two aspirin and a glass of water, but no sooner had I swallowed them than I vomited them up again. I felt awful, I was making such as nuisance of myself. But Maggie was an angel and she set about cleaning me up without a word of complaint or irritation.

'A doctor will be along to see you first thing,' she said as she tucked the clean blanket over me. 'Try and get some sleep.'

But I couldn't sleep: my headache was extreme. I felt I was going to die, but then I told myself to pull myself together: if I was going to die, then the doctor would have to be disturbed from his bed. How I got through those next few hours I'll never know.

I felt even worse by the time the doctor did come. He was a good-looking chap, with a quick smile, neatly combed hair in a side parting, a thin Errol Flynn moustache and a gentle bedside manner. He studied my notes and asked me a few simple questions. He put his hands to my neck to feel my glands.

'Sore throat?'

I nodded softly.

'Headache bad?'

I nodded again.

'And you've been nauseous?'

'Yes, Doctor.'

'Unbutton your nightdress, please.'

I did as I was told. The doctor peered closer and smiled wryly.

'That's a beautiful rash, Nurse.'

I glanced down. He was right: there were red blotches all over my chest.

'Well, Nurse Elsworth,' he smiled. 'I believe you have scarlet fever.'

'But how ... ?' I started to say, but he had already turned to the ward sister.

'I'm afraid, Sister,' he said, 'she'll have to go into quarantine, along with the rest of the ward. Three weeks.'

I was stunned.

'But sir,' one woman piped up, 'I was due to be discharged today.'

'I'm sorry, madam,' the doctor said, 'but this is very contagious, and as a precaution I would insist that you stay until declared free from infection.'

The doctor marched out, to shocked silence. As soon as the ward doors closed after him, the women began to moan and curse and fret as one.

I shrank down lower in my bed, glad the screens were still up around me, as my mind puzzled over how I had contracted scarlet fever in the first place. Surely it was a misdiagnosis?

However, it was confirmed when the Assistant Matron came to visit me.

'Hello, Nurse Elsworth. How are we feeling?'

'Dreadful, Miss Ward. I feel so awful having caused so much—'

Miss Ward tut-tutted. 'No, Nurse, in yourself, I meant. You really mustn't blame yourself for the quarantine. These things happen.'

I tried to smile, but I knew how bitterly disappointed the patients in the ward were feeling.

'Now,' Miss Ward said, 'we are going to be transferring you to the Fever Hospital across the way, where you will remain for six weeks. Your personal belongings and anything of value will be kept in a safe place until your release. Your parents will be notified. But you mustn't worry. You'll be well cared for.'

The Fever Hospital. That was like a prison. I would be alone, unable to leave, unable to have visitors. Miss Ward left, and I slumped back in my pillow and began to weep in despair. How wretched I felt. I was supposed to be nursing, not being nursed.

The six weeks of my incarceration were tedious and seemingly endless. Yes, I had my books to study, and yes, I sent and received lots of letters – particularly from George, who was very sweet and concerned for my well-being – but I felt at such a loose end. The other patients were friendly enough, but I felt so different from them. Thankfully, after a few weeks of being bedridden, I was able to get up and about and put myself to good use, helping the nursing staff in any way I could. I think the ward sister was glad when the day came for my release.

Another shock was in store for me, though. I still wasn't allowed back into the main hospital, and was instead being sent home to Dovercourt for a further four weeks sick leave, under strict instructions to do no nursing whatsoever. They even gave me an escort to the station, a second-year trainee, to make sure I got on the train. Why Mac or Eddie wasn't allowed to escort me, I didn't know – perhaps Home Sister thought they'd lead me astray and we'd end up in a pub, celebrating my recovery!

Nurse Mitchell didn't stop talking for the entire bus journey from Homerton High Street to Liverpool Street Station. I was glad to hand my ticket in at the gate and climb aboard the train to finally get away from her arrogant and overbearing bragging.

As the train finally pulled away from the station and I settled down for the two-and-a-half-hour journey, I was amazed to think that since I'd started my training, I'd only been back home twice. I was actually quite excited, to be honest, summer being the best time to be in Dovercourt Bay.

I had bought a newspaper for the journey but once I opened it, I wished I hadn't bothered. It was full of news that Prime Minister Neville Chamberlain had publicly reaffirmed his support for Poland and declared Britain's promise to intervene if Germany threatened Polish sovereignty. With Hitler's troops massing on Poland's borders, things looked bleak. The editorial was in no doubt: war was coming.

12

The worst thing about being back home isn't my parents, who fuss and run around after me no matter how much I protest and assure them I am on the road to recovery, or the fact that it is high season and the town is busy. No, it is the rotten luck that George has recently been back from France for a brief visit, but is now overseas again. There is a letter from him waiting for me on the mantel – he knows I've been ill, and indeed came up to London to see me, but of course he was refused permission as I was still in isolation. Oh, how cruel Cupid is to us. I tear open the letter; even though it touches my heart, his feelings towards me are somehow lacking the sweetness I felt when we were together in person. I curse softly to myself. All I know for certain is that I am fed up with words. I want to see the man, to hold him, to touch his rough cheek, to feel his lips on mine once more.

July turned into August, the weather got hotter and the crowds got thicker. One afternoon Father and I sauntered down to the beach together. As I lay with the hot sand at my back and the sun blazing down upon my face, I just couldn't believe in all the talk of war.

'I'm frightened, Father,' I said, squinting up at him.

But, like a good many others, Father was optimistic. 'If we do go to war, Phyll, it can't last long. Six months at the most. No one really wants war, not even the Germans. Not after last time.'

He pulled himself to his feet and smiled down at me; but I could see the worry in his eyes. He'd fought in the Great War alongside Lawrence of Arabia, he'd faced the horrors of battle. I knew he was just trying to protect me, but I wished he would be honest with me.

'In any case,' he said, 'you shouldn't be worrying your pretty young head about this now. You're supposed to be recuperating, remember?'

I gave him my best smile and he nodded, satisfied.

'Good, now come along,' he said, 'I'll race you down to the sea.' He pushed me playfully and sped off.

I raced after him, my mind empty of worry for the time being.

Returning home, though, our happy mood soon darkened. Mother was sat at the kitchen table, an open letter in front of her. She was agitated and had clearly been crying.

'Violet?' Father said, dropping his bathing gear in the hall and rushing to her. He looked from her face down to the letter. He scanned it, then, 'There, there, dear,' he said soothingly. 'It's just precautions. Better to be safe than sorry. I should know, hey?'

I stepped into the kitchen and picked up the letter. It was on official government headed paper and just stated that all citizens were to be issued with gas masks.

What a horrible thought. Surely no one would be so callous as to drop poisonous gas on innocent victims? Of course Father had been gassed during the war, so he knew all about this kind of threat. He'd been lucky to escape: many of his friends had died a shocking death. He never really spoke of it, but if it was a damp, cold or foggy day, he'd cough for hours. He was silly to smoke, of course, but there was no telling him. 'I survived Johnny Turk's gas, I'll survive Mr Player's tobacco,' he would jest.

I reread the letter. 'It says at the bottom that residents in our area are to be issued with the masks at the Second Avenue Infants School from this afternoon. That's just around the corner, isn't it?'

'Come along, Violet,' Father said, helping Mother to her feet. 'Let's all go together.'

Mother never really got used to having to carry that little square box wherever she went, slung over her shoulder like a cheap bag. But she was even more devastated later that week, when we were all issued with an Anderson air-raid shelter to erect in the garden.

'What about my roses?' she said with a shake of her head.

Father gave her a winning smile. 'I'll move them to the front.'

'But I don't want them at the front. I want to see them from the kitchen window.'

I helped Father erect the thing. It was ghastly, just like a hot-air balloon sliced in half and sunk into the ground. Father placed two huge oildrums filled with earth at the entrance to act as a blast wall and, to appease Mother, planted some Sweet Williams in the tops of them.

When it was finally up, we stood back, tired, hot and grimy, to 'admire' our new addition to the home.

'An eyesore,' Mother said.

'Ghastly,' I said.

'Pug-ugly,' Father said.

And we all laughed.

Sunday, 27 August, the last day of my 'recuperation', arrived and with it a National Day of Prayer, called for by the Archbishop of Canterbury. We attended church but it was a very depressing service. Hope, it seemed, was running out. Then Mother and Father walked me to the station. Along the way I noticed that many of the pavements had now been painted with intermittent white squares, and that the road signs had been fitted with black cowls.

'It's all just precautionary, Phyll,' Father said with a cheery smile.

But I no longer subscribed to that way of thinking. Without doubt, we were expecting war. It was just a case of when.

Father slipped me some cash as usual, and I gave him and Mother a tremendous hug. They'd both been so wonderful.

'I shall miss you.'

I wondered when I'd get to see them again, and stayed at the window until they vanished from sight.

It was good to be back in London, but as with Dovercourt, everywhere I looked there were war preparations, only on a much larger scale. The taxis and buses had cowls fitted over their headlights now, and many buildings had sandbags piled up outside their entrances. And the servicemen! Everywhere I looked there were soldiers, sailors and airmen. Oh, how I worried about George.

Home Sister gave me a rather forced smile in greeting. 'Ah, Nurse Elsworth,' she said, 'back amongst the living.'

'Yes, Miss Lee.'

'Well, I hope you are fit and ready to return to duty?'

'Yes, Miss Lee.'

'Good. You are to report to Matron in the morning, then return to bed in readiness for duty on Monday night at eight-thirty. Female Outpatients.'

'Yes, Miss Lee.'

'And your room is now on the fifth floor. All the night nurses are on the upper levels. Here.' She handed me a few envelopes and my new door key.

'Thank you, Miss Lee.'

'That is all, Nurse. Good evening.'

I turned and left, clutching my post, seeking out a letter from

George. There was one. Inside was a photograph; how handsome he looked in his uniform. He confirmed he was overseas but obviously couldn't say exactly where, but promised that the first leave he got he would arrange to meet me in London. That made me feel so much better about our relationship.

My new room and all my belongings looked no different from when I'd left them – what?, nearly three months previously – only now the view out of my window was a little more panoramic. I could see over the hospital walls for the first time. I watched the traffic moving up and down Homerton High Street for a moment then, pinning George's photograph to the wall above my desk, began to unpack. I wanted to go and find Mac.

But she was nowhere to be found, and Eddie's room was locked. Disheartened, I decided to try the lounge. That was empty. Where was everybody? I checked my watch. The dining room too would be empty until teatime, so I decided to sit down at the piano and began to play Debussy's 'Claire de Lune'.

I don't know how long I was there for, but when I finished, I was startled by a polite, solitary round of applause. It was Matron. She must have been sat in the wing-back armchair facing the hearth, hidden from view. I felt terribly embarrassed.

'You play beautifully, Nurse ...?' she said, walking over to me.

'Elsworth, Matron,' I said, getting to my feet. 'I'm sorry if I disturbed you. I didn't realise there was anyone in here.'

'Not at all,' Matron said. A handsome woman with a good figure for her age, she was, I would guess, a little younger than my mother, perhaps in her late thirties. She had lightly curled brown hair, brown eyes and a soft, rounded face. 'Elsworth? Ah, yes. The scarlet fever case.' She smiled. 'You gave us quite a scare.'

'I'm sorry, Matron.'

'Don't be silly. These things happen,' she said. 'All good practice, you know. For the medical staff who looked after you.'

'I . . . Yes, Matron.'

'Tell me, do you think you'd be prepared to play for us – the
hospital, I mean – in our forthcoming concerts?'

I didn't hesitate. 'I'd love to, Matron.'

'It mustn't interfere with your studies, mind.'

'Not at all, Matron. I love to practise – in my own time. As you
can see, I'm not on duty at the moment, not until tomorrow
night.'

Matron nodded in satisfaction. 'Very well, I shall put your
name forward to the entertainments officer. So, I shall see you at
nine o'clock tomorrow morning in my office?'

'Yes, Matron.'

'Good evening, Nurse.'

'Good evening, Matron. And thank you.'

I waited until she'd left the lounge, then sat back down at the
piano. I paused, beamed with delight and played a quick little
ditty. Then I made my way to the dining hall, glad to see Sammy,
Moody and a few other familiar faces already there.

'Phyll!' Sammy said, running up to me. 'Boy, did you give us
a turn!'

'Yes, Matron just said something similar.'

'Matron?'

'She was in the lounge. Anyway, how is Hackney coping without me?'

We chatted and caught up with all the gossip. Mac, it turned
out, was on holiday, and Eddie was out with her boyfriend.

'Boyfriend? In the singular? Eddie?'

Sammy laughed. 'Yes, he's in the Medical Corps, wouldn't you
know it, but he's being posted to Hong Kong tomorrow.'

Oh, poor Eddie, I thought. At least George was only across the Channel, not on the other side of the world.

'How long's that been going on?' I asked.

'A couple of months. Hardly see her now. She's always off out with him.'

'Good for her. And Mac?'

'Mac's Mac, you know?' Sammy said.

After supper we decided to head out, but instead found ourselves drifting with many other nurses and medical staff towards the hospital chapel. We sat through the service, lost in our own thoughts about what the impending war might mean for us all. Afterwards we went for a walk in Victoria Park. It was a balmy night, the stars were out, and it was all just so peaceful. *War? Surely not*, I thought.

The next morning, back in my uniform, I arrived promptly at Matron's office. She smiled, but gone was the informality of the previous afternoon in the lounge.

'Nurse Elsworth,' she said. 'Now, despite your unfortunate illness, your ward schedule report has so far been satisfactory, with, I'm pleased to tell you, no complaints from the Sisters. Therefore your probationary period is up, and so . . .' she pulled a document from the tray on her desk and pushed it towards me, 'I've had your contract of nursing drawn up, along with a copy for your father to sign.'

I took the contract in my hands as if it were a priceless artefact. It stated that I agreed to complete three years of training, plus a fourth year as a staff nurse.

'When it is signed, Nurse Elsworth, it is binding,' Matron said. 'Only marriage can legally break it. Is that clear?'

'Crystal, Matron,' I said, barely able to conceal my delight. This was a momentous occasion.

Marriage? I thought. *Well, I can't see that being George, not with how things have been between us*, in that there'd hardly been any intimacy. I cared deeply for him, I always had and I always would, but in my heart I knew he wasn't 'the one'. I realised at that moment that there was nothing I wanted more in the world than to be a nurse, and only a nurse.

'Thank you, Matron,' I whispered.

My chest swelled with pride and I floated out of that office and back to my room. I was a nurse! A proper, bona fide nurse.

13

Sunday, 3 September. I come off night duty and emerge from the hospital block to a beautiful sunny morning, with not a cloud in the sky. The hospital authorities declared a few days ago that there is to be a mass evacuation of patients and staff, 'as a precaution', they assured us, to a leafy suburb of north London. Only a skeleton staff will remain at Hackney, but this doesn't include any trainee nurses. It is disturbing news without a doubt, yet this morning I feel strangely hopeful that peace will prevail after all.

Mac and Eddie were in the dining room already, and I sat down with them just as a plate of scrambled eggs and toast was put in front of me.

'Have you heard, Phyll?' Mac said, wiping her plate clean with a slice of buttered bread.

'Heard? No, what?'

'The Prime Minister is making some announcement at eleven this morning.'

I glanced at my fob watch. It was only a little after seven. 'Let's hope it's good news,' I said.

'You packed and ready?'

'Yes, finished yesterday afternoon,' I said between mouthfuls of egg. 'What time does the bus leave?'

'We're on the nine o'clock,' Eddie said.

'Good, time for a quick bath and maybe forty winks,' I said, taking a big bite of toast. 'Hang on, I'll come up with you.'

I was too excited to sleep, so I spent the time after bathing by writing to Mother and Father to tell them what was happening and that I'd be in touch as soon as we were settled in our new digs.

Three double-decker buses marked PRIVATE were waiting for us outside the main gates, and a queue of nursing staff was waiting to climb on board. Assistant Matron and Home Sister were there with clipboards, ticking everyone off.

'This is all really rather daft, isn't it?' Eddie said, joining Mac and me in the queue for the third bus.

I had to agree. Here we were, wondering what the Prime Minister was going to say, whether we would have peace or war, and we were about to go off on a bus excursion to the countryside! Some of the girls started to sing and it really did feel as if we were off on holiday.

We headed north, and busy London with its war preparations soon gave way to leafy suburbia. Within an hour, we had reached Woodford and were turning into the grounds of Claybury Asylum.

'Cor,' Mac said, sitting forward, 'will you look at this place!'

'Apparently,' Eddie said, pointing to the mid-Stuart part of the building, 'this was where the Merry Monarch "entertained" Nell Gwynne.'

The hospital was a grand manor house, built over three floors, with cut-stone windows, turrets and tall chimney stacks. The gardens were well maintained and were ablaze with colour against a background of evergreen bushes. What a contrast to Hackney Hospital, imposing and gloomy, more like something that would be used in a Bela Lugosi picture.

'Keep your voices down, girls,' Miss Lee said as we filed off the bus. 'This is primarily a place for epileptic patients, but there are to be two or three wings made up in readiness for war casualties.'

We had to walk past the psychiatric exercise garden, which had a high railing around it. I could see some patients walking in endless circles, while others sat on the ground or huddled in a corner, staring vacantly into space.

'Do you think they've taken a vow of silence?' Mac hissed, making Eddie giggle.

The entrance lobby was rather stunning, a large echoing chamber with wooden floors and a huge sweeping staircase. I gazed in awe at the walls, lined with portraits of forgotten dignitaries and landscapes of hunting scenes.

'Would you just look at this place,' Mac repeated, this time with a low whistle.

'Into the main hall, nurses. Quickly and quietly please,' Miss Lee said, her face looking rather drawn.

If we thought the lobby was impressive, then the hall was even more breathtaking.

'Would you—'

'Shut up, Mac,' Eddie said.

The grand room probably used to be a ballroom, judging by the large windows running along both walls and the opulent chandeliers hanging above. At the far end there was a platform, and here Matron sat with a few members of the senior staff, at a table on top of which was a wireless. Already there was a large gathering of doctors and porters in front of the platform, chatting amongst themselves. I glanced up to my left and spotted a large Victorian clock. It was close to 11 a.m.

Matron pushed her chair back and stepped to the edge of the platform. She raised her hand and the hall fell silent.

'Thank you,' Matron said. 'First of all, welcome to Claybury.

This shall be our hospital for the time being. Hopefully not for too long. But now I must ask you all to remain calm and quiet while we listen to an important announcement.' She nodded to one of her colleagues, who rose from his seat and turned the volume dial on the wireless.

There was an audible hush all around me and I swallowed hard as my heart began to race in my chest.

A hiss of static erupted from the wireless, then the chimes of Big Ben echoed through the hall. Eddie grabbed my hand and I turned and gave her a reassuring smile. Mac stepped closer and slipped her arm through mine.

From the wireless, the thin cool voice of Prime Minister Neville Chamberlain spoke:

'*This morning, the British Ambassador in Berlin handed the German government a final note, stating that unless the British government heard from them by eleven o'clock that they were prepared at once to withdraw their troops from Poland, a state of war would exist between us.*'

A sob of despair broke out somewhere behind me, followed by an angry snap of 'Hush!'

'*. . . I have to tell you now that no such undertaking has been received, and that consequently this country is at war with Germany.*'

Tears and cries broke out all around the hall. One maid screamed, a nurse fainted, a doctor began to sob. It was so shocking, the level of grief and disbelief that filled that room, each room in the country, my parents' kitchen at home. My mind seemed to go blank and, although I was aware of Eddie weeping next to me and Mac cursing and shaking her head in disbelief, I felt as if I wasn't in my own body, but watching from above. I didn't hear what else came from the wireless, but what did that matter now? War had been declared. Oh, dear God, what was to become of us?

Matron was still standing at the front of the platform. She looked rather ashen and had her hands raised once more.

'Please, calm yourselves.'

She waited until eventually she had everyone's attention.

'We must be brave. We must do our duty. But most of all we must remember who we are. We are British and we are strong. We are all members of this great nation and together we will get through this terrible, terrible calamity that has befallen us today. But, most of all we are members of the medical profession, and it is our calling and our duty to help those in need. And I feel that we shall soon be needed more than ever.'

She paused, and cast her eyes over us all.

'Now, after lunch those of you who haven't already been seen to will be taken to your various billets. Those who cannot be accommodated here at Claybury have been housed with private families in the area. I don't need to tell you this, but respect their homes and their hospitality. Rotas will be posted in the main entrance; duties proper will begin tomorrow morning. God save the King. Dismissed.'

Later that afternoon, having tried but failed miserably to eat, Eddie, Mac and I were directed to our billet. We were going to be staying in one of the private homes in the village, and it was a real stroke of luck that we were all placed under the same roof.

Woodford was a pretty, quiet little place, with a post office-cum-general store, a small café-cum-chip shop and an antique shop next door to what appeared to be a haberdashery. There was a telephone box on the village green by the shops, and then woodland. Our digs were along a leafy road that ran off the green.

'Little Woodford House. Here it is,' I said, stopping at an iron gate set between two clipped box hedges.

'Really?' Eddie said. 'Are you sure?'

'That's what it says on the chit,' I said.

'Golly,' Eddie gasped.

The house was little in name alone. It was a rather grand, double-fronted property set in ornate, well-kept gardens. A path ran from the iron entrance gate, through a line of cherry trees to a polished oak door with brass fittings. Ivy covered most of one side of the house, and rosebushes were planted in borders under the windows.

'What shall we say?' Mac said, looking about her uneasily.

'About what?' I said.

'Who we are?'

'We're not salesmen, Mac,' I said with a smile. 'This is where we've been billeted, so—'

The door opened and a maid blinked back at us. 'Can I 'elp you, ladies?'

'Yes, good-evening. We're from Claybury Asylum.'

'We're not escapees,' Mac blurted out.

'Mac!' I said, trying not to laugh.

'Sorry. We're part of the nursing team sent—'

'Oh, yes,' the maid said, stepping aside. 'Please come in. Mrs Mason is expecting you.'

'Thank you.'

I prodded Mac in the back and we stepped through the door. The maid led us to a living room and asked us to wait.

The room we found ourselves in was like nothing I'd ever seen before. It was like an Aladdin's cave, like an illustration from *Arabian Nights*. Every surface was covered with some *objet*, decoration or ornament. There were brasses Mother would die for, exotic pot plants of varieties I'd never seen before, as well as stuffed birds and mammals placed here and there. Richly coloured Persian rugs carpeted the floor, and the walls were covered with paintings of foreign landscapes and photographs of a beautiful woman in movie-star poses. In one corner there was an elaborately carved screen, which partially masked a bookcase bulging with dusty volumes.

The room had an intoxicating smell of spices and sweet tobacco. A lit cigarette was smouldering away in an ivory ashtray, which was perched on top of an elephant-leg stool. On a small card table next to the marble fireplace, above which hung an old hunting rifle, rested a gramophone player, records stacked haphazardly on the floor beneath it. Inviting, deep armchairs and sofas of leather and wood filled the room, most covered with bejewelled cushions and fabrics. But what made my eyes open widest of all was the grand piano which sat just within the slightly open French windows. Oh, how I wanted to sit there and play as I watched the birds and insects dance in the golden light of the early-evening sunshine that spread across the carefully tended lawns.

'Golly, Eddie gasped, 'it's like the Egyptian room at the V&A.' She tentatively reached out to touch a stuffed parrot. It squawked suddenly and she jumped back. Mac and I laughed as the bird began to chatter away, flapping its wings and strutting up and down on its perch.

As I turned to look at the piano once more, I saw a handsome, elderly woman standing in the doorway watching us. I pulled myself together quickly.

'Mac, Eddie,' I hissed.

The woman was very slim and tall, with her silver hair cut just above the neck in the old-fashioned way. She was wearing an elegant dress of black lace, with jewellery on her wrists, neck and fingers. Beneath subtle but meticulous make-up, her blue eyes sparkled back at the three of us with warmth. She stood there smiling, holding herself as if posing for one of the photographs behind her on the wall.

'Good evening, girls,' she said, her voice clipped and surprisingly deep and rich. 'My name is Mrs Mason. I see you are enjoying my boudoir.'

'Good evening, Mrs Mason,' I said. 'Yes, sorry. Eddie was startled by your parrot. It quite made us all jump.'

'What? Algernon? He's harmless, my dears,' Mrs Mason said, 'harmless.'

'I—' But no sooner had I started to speak than Eddie butted in.

'Excuse me, Mrs Mason, were you an actress?'

'Of sorts, my dear,' Mrs Mason beamed. 'I was a mannequin.' She then gave an elaborate flourish of her arm.

'A mannequin?' Mac all but laughed.

'A model, my dear. Fashion!'

'Golly!' Eddie gasped.

'Come, let me take you to your rooms, and after you've unpacked I'll show you my wardrobe.'

'Oh, super!' Eddie said.

Mrs Mason turned with a flourish and exited like a wisp of smoke on the wind, as if leaving the stage.

That night, after a pleasant evening sat listening to Mrs Mason's stories about the wild parties she used to attend in the 1920s, I settled down in the comfy bed I had been given in the attic. It must have been a nursery at one point, because there was the largest wooden doll's house I'd ever seen in the far corner, as well as an old rocking-horse, and a vast collection of dolls staring back at me from their place on the floor beneath the window. Mac was just down the hall, and Eddie next to her before the stairs. I wondered how my parents were and how they and sleepy Dovercourt Bay had taken the ominous news about being at war. Poor Mother, she would be worrying so, although they would soon get my letter telling them that I was safely out of the city. Perhaps I would write again in the morning and tell them all about Mrs Mason and our new digs, which were certainly a few classes up from the nurses' home. Just as I felt myself drifting off, a sudden shrill whining noise made me sit bolt-upright.

'Good God. An air raid!' I said aloud, fumbling for the light. 'Blast!' I cursed and switched it off again. I'd left my curtains open, and I'd be for it if an ARP warden happened to be passing.

I felt for my slippers and dressing gown in the dark, and then rushed along the hallway to Mac and Eddie's rooms. I banged on their doors.

'Mac! Eddie! Get up! An air raid! An air raid!'

Eddie burst out of her room, all in a fluster.

'Mac? Mac?' I opened her door to the sound of gurgled snoring. I rushed in, stubbed my toe on something, cursed and all but fell on to her bed.

'Mac! Get up!'

There was a groan and a sleepy 'Whaat . . . ?'

'An air raid! Can't you hear the bloody siren, girl?' I hissed, dragging her up.

The three of us tumbled down the stairs, to be greeted by the glow of a candle. Mrs Mason looked positively frightful, in a hairnet and her face covered in a mud pack.

'Come along, girls,' she barked, 'to the Anderson shelter.'

The housekeeper, a frumpy woman by the name of Molly, was waiting for us in the kitchen, a cowled lantern in one hand, a hot kettle in the other and blankets over her shoulder. We marched as quickly as we could to the other end of the garden, glancing nervously up at the cloudless sky. But I could see no lights, let alone hear any aeroplanes. Mrs Mason's shelter was built in the standard way, with the entrance masked by a wall of sandbags, but the inside was nothing like the basic simplicity of the one I'd helped my father construct in Dovercourt. There were soft furnishings of fine materials, a standard lamp with a frilled shade, a drinks service and even a Persian rug on the floor. It was like stepping into a gipsy caravan.

'Where's the crystal ball?' Mac whispered, setting Eddie off into a fit of giggles again.

Molly served us all hot tea, and we spent the next hour listening to another of Mrs Mason's society tales. At one point I could see Molly roll her eyes as she worked on some mending. I suppressed the urge to laugh, guessing that she'd heard these stories a million times over.

Soon afterwards, the all-clear sounded.

'Well, my dears,' Mrs Mason said, 'a false alarm, it would appear. Probably a wag at the town hall wanting to keep us on our feet! There'll be time enough to sit through the real thing. I remember the Zeppelin raids during the Great War. Horrid, horrid!' she exclaimed. 'But life shouldn't be taken too seriously, even in our darkest times. Humour will get us through. Remember that.'

14

L ife at Claybury soon settles into a routine. Our duties are rather tedious, with only a few patients to deal with, and all the while our studies have to continue. After all, the hospital exam is looming and, what with my illness, I am already quite a way behind the others.

Mac, Eddie and I would tune into the wireless every night to listen to the news from Europe; but it was like an endless overture, with no drama unfolding at all. Very soon we began to hope, even to believe, that it would all blow over.

'Like I said all along,' Mac announced rather sniffily, 'it's a load of hot air.'

'*You're* a load of hot air, Mac,' Eddie smirked.

Even Mrs Mason smiled at that. But then she was just as quick to put the wind up us again.

'My dears, the BBC can't tell us the truth, can it? After all, there are spies and saboteurs everywhere, no doubt listening in, ready to pass secrets back to Berlin. The war is coming to us all and these days may be the last real peace we shall know for … Heaven knows how long.'

Then one morning, less than a month since we'd arrived at

Claybury, it was announced out of the blue that we would be returning to Hackney.

'What did I tell you? It'll—' Mac said.

'It'll all be over by Christmas,' Eddie and I interrupted.

The journey back was somehow less exciting, and we sat in silence as the bus trundled along, all lost in our own thoughts, the words of Mrs Mason's warning of worse times to come echoing round my head.

A lot had changed by the time we returned to the East End. The roads were busy with traffic and people, as always, but everywhere one looked there were signs that we were at war. Servicemen, sandbags, blackout cowls, recruitment posters, warning posters, ARP wardens, and the skyline littered with huge barrage balloons, as if there was a giant children's birthday party being held all over the capital. But children themselves were noticeable by their absence. Many had been evacuated to the countryside and the streets were eerily empty. One poster that caught my eye showed a ghostly Hitler trying to entice a doubtful mum to take her kids back to the city, and advising: DON'T DO IT, MOTHER – LEAVE THE CHILDREN WHERE THEY ARE.

Back at Hackney Hospital, we settled down to our studies, with anatomy proving to be a particular stumbling-block for me.

'Do you know how many small bones there are in the human body to memorise?' I groaned to Mac. At times I felt so frustrated I wanted to scream.

But, as always, Mac would reassure me. 'After all,' she said, 'you're top of the class in physiology and hygiene.'

'What else could one expect from Etiquette Elsworth?' said Eddie.

Ah, the book Father had given me nearly a year previously. How time had flown.

*

Come November, having discarded my 'white coat' for a proper nurse's uniform, and proudly bearing a first-year's blue chevron on my sleeve, I began to feel much more confident in my work. In between nursing and studying, I flatly refused to go out with Mac and Eddie, heeding Miss Lee's words about knuckling down after my sick leave. However, it wasn't all work and no play: one day I was approached by the entertainments officer, a Dr Clark from Orthopaedics, eager to sign me up for the Christmas concert. I practically bit his hand off, I was so desperate for some light relief from my textbooks.

I wrote letters too, but from George, whom I had to write to via the War Office, I heard not a word. I was aware that he was doing his duty, so I accepted his silence, however reluctantly. I tried to put any thoughts I had for myself and my own silly little worries to one side: I was more concerned for Mother and Father's welfare, for all I had heard on the news of late was how the Essex coast was being fiercely attacked because of the importance of the docks and submarine stations to our Navy. I was full of dread, always waiting until the next letter from them. It was an awful worry, and I could read between the lines of their everyday news just how frightened Mother was.

'Well,' Mac said, 'there *is* a war on. Poor Eddie hasn't heard from her Bobby in an age, either. Tell me about this Christmas concert. What's the lark?'

'Lark?'

'Oh, come on, we'll have to do a skit or something,' she insisted.

'With you singing?' I raised an eyebrow.

'Why, of course, Phyll,' Mac grinned. 'It wouldn't be a show worth seeing unless I unleashed my magnificent voice for one and all.' She then broke into a few lines from *The Mikado*. 'Three little maids from school are we ...'

*

The next few weeks were rather taxing to my memory. All my free time was spent revising, or rehearsing for the concert, with the theme – remarkably, given Mac's earlier rendition – being a medical skit to the music of *The Mikado*. It was mainly doctors and male nurses taking part, but Mac was to take the lead in the spirituals, whilst Sammy and Moody would do some comedy sketches. Eddie offered to do a strip-tease, but was turned down flat by our director, Dr Johnny.

With the concert music constantly in my ears, and the words to such lively numbers as 'Alexander's Rag-Time Band' and 'Oh, Johnny, Oh, Johnny, Oh!' as well as the song that brought the house down (with even, it was rumoured, Miss Lee singing along), Kennedy and Carr's 'We're Going to Hang out the Washing on the Siegfried Line', I was finding it hard to concentrate on my studies.

Once Christmas was done and dusted, the day after Boxing Day saw us being transported to Middlesex Hospital to sit our hospital exam. Pass that and we would earn our 'square caps'.

It was awful. My stomach churned with nerves in the reception lounge as I fretted over what the questions would be. After what seemed like hours, my number was called and I was directed to the examination room.

I opened the door to find a cold, clinical office, with an elderly doctor sat behind a desk.

'Come along, Nurse. Take a seat.'

He nodded, glanced at his watch, made a quick note next to my number on the list in front of him, then fired off a series of questions on physiology. Only once did my mind seize up, but he allowed me time to think and I answered eventually. Then, before I knew it, fifteen minutes had passed and I was excused.

'Very good, Nurse. Off you trot,' he said with a warm smile.

Once again I was sitting in the reception area, but I felt a little more relaxed. The examiner had smiled. That was a good sign. Wasn't it?

Anatomy next, I told myself, and suddenly I found myself softly humming the tune of 'Dem Bones'. *The toe bone's connected to the foot bone, the foot bone's connected to the ...*

Mac! I could kill her. It was one of the spirituals she had sung in the concert. It was such a catchy tune, I just hoped I didn't start relating it to the examiner. I frowned and tried to clear my mind.

Now hear the word of the Lord!

Blast! I thought.

My number was called again, and this time the doctor testing me had eyes of steel that glared back at me as soon as I sat down in front of him.

Without a word of greeting he picked up a femur from a tray in front of him and thrust it under my nose.

'Tell me all you can about this,' he growled.

By the time the day was over, I was exhausted. My heart was racing and my head was splitting. For a moment I feared the scarlet fever had returned, and I pulled open the top of my dress, looking for signs of a rash on my chest.

The following day I had the written paper, but at least it was taken in our own lecture room at Hackney. Oh, how I hated exams. I just wanted to practise nursing. *Put me in a ward*, I thought, *and I'll show you what I'm capable of.*

A knock at the door roused me from my troubled slumber and I pulled myself wearily off the bed. I opened the door to see Mac's grinning round face.

'Hello, Phyll. Got a letter here for you,' she said, handing me an envelope. 'Looks like it's postmarked Harwich Town. Say, how did you get on? That doctor who took anatomy ... phew, what a horrid man he was. At one point I felt like shoving his tray of bones where the sun doesn't shine. "Tell me all you can about that!'" she added, doing a good imitation of the doctor's nasal voice.

I sat down at my desk-cum-dressing-table and tore open the letter. I read the words, then reread them just to make sure.

'Everything all right back home, Phyll?'

'Yes and no,' I said. 'It's from Father. He says they've been suffering such heavy bombardment at the docks and all along the Essex coast of late that his work is being transferred to London.'

'But that's good news, isn't it?'

'Yes, but poor Mother,' I said. 'It means they have to leave and let their house out to the War Office. For soldiers and sailors, I presume. Mother and Father are going to have to move in with my aunt and uncle on the outskirts of Sydenham.'

'Well, that makes it pretty easy for you to visit them on your days off.'

'Yes,' I nodded, 'I suppose it does.'

'Great! Then let's hope we get invited for tea.'

'We?'

'Of course. I couldn't possibly miss an opportunity to sample your mother's baking,' Mac grinned. 'They do have a kitchen, your aunt and uncle?'

PART THREE

1940

Daily Express
Monday, September 9, 1940

"Come then, let us to the task, to the battle
and the toil. Each to our part, each to our
station . . . Guard the streets, succour the
wounded, uplift the downcast, and honour
the brave. Let us go forward together."
– MR. CHURCHILL

BLITZ BOMBING OF LONDON
GOES ON ALL NIGHT

Two buses hit: Hospital
ringed by explosions

EAST END AGAIN: MORE FIRES

WHY BE GREY?

BLACK-OUT ZERO HOUR TO-NIGHT UNTIL 5.56 A.M. MOON RISES

ASTOL No. 12,573

Daily Express

Monday, September 9, 1940   One Penny

BOURNVILLE **COCOA**

"Come, then, let us to the task, to the battle and the toil. Each to our part, each to our station . . . Guard the streets, succour the wounded, uplift the downcast, and honour the brave. Let us go forward together."—MR. CHURCHILL.

BLITZ BOMBING OF LONDON GOES ON ALL NIGHT

Premier sees for himself

MR. CHURCHILL toured the East End of London late yesterday

Two buses hit: Hospital ringed by explosions

EAST END AGAIN : MORE FIRES

GOERING RESTARTED HIS GREAT BLITZKRIEG ON LONDON LAST NIGHT PROMPTLY AT BLACK-OUT TIME—ONE MINUTE TO EIGHT. HALF AN HOUR BEFORE THAT TIME HE MADE A GLOATING, BOASTING BROADCAST TO THE GERMAN PEOPLE.

"A terrific attack is going on against London," he said. "Adolf Hitler has entrusted me with the task of attacking the heart of the British Empire.

"From where I stand [presumably his headquarters] I can see waves of planes headed for England."

Six minutes after the news of his broadcast reached the Daily Express office the sirens howled the Alert.

Bombs began to fall almost immediately. High explosives. Screamers. Incendiaries.

German airmen, evidently using the smouldering fire of Saturday night's raid to guide them, made at first for the same targets—London's dockland. Later they dropped bombs indiscriminately in many parts of London.

While the work of succour went on among the wreckage of the little houses of the East End, while the people still searched the ruins of their homes, the Germans droned overhead, dropping more bombs, adding to the destruction.

The outer defences, blazing away at the raiders, were joined by the guns in inner London.

The noise was deafening. Bomb flashes and bursting shells made a pattern in the darkening sky.

London's fiercest gunfire

Three-quarters of an hour after the Alert a second wave of bombers circled the East London area. But they were fewer than came over on Saturday. The continuous barrage, from the coast to London, had held off the main forces.

For ten minutes there was silence. Not even the sound of all-engine.

Then, as new, London's guns roared again into the heaviest A.A. bombardment of the war. The raiders were back. The screaming of the bombs as they fell, the dull crumps as they exploded formed a frame of bursting shells at the intersections of a score of searchlights unleashed ten bombs on a London suburb.

One fell in a road of big houses where a King's French judge lives. Others fell near by.

Five screaming bombs dropped around a London hospital—the third in the London area damaged in two days.

➤ BACK PAGE, COL. FIVE

A.A. GUNS BAG 21 IN NIGHT

Daily Express Air Reporter

NO matter how inhuman the German air attack on Britain may become, a high authority is confident that our reserves of machines and men can stand up to it.

London's Saturday night raid was a setback for the R.A.F. bombing of Berlin: it delayed a thousand-for-the-sweest German blitz attempts to prepare to invade.

But it was not the biggest concentrated attack made on this country in the night raids but more than 200 machines. Enemy raiders were turned back or reached us in ones and twos.

Will get through

At night time many Germans will continue to get through. Civilians can be prepared for that. Enough A.A. guns abut with great accuracy of fire reports suggest ...

BLOW FOR BLOW

GREAT attacks by British bombers on Hitler's "invasion zone" in France and Belgium and on big armaments works in Germany—including Krupps—were announced last night.

Aircraft of the Bomber Command made a series of raids from dusk until nearly Saturday midnight on docks at Ostend, Calais, Dunkirk, and Boulogne.

8 bombs hit barge fleet

The OSTEND docks, in which a large number of Italian barges were concentrated, came in for the heaviest attacks.

In two hours of almost continual bombardment many tons of high-explosive were scattered. Several tankers, set alight, were seen from nine feet to make sure of hitting their targets.

Buildings adjoining Boulogne dock, and others used to shelter barges, were damaged. Another target flung into the air from the harbour was a moored barge.

THE COCKNEYS ARE IN IT

Homes shattered—but not their hearts

Daily Express Staff Reporter HILDE MARCHANT

THE civilian population is taking its batterings well.

Through the East End yesterday there trekked a ragged, sleepless army whose homes had been smashed through the night.

They pushed perambulators, carts, or took the best of their homes on their backs, climbing through streets that had once been two neat rows of houses and were yesterday like a dimpled field.

The very toll under their houses had been ripped open, scattered with brick and tile across their path.

Little homes, four rooms and a bath tub, eight shillings a week, had taken but attack.

All through the night they welter in their anthem while bombs clapped into the houses and streets around them. At daylight they came up and many saw the ruin of their homes turned to the sky.

Great troop convoy beats Duce

Daily Express Staff Reporter ALAN MOOREHEAD
CAIRO, Sunday

FOR two days I have been watching a British convoy arriving with the largest reinforcements we have had here since the war began. It is the good news we have been waiting for and the answer to No. 1 question about the future of the Middle East war.

THE TREK

They dusted and shook with the loss of wives, children, money and belongings. The elderly did not grumble....

GUNS WITH THEM

This convoy makes a difference in the situation now; it has brought more ...

HOW TO GET TO WORK

EVERYTHING possible is being done to help you get to work today, despite week-end week-end damage to railways.

Marked improvement in the affected services was reported by the London Transport late last night.

Plane down to 80 ft.

The exploits of this German aircraft have, after its machine was hit, it dropped and turned to dive on an anti-aircraft position and crew, its engines silent, three machine-guns blazing.

Soldiers manned a Bofors gun, aimed it point-blank range and as he neared the gun and swooped to about 80 feet the guns roared.

Revenge at Dunkirk

At DUNKIRK the assault was up to the Medic of English big bombs, and then broke. Our aircraft and fighters had been concentrated on the docks by the return of barges.

One searchlight which was particularly prominent was put out of action.

A simultaneous raid, but not so heavy, was on the docks at Boulogne.

Big fires in forests

WHILE these attacks were going on, forces of heavy bombers were hitting targets in Germany. A big fire was caused in one forest, believed to be ammunition, and a fire at Krefeld started in the dock area at Hamburg.

At attack on the docks at Emden, the broad bore slopes through Hamburg. Other bursts apparently took the Germans by surprise.

DOCKS CARRY ON

Food losses small

Historical but slight hit aid effected at the Port of London Authority: "While damage to fire at docks is considerable, the sheds and loading berths are intact, and all services of the port will be maintained."

Though some warehouses have been burned, the board of handling of goods is quite normal.

A Dock District traffic inspector said, "We have cleared the damage of military..."

36 French planes join Britain at Gibraltar

A message from Algeciras received in one Vine last night said that eighty-five French warships have joined forces with the British near Gibraltar.

Fire in U.S. destroyer intended for Britain

BOSTON, Sunday.—Fire broke out in the destroyer Mackenzie, one of American vessels to Britain, Fire was confined to one cabin.

Why did they ring the bells?

IN south-west and north-east England, in Wales, and Scotland church bells—warned of attempted invasion—rang out on Saturday.

Officials were trying to find out yesterday why they were rung.—EXPRESS PAGE SIX.

HOSPITAL ATTACK

I fall down flat with doctors—and we all escape

Daily Express Staff Reporter NORMAN SMART

WHILE I was in an East London hospital last night it was bombed by German airplanes. Along with doctors, porters and members of the hospital A.R.P. squad, I flung myself flat on the clear floor of the casualty hall as three bombs, with unearthly melody, crashed into the hospital grounds.

I went to the hospital to inquire ...

NURSES' HOME

I was learning about these bodies and had been told that the old nurses' home was being used as a casualty station. But the report was not true ...

Transfusion given by light of candles

People hurt in Saturday night's raids were being given transfusion in the light of candles and wireless sets late last night.

A Cray nurse, Ruth, explained several times to me how the staff carried on despite a raid, the lighting system.

Lady Borden dead

OTTAWA, Sunday.—Lady Borden, widow of Canada's first War Premier, Sir Robert Borden, died to-day in Ottawa. She was seventy-seven years old.

STOP PRESS

LONDON BOMBED FOR 8½ HOURS

Bombs were still dropping on London eight and a half hours after last midnight.

Raid was of even greater intensity than that of Saturday night.

Several new fires were started. Others already ranging. It was the longest London bombardment yet experienced.

It was the longest London bombardment yet experienced.

Throughout the afternoon, and spent a considerable time talking to people made homeless by Hitler's bombs and inspecting the damage.

➤ BACK PAGE, COLUMN ONE

COLD FACT

A cold chilly body is not only the easiest target for winter complaints, it is the surest prey to depression and discouragement. The first duty of every good housewife should be to keep the family warm this winter. Not by relying on outward heat—but by providing the sturdy inner warmth that comes from wearing soft, light wool underwear.

While other great firms are producing guns and shells to protect our shores, it falls to our lot at Wolsey to defend men and women from the cold, up to the limit which rationing permits. Experience has taught us how to make the most of limited stocks of wool. We have eliminated all out-moded styles—and are concentrating only on those which are most practical, good-looking and efficient. And we shall do everything in our power to keep prices down.

We have faced wars before at Wolsey—more than a hundred years of them. And we have never failed to supply the nation with vital warmth yet. We shall try not to do so now.

WOLSEY MUNITIONS FOR WARMTH: Underwear for men. Underwear for women (MAYFAIR): CARDINAL SOCKS and pullovers. ELDERSKIN silk stockings. Wolsey, Leicester.

Iron Guards fire on fleeing Carol

Ex-King Carol of Rumania arrived at Lugano, Switzerland, late last night. He was fleeing to exile with his mistress, Magda Lupescu, and his son, Michael. His train was fired on by his own Iron Guards as it crossed into Switzerland.

15

As 1940 marches on, so does Hitler. In Europe the German war machine seems unstoppable. The Phoney War is finished once and for all as Denmark and Norway, both neutral, fall to the might of the jackboot. Neville Chamberlain, now derided as the great appeaser, finds his position untenable: having lost the respect of Parliament, with shouts of 'Go! Go! Go!' ringing in his ears, he heads off to Buckingham Palace to resign. Lord Halifax, the Foreign Secretary and favourite of many politicians, as well as the King, has politely excused himself, and therefore it is Winston Churchill who is summoned to the Palace on 10 May and asked to form the next government.

Mac, Eddie and I huddled around the wireless, listening to Churchill's first speech, and wondered just what would happen next.

'Father believes he's exactly what the country needs,' I said.

'I don't know, Phyll,' Eddie said. 'He's a bit ... garrulous, don't you think?'

'Garrulous? What's that? A tropical disease?' Mac said.

'Hush!' I said, adjusting the dial against a sudden hiss of static.

'*... I have nothing to offer,*' Churchill was saying, '*but blood, toil, tears and sweat.*'

'Hear, hear!' Mac shouted. 'Because, Mr Churchill, sir, that's bloody well all us nurses have to offer too!'

I switched off the wireless and we returned to our duties on the wards.

'Have you heard?' one of the porters said as he wheeled in the lunch trolley.

'No?'

'France. Bloody Jerry's only gone and pushed past the Maginot Line.'

My thoughts went straight to George. It had been a while since I'd heard from him, and he never did get to see me on his last leave as it coincided with my posting to Claybury. He'd had barely enough time to visit his own parents in Dovercourt before returning to France. And now the Germans were there too.

But by the end of May the small Allied counter-attack had done only enough to delay Hitler's advance, though at least British and French troops had time to evacuate Dunkirk. It was truly stirring, listening to the wireless and reading the newspaper reports about how countless citizens risked their lives and livelihoods by crossing the Channel and helping to bring back our boys in whatever they could make float, from rowing boats and pleasure yachts to trawlers and tugs. I prayed that George was safe among them. Although he was in the RAF, he was only ground crew, and I doubted he would get a place on an aeroplane.

Later that evening, as had become routine, we gathered in the lounge to listen to the nightly news and to the BBC announcer as he read out sections of what the PM had said that very afternoon. Parts of Churchill's latest speech were stirring, undoubtedly, but on the whole it left us all rather depressed and forlorn.

"' . . . Even though large tracts of Europe and many old and famous states have fallen or may fall into the grip of the Gestapo and all the odious apparatus of Nazi rule, we shall not flag or fail. We shall go on to the end."

'Mr Churchill then went on to say:

"'We shall fight in France, we shall fight on the seas and oceans, we shall fight with growing confidence and growing strength in the air, we shall defend our island, whatever the cost may be. We shall fight on the beaches, we shall fight on the landing grounds, we shall fight in the fields and in the streets, we shall fight in the hills; we shall never surrender."

'There was a mixed reaction in the House,' said the BBC announcer, *'with many members sitting in silence, while others, notably on the Labour benches, were in tears. Mr Churchill then ended his speech thus,*

"' . . . and if, which I do not for a moment believe, this island or a large part of it were subjugated and starving, then our empire beyond the seas, armed and guarded by the British fleet, would carry on the struggle, until in God's good time, the New World, with all its power and might, steps forth to the rescue and the liberation of the old."

'In other news, the War Office has—'

The radio was abruptly switched off.

'My, that was rather grave?' one of the junior doctors sat by the fire said, as he got to his feet.

'Well, if that was supposed to cheer us up, it failed miserably,' another said.

Later on in June, to round off a disastrous series of events, the dreadful news came through that Paris had fallen. Britain was alone.

'Surely it's just a matter of time now,' Eddie said, voicing the thoughts of many, that the Germans would be knocking on our door any day now.

'Come on, old girl,' I said softly, 'chin up.'

'Now I'll never get to Paris,' Eddie sobbed. 'Beastly Germans.'

'One day, Eddie,' I said, 'one day it will be free again. You'll see. Then perhaps Bobby will take you.'

'Balls to Bobby,' Eddie said angrily. 'Bugger's gone and left me for a bloody Wren.'

'What a coward,' Mac said. She handed Eddie a handkerchief. 'Or do I mean cad? Hey, let's go for a pick-me-up at the Adam and Eve. What do you say?'

Eddie sniffed and smiled as she dabbed at her tears. 'But I must look so ghastly.'

'You could never look ghastly, Eddie,' I said.

But now that she was single again Eddie had no end of suitors vying to take her dancing, which rapidly cheered her up. Mac seemed happy enough with her own love life, not that she ever talked about it, and was soon off on holiday to 'visit a cousin', she told us rather mysteriously, in Aberystwyth.

As for my own romance, I still wasn't sure that I had one; or, for that matter, if I ever really had one at all. I hadn't heard a peep from George, neither had his parents, and all our enquiries to the War Office remained unanswered. I did what I could to lose myself in work, all the while keeping one ear out for news of events across the Channel, and the other for the dreaded air-raid sirens. They had been silent ever since that false alarm back at Mrs Mason's house in Woodford, but the threat of invasion was on everyone's lips, especially following the terrifying news on the first day of July that the Channel Islands had been invaded. The Germans were finally on British soil. Just nine days later the skies darkened, and the Battle of Britain began.

Much of the early conflict took place over the Channel, and what news we got was, as always, from huddling around the wireless or from the Pathé newsreels at the picture house. As it was reported, our boys were giving Hitler's Luftwaffe a bloody nose daily. My ears pricked up to hear that a Messerschmitt had been shot down over Harwich; how glad I was that my parents were in Sydenham now. Scotland came under attack, as did Wearside, Norfolk and Kent, but not London. But for how long?

A few days later I had the night off, the first evening to myself in over two months. I was struggling to concentrate on the notes from the previous week's lectures when there was a knock and Eddie popped her smiling face around the door.

'What ho, Phyll,' she grinned. 'Fancy coming out tonight?'

'No thanks, Eddie. I'm a little pooped.'

'Oh, come on old girl,' she said. She was wearing a quite stunning figure-hugging double-breasted tea gown in pale pink.

'Wow! Eddie,' I said.

'Thanks awfully.' She shrugged as nonchalantly as ever about her remarkable wardrobe. 'Please do come out. I've a date, you see.'

'Then you won't want me as a gooseberry,' I said.

'But that's just the thing – *I'm* the gooseberry.'

'What do you mean?'

'Tim – that's my new chap – well, he's got a pal and he's gone and invited him. Asked if I knew anyone who fancied making up a foursome. Oh, do say yes, Phyll.' Eddie grabbed my hand, blinking her blue eyes coyly back at me. 'I'm sure he's a dish.'

'What about George?' I said, feeling guilty at the very thought of going out with another man.

'Balls to George, Phyll,' Eddie scoffed. 'He doesn't deserve a girl like you. Besides, when did you last hear from him?' She jumped up and pulled open my wardrobe. 'Now, let's see what you should wear ...'

Eddie not only knew how to dress up, but how to cheer me up too. I felt so much better as we sat on the bus heading into town. It was getting dark and the ARP wardens were already out and about. How strange it was to be at Piccadilly Circus, with all the advertising hoardings still showing signs of normality with their huge adverts for Bovril, Wrigley's and Schweppes, and, of course, the 'Guinness is good for you' clock.

'Oh, Eddie,' I said, looking around me, 'how I wish the black-out would end and we could see them lit up again.'

'I'll light 'em up for you, darlin',' a sailor said with a saucy whistle as he and his two colleagues passed by.

'Need any company tonight?' another said, stopping short.

'No we don't,' Eddie sniffed, grabbing my arm. 'We have dates, thank you very much.'

'Ooh, la-di-da,' the sailor said.

Eddie giggled as we pushed through the busy evening crowds and headed towards Coventry Street.

'You are a one, Eddie,' I said, glancing back over my shoulder.

'Come along, Phyll,' Eddie said, 'we'll be late.'

The Lyons Corner House was as grand as it had been the last time I was there, with its wonderful Art Deco style a tonic to my eyes. We made our way through the food hall, to the restaurants upstairs.

'Where are we meeting?' I asked.

'In the Brasserie.'

Here there were more tables covered with white cloths, attended by uniformed waiters and waitresses. Elegant lamps hung down from the ceiling, casting a cool light over everything, and there was a band in the corner.

Eddie was craning her neck, trying to see her boyfriend, when I spotted a soldier waving to us.

'There, Eddie,' I said.

We weaved our way through the tables and as we approached a sergeant and a corporal rose to greet us.

Eddie gave her boyfriend, the sergeant, a quick kiss.

'Phyll, this is Tim,' she said.

Tim held his hand out. 'Pleased to meet you,' he said. 'This is my friend and colleague, Corporal Alistair Ross. He's with me in the RASC.'

'RASC?' I said, raising an eyebrow as I turned to greet the handsome man with a head of neatly combed, slicked-back fair hair.

'Royal Army Service Corps, miss,' Alistair said.

'You don't look like taxi drivers,' I said, keeping a straight face. 'And please call me Phyll.'

'Sit down, please,' Tim said, pulling a chair out for Eddie.

As I removed my coat, Alistair followed Tim's example by pulling my chair out for me. *What a gentleman*, I thought.

'We do a little more than transport, miss – I mean Phyll,' Alistair said.

'That's correct,' Tim added. 'We're responsible for the supply of food, water, fuel . . . that sort of thing.'

'I see.'

'Faithful in adversity, that's us.' Alistair said.

'Hear, hear!' Tim said.

A waitress approached and with a warm smile asked if we were ready to order.

Alistair scooped up the menu and, with a flourish, opened it up and passed it to me.

'Now, ladies, what shall we have?' Tim said. 'I'm afraid Alistair and I are on duty later tonight, so no alcohol for us. But you can have a drink if you like.'

'I have studies to do,' I said. 'So I think I shall have coffee.'

'And cake,' Alistair chipped in. 'You must always have cake with coffee, it's the law.'

'Admirable choice. Cake and coffee for four please,' Tim said to the waitress.

'Now, tell me, what news from the front,' Tim said.

'Front?'

'Hospital. The medical battleground. I hear you have a dragon?'

I had to admit that Alistair was very charming and attentive, and funny too. But I found my mind wandering at times to George. I couldn't help but feel awkward and a touch guilty about being out with another man. How I wished I would just hear from him.

When our cake was put in front of us, I picked up my fork and out of the corner of my eye I saw Alistair pick up his piece with his hand and take a huge bite. I glanced about at the nearby tables and hoped no one else had noticed.

'Whatever's the matter, Phyll?' Eddie said, a frown of concern on her face.

'I . . . nothing. Nothing at all.' I smiled back sweetly and continued to eat my cake.

Afterwards, we decided to pop into a news theatre. It was rousing stuff and we sat there captivated by the images of Churchill on walkabout, and of our RAF boys repulsing the waves of German fighters and bombers. It really did look like we had held off any invasion. I half expected to see George wave at the camera when the images showed ground crew at one airfield. Then the news turned to the invasion of the Channel Islands.

Alistair leaned in close. 'I'll take you there one day,' he whispered.

I turned to stare back at him.

'To the Channel Islands,' he explained, totally misreading my reaction. 'To Guernsey. It's a beautiful place.'

He sat back in his seat and I watched the flicker of the projector reflected on his face for a moment.

My, but he's a fast worker, I thought. *How presumptuous of him. Whatever makes him think that we'll be an item at all? I do hope Eddie hasn't given the wrong impression of me.*

'Eddie,' I hissed into her ear.

'Yes?'

'What did you tell Alistair about me?'

'Nothing. Why?'

'He wants to take me to Guernsey!'

Eddie giggled. 'How sweet.'

'But Eddie, what about George?' I whispered back.

'Oh, Phyll, forget George. Don't you think Alistair is handsome?'

'Yes ... But ...'

'But what, Phyll?'

I hesitated. 'He eats cake with his hands!'

At this Eddie burst out laughing, which made the audience hiss at us to be quiet.

'Oh, Phyll,' Eddie sniggered. 'Etiquette Elsworth will be the death of me!'

16

August draws to an end and the RAF continue to valiantly repulse the waves of Nazi planes. More cities, though, come under attack at night, as well as airfields in Kent, Surrey and even Croydon. The German bombers are getting closer to London. And on the night of 5–6 September, Thames Haven is set ablaze.

My three months' night duty had finally finished, and to my delight my next ward was to be Casualty. With air raids expected at any moment, it was necessary to be detailed with an individual responsibility, and mine was the setting up of sterile trolleys, ready for use by the medical team for any casualties requiring immediate treatment.

Barely had I hung up my cloak in my new ward when the siren sounded. I felt the colour drain from my face.

Please be a false alarm, I prayed, glancing at my watch. It was 4.56 p.m.

The Sister clapped her hands for attention. 'Those detailed with specific tasks, now is the time. Those—'

The doors to the department crashed open, cutting her short. Two ambulance men rushed in, carrying a moaning, writhing young woman who was well into labour. I immediately forgot the air raid and set about helping them escort her to one of the examination rooms.

The ambulance men lifted her gently from the stretcher and onto the bed, and then quickly exited again.

'We'll get her to a ward right away, Nurse,' Sister said. 'Just hold on.'

She disappeared again and I was just getting the poor woman as comfortable as could be when I heard something from outside the blackout windows. It was like a rushing whistle, as if a distant train was rapidly approaching.

'What's that?' the woman gasped between contractions.

'I don—'

A thundering explosion suddenly shook the hospital. The expectant mother screamed, and I threw myself over her just as a second explosion rocked the room, shattering the windows. Glass and light debris fell around us and pattered across my back. I held myself over the trembling, hysterical woman until I was sure that it was over. Coughing and waving away the cloud of choking dust, I quickly patted the mother down, checking that she wasn't cut or injured in any way.

'There, what a mess!' I said, surprised at how calm my voice was.

The woman's eyes were wide with shock as she coughed and blinked back at me, tears streaming down her cheeks. 'Are ... we ... d-dead?' she trembled.

'Don't be daft, madam,' I said. 'You've got a baby to deliver. You can't be dead.'

She blurted out a bark of laughter, then began to sob.

'Let's get you to the ward,' I said gently.

Two porters rushed in with a trolley, their faces white with shock. But they calmly lifted the woman on to the trolley.

She held her hand out to me and I briefly clasped it with my own.

'Thank you, Nurse,' she said, and was rushed away.

I brushed myself down, picked pieces of plaster and glass from my hair, amazed that I wasn't cut, and slowly crunched my way over to the shattered window.

Across the road, the Adam and Eve was ablaze and the buildings either side reduced to piles of flaming rubble. The sky above was alight with ack-ack fire and sweeping searchlights, and I could hear the heavy drone of distant aircraft.

The bombing seemed to be on the other side of London now, so how we'd been hit I didn't know. Perhaps it was a stray aircraft?

Suddenly the department doors burst open, and I turned to see a young man stagger in. He couldn't have been much older than I was, but he was covered from head to toe in grey dust. He looked like a ghost.

'My eyes! My eyes!' he screamed, holding his hands up to his face.

I stood gawping, frozen to the spot for a moment. Then the doors crashed open again and more and more men and women, ordinary civilians of all ages, dishevelled, cut, bleeding, bruised, nursing head-wounds, holding broken limbs, crying and moaning, followed. I pulled myself together, grabbed hold of the first young man and helped him to a seat. Blood was oozing from a deep cut in his hairline. More ambulance men arrived with stretchers bearing the injured.

'Got a shrapnel wound 'ere,' one of them said.

'This one's lost a leg,' another stated grimly.

The doctors rushed around directing who should receive care first, who needed to go to the theatre and who to the morgue. I realised that many of the people coming in on stretchers were already dead or on the point of dying.

The department soon became a stinking, stifling, claustro-phobic place and the smell of burnt flesh, of sweat and fear, of blood and bodily excretions, all coated in choking dust, was over-powering. Gagging, I had to breathe through my mouth as I worked, ignoring the cacophony of curses, sobs and moans, and the cries of despair as the rumble and shudder of nearby explo-sions continued.

I moved from one patient to another, cleaning up cuts, cutting away hair and applying temporary dressings to the deeper wounds. A lot of the time I was holding a hand, comforting those too far gone to help. Blood transfusions were needed con-stantly, and at one point a terrific *crump* shook the floor under my feet, followed by an enormous thud that made the wall shud-der. All the lights went out and people screamed. But as quick as striking a match, candles were lit and torches turned on, and we worked on, in the kind of conditions my heroine Florence Nightingale must have had to endure. And all the while I could feel the acid build in my stomach and the anger swell in my chest.

How can this be? I thought. *How could this be allowed to happen?*

After about an hour, the relentless crack and thump of the raid stopped. Was that it? The end of the world?

The all-clear sounded.

I checked my watch: 5.59 p.m. There followed a moment's silence and then the distant clang of sirens.

'Please, please ...'

Another young man with a deep wound on his cheek was pulling at my sleeve. I narrowed my eyes and was about to exam-ine his injury when he waved me off.

'I'm all right, Nurse,' he gasped. 'It's nothing. But my wife – she's not moving ...'

He led me over to the next cubicle, where a young woman was lying as if crucified on a broken and charred door. She had clearly been thrown against the door in a blast, and all but her underclothes had been blown off.

'The amb – ambulance men brought her in,' the young man said, his voice wavering with emotion, 'on the door. We were in the pub, you see.'

A doctor pushed past me and leaned over the woman. He examined the back of her head tenderly and felt her pulse. He hesitated, then turned and looked at me gravely with a soft shake of his head.

'Oh God,' the man sobbed. 'Don't tell me she's dead.'

'I'm sorry,' the doctor said, and moved on to the next cubicle.

It was so heartbreaking to see the young man touching his dead wife's bare feet, his body shaking with uncontrollable grief. I put my hands to his shoulders and just held him like that for a moment, not saying a word. What could one say?

'Let me, Nurse.'

I looked up to see a WVS worker in her distinctive grey dress with its breast badge of cream and red step forward. She gave a gentle smile and quietly and calmly led the sobbing man away.

It was awful, but the scene was repeated so many times throughout the course of the evening, and all one could do was get on with it. We patched up and saved those we could. Eventually the injured stopped coming and we were left with clearing up the department, which now resembled a battlefield more than a hospital ward. I began to automatically go through the process of resterilising and setting up the trolleys for the next shift.

'You go and get some rest now, Nurse,' said the ward sister, taking the instruments from my shaking hands.

As I walked wearily across the forecourt back to the nurses' home, glass and debris crunching under my feet, the first rays of dawn were lighting up the sky. I hesitated, confused, and looked at my watch. It wasn't dawn; it was still evening, a little after 7.30 p.m. The sky was red and flickering all about me.

London was on fire. Pillars of smoke were rising into the pulsating red and orange sky. Beyond the main gate I could see that the pavements were covered with glass blown from windows by a bomb that had torn a huge cavity in the centre of the road. Two buses, their sides smashed in by the force of a blast, were standing abandoned at the side of the road.

Everywhere I looked, nurses were helping to sweep up the mess. I wanted to join them, but I could barely stand, I was dead on my feet.

Just a few minutes lying down, I thought. *Just a few. Then I'll come back and help.*

I reached the haven of my room and collapsed, exhausted, on my bed. There was a soft knock at the door and I opened my eyes to see Mac pop her head in.

'Brought you a cup of tea, Phy—' She was staring at me, a look of utter shock on her face.

'What?' I said, glancing down at my apron. It was smeared with blood.

I'd been so caught up in caring for the injured that I hadn't noticed the state of my uniform. I peered at my face in the wardrobe mirror. It was caked in dust, streaked with sweat and spattered with blood. I looked like something from a horror film. I began to shake, and then to laugh.

A sudden sharp smack hit me across the cheek and, stunned, I put my hand to my face. I looked up at Mac, bewildered, then burst into tears.

'Oh, Phyll,' Mac said, taking me in her arms and holding me tight. 'It's over now. It's over now,' she said, rocking me gently.

I sat there, feeling safe in my dear friend's embrace, as I cried my heart out.

Then the air-raid warning sounded again.

After that, despite my stomach doing a flip each and every time the siren sounded, I remained calm on the outside and kept my emotions in check. It was hard, so hard, but that's what I had to be, that's what we all had to be: hardened to the horror, hardened to death. That breakdown after my first stint in Casualty was the last time I let my feelings show to anyone. If I felt the need, I would take myself off and weep silently into my pillow, thank God that I was still alive to help others, and ask Him to protect us all and end this foul war.

The lighting system that suffered during the raid was quickly repaired. Apparently, a huge piece of granite had been thrown against the wall, affecting the circuits. However, it would be quite a while before the glass was replaced in the windows.

It was incredible to think that so many bombs had fallen that night yet none had hit the hospital and not one member of the medical team had been seriously injured.

All about us, though, the effects of the German bombs were devastating. Walking down to the High Street was like picking your way through a builders' yard, only a builders' yard where ARP workers and troops were busy digging amongst the rubble, sticking bravely to their grim task of bringing out the dead and injured.

One day I saw an Army lorry pull up by the main gate. Two doctors whom I recognised from the entertainments committee jumped up into the back. *Whatever are they doing?* I thought. Then I realised. *Oh, of course, they're certifying the dead.* It was a common sight for many months to come, living as we were with a time bomb, wondering if each day was to be our last.

'A penny for them, Phyll?'

I turned away from the window to see Eddie's pretty face smiling back at me.

'Oh, nothing,' I said, 'just thinking on all this . . . destruction. How are you?'

'Very well. Things are going swimmingly with Tim. But . . .' She hesitated, and I detected a hint of sadness in her face. 'Fancy a cup of tea?' she said.

I checked my watch. It was already well into my morning break. We linked arms and made our way to the dining hall.

'Everything is all right between you and Tim, isn't it?' I said.

'Smashing. It's just this damned war,' she said. 'It's such a nuisance.'

'That's one way of putting it,' I scoffed.

'You know what I mean, Phyll,' Eddie said. 'How's a girl supposed to have a proper love life if they keep sending our men away?'

'Has he been posted then?'

Eddie shook her head. 'Sent away on manoeuvres. To Yorkshire.'

'Well, that's better than Europe,' I said.

'I know. It's just such a bother!' she said. 'But at least he has his pals.'

'How is Alistair?' I said, more out of politeness than curiosity.

Eddie stopped. 'I say, Phyll, do you like him then?'

'Not at all.'

'You *do*!' Eddie said, sensing my awkwardness. 'I'll let Tim know next time I write.'

'You dare!' I said.

'Dare what?' Mac said, appearing from around the corner.

'Phyll has taken a shine to Tim's friend Alistair,' Eddie said.

'I have not,' I insisted. 'I'm with George, as you well know.'

'And just when was the last time you heard from George?' Mac said.

'I . . .' But I couldn't say. They both knew already it had been an age.

'Listen, Phyll,' said Mac, her face serious. 'Isn't it time you moved on? I mean to say, he could be . . . you know? I mean, I fear for his . . . fate.'

'Mac!' I said. 'How could you?'

Mac shrugged. 'I'm sorry, but it's true. There's a war on. He's in the services. And he's gone AWOL. From you, I mean.'

Eddie nodded her head. 'That's very true, Phyll.'

I stared back at both of them for a moment, then turned on my heel and stormed off.

'Phyll? Phyll?' Eddie shouted after me, but I ignored her and headed back to the ward.

How could they be so insensitive? They knew how I fretted about George, that even his parents had had no word from him in months. Yes, of course, he could be dead, I realised that. But to be so cold about it . . . They were supposed to be my friends. Bloody Eddie and her boyfriends. I wished I'd never agreed to go on that damned double date now.

Sod them, I thought, *and sod tea*. 'And sod bloody Alistair,' I muttered aloud.

'Nurse Elsworth? Nurse Elsworth?'

It was the casualty sister.

Now what? I thought.

'I'm sorry, but you're on emergency ambulance.'

'But Sister, I'm supposed—'

'Don't argue with me, Nurse,' the sister snapped. 'We are overwhelmed with the last air raid and I need all the junior staff to assist with minor call-outs.'

'Where—'

'Just grab your cloak and get to the ambulance station. Move!'

I hurried to fetch my cloak, then made my way to the emergency entrance where three ambulance men were sitting smoking. They were wearing their distinctive navy serge tunics and trousers, with white satin satchels across the shoulder and hard hats with the letter 'A' painted on in white.

'About blooming time,' one said, tossing his cigarette end aside. He scowled back at me and then jumped up into the driver's cab.

'Charming,' I muttered.

The second ambulance man opened up the back. 'Come on, Nurse,' he said, but with a friendly tone.

The ambulance was little more than a converted box van with the word 'AMBULANCE' daubed on the front and rear, and 'LCC AMBULANCE' on the sides. There was a drop-down step to the rear, with double doors that opened up to reveal two benches, under which were stored stretchers, a first-aid kit and a metal receiver tray. The engine coughed into life, and the third ambulance man ran round to the front passenger seat. I climbed into the back and as the second ambulance man jumped in with me, he pulled the door to. We shot off and I was thrown back hard on to the bench seat. The ambulance was uncomfortable and noisy and shook like a rattle.

'Where are we going?' I said, rubbing my elbow.

'The Marshes. Threatened miscarriage.'

'Couldn't she get to the hospital?'

The ambulance man shrugged. 'One of the mites was sent to fetch the ambulance. Said his ma's bleedin' all over the kitchen.'

There was a sudden screech of brakes and a blast of the horn as the ambulance swerved left and right. I could hear muffled curses coming from the cab.

'I'm Tom,' the ambulance man said, holding out his hand for me to shake.

'Phyll,' I said.

'Other bloke's Frankie,' Tom said. 'Driver, well ...' He paused and shrugged. 'Don't mind Jack. His house got flattened last night.'

A few uncomfortable minutes later, the ambulance shuddered to a halt in a bleak and festering street of terrace houses. There were quite a few people about, craning their necks to see what we were up to. Outside the house we'd pulled up next to, a number of grubby children were shouting and jumping in excitement.

'This way!'

'Cor, a nurse!'

'Put yer siren on, mista!'

'Here it is, mista!'

Jack the driver stayed where he was, while Tom and Frankie grabbed a stretcher from the back of the ambulance, and followed me. The house itself was a filthy, grimy slum, with ragged net curtains at the windows. There were more children inside, snotty-nosed tykes with dirty faces, all hollering at the top of their voices.

'Da? Da?' one shouted. ''Ospital men's 'ere!'

A door swung open to reveal a big burly fellow in shirtsleeves.

'What kept ya?' he said gruffly. 'She's in 'ere.' He stepped aside to let me and the stretcher party through.

The kitchen was hardly bigger than an outside privy. It was hot, claustrophobic and filthy and smelled of rancid cooking fat and burnt toast. There was a kettle on the stove, boiling away to steam, and in the middle of the floor, hair bedraggled, cigarette dangling from her mouth, sat the pasty-faced mother. She was probably only in her thirties, but looked much older.

Wincing up at me through a trail of tobacco smoke, she suddenly dropped her cigarette. ''Urry and get me up off a this bleedin' bucket.'

'I'm going to have to take a look first,' I said, with as reassuring a smile as I could muster.

She nodded nervously and hitched her apron up above her thighs. There was blood everywhere. The poor woman had aborted in the bucket. I could see that the umbilical cord was still attached, and it was clear that the placenta was still in her womb, too. We needed to get her to the hospital, fast.

My God, this is horrific, I thought, as my mind raced through all the relevant information I'd learned over the past two years.

'Da? Da?' one of the children screeched. 'What's that nurse doin' 'ere with the funny 'at on? What's she doin' wiv our ma?'

'Shut up, Billy. Let the woman work,' the husband barked.

The only instruments I had with me were artery forceps, so I clamped the cord, carefully cut the end and then gently placed the tiny foetus in the metal receiver. I wiped my bloodstained hands on my apron and stood up.

'Right,' I said, surprised at how authoritative and calm my voice sounded. 'Frankie, Tom, get her on the stretcher as gently and quickly as you can. Mrs ... ?' I raised an eyebrow at the woman.

'Mrs nothing, ducks. Call me Agnes,' the woman said. 'Is it ... ?'

'I'm afraid so, Agnes,' I said.

As Frankie and Tom helped her up, I grabbed the cleanest towel I could see and placed it under her on the stretcher.

'I didn't want the bloody kid,' Agnes said, her voice quivering. 'I kept jumpin' off the bloody table to get rid of it ... I didn't want it, miss,' she sobbed. 'Got enough bleedin' kids to feed. Rations are stretched as it is ... Bloody man.'

We laid her down and I put my hand on her forehead. 'It'll be all right,' I said. 'We're off to Hackney now.'

She nodded weakly, then Frankie and Tom carried her out.

Outside, the neighbours had crowded round for a better gawp, and I had to push them aside as the men carefully loaded Agnes into the back of the ambulance. Tom jumped in with me, quickly followed by the husband, who turned and bellowed out to the kids, 'Tell Mrs Pike next door to fix yer tea. I'll be 'ome w—'

Frankie slammed the back doors shut, Jack started the engine, and with a crunch of gears and a clang of the siren we sped off.

I covered Agnes in blankets and reached for her pulse. It was weak, but steady.

She blinked up at me, tears in her eyes. 'I didn't want the bloody kid, miss,' she said through choked sobs.

'Just keep calm, Agnes,' I said, patting her hand.

''Ere, miss?' the husband said, pulling at my sleeve.

'Yes, sir?'

'What d'you want doing with this?' He held up the bucket that his poor wife had been sitting on.

The ambulance made good time back to Casualty, and Agnes was quickly rushed to theatre.

''Ere, Nurse,' the husband said to me as he stood looking rather lost in reception. 'She'll be all right? I nevers meant 'er no 'arm. We love our kids.'

'I'm sure you do, sir,' I said, looking up at Agnes's husband. He was a gruff fellow, but I could tell by the concern in his voice that he cared for his wife.

'She'll be fine,' I said. 'When women lose a baby it's normal to sedate them, ready for theatre and a D.C. op.'

'Eh?'

'Just an operation to fix her up again,' I said. 'She'll be right as rain soon enough.'

He nodded briskly. 'I'll just sit and wait . . . if I may.'

'Can I get you anything?'

'Cuppa be right fine, miss,' he said with a sniff.

'It's Nurse Elsworth, sir.'

'Nurse Elsworth,' he nodded back. 'Call me Bert.'

Later that afternoon, exhausted and emotionally drained, I made my way to the dining hall for a good cup of cocoa and automatically sat down with Eddie and Sammy.

'Still mad at me, Phyll?' Eddie asked rather pensively. 'I'm sorry if I upset you.'

I frowned back at her, then suddenly it clicked. I'd forgotten my falling out with her and Mac over George and Alistair, such was my hectic ambulance trip. I shook my head and gave her a smile.

'Forget about it. I have.'

It was true, I had. And I'd told myself before that it was nigh on impossible to fall out with Mac for too long. Even Eddie, I knew, had her heart in the right place. Some man's place usually, I scoffed. So, any damage done is soon repaired.

'Look what I've got,' Mac said as she rushed into the dining room the next afternoon. She was brandishing what looked like bus tickets in her hand.

'A full house?' I smirked.

'No, three passes signed by Matron.'

'Who for?' I said.

'Us, silly,' Mac said.

'For what, though, Mac?' Eddie said.

Mac slumped down in the seat next to me, jolting my elbow and spilling tea across the table.

'The Mayoral Ball next month.'

'Ball? Really?' Eddie's face lit up like a child's at Christmas. 'Oh, how super.'

'Why?' I said with a touch of doubt. 'What's the catch?'

'No catch,' Mac said. 'Matron can't attend and I just happened to be passing when she was bemoaning the fact to the Dragon.'

'So you volunteered?'

'I most certainly did!'

'But why you? Why us?' I said. 'We're not model nurses by a long chalk.'

'Ho, ho. That's where you're wrong, Phyll.' Mac beamed. 'You are.'

'What?'

'It's true. Well, your piano-playing is. I sort of told a white lie.'

'Meaning ... ?' I was beginning to feel more than a little irritated with Mac's mysterious behaviour.

'Meaning the Mayor is musical. You are musical. And Matron needs funds for the Christmas concert.'

'I don't get it.'

'Butter him up, silly,' Eddie said.

'Oh, you don't mean ...'

'No, Phyll!' Mac said, getting what I was thinking. 'That's more Eddie's department,' she smirked. 'No, he's a sweet old man. Matron just wants you to talk music, say how much you love playing and what grand plans we have for entertaining patients and medical staff.'

I put my hand to my mouth to stifle an embarrassed laugh. 'I see. Well, that's all right then I suppose.'

'Whoopee,' Eddie clapped. Then her face dropped. 'But I haven't a thing to wear!'

Mac and I rolled our eyes at each other.

'Eddie,' I said, 'I'd wager that you have more dresses than the rest of us nurses put together.'

17

When the night of the ball arrives, I am not enthusiastic as I gaze critically at myself in the mirror. Although my hair, falling to my shoulders in ringlets, looks quite becoming, I am not so sure about the pale pink satin dress I am wearing. It isn't Dior by any means, but I have trimmed the sweetheart neckline with swansdown. I check my seams are straight, place a diamanté necklace around my throat and then smile.

'You'll do, Phyll,' I said to myself.

It turned out that six of us had been given the task of representing Matron that evening: myself, Mac, Sammy and Eddie, who looked absolutely breathtaking in her cream crepe evening dress, and male nurses John and Bill to act as our chaperons. They both looked very smart in their three-piece suits and trilby hats.

We checked our torches then set off into the cold, dark night. A chill breeze rustled the dying leaves in the trees, and the atmosphere felt strangely sinister, with nothing visible but the slit headlights of the passing buses and taxis and the red glow from Bill and John's cigarettes.

Huddling together, we followed the kerb carefully with our torches. If the dreaded air-raid warning sounded, heaven only knew where we would run to. But since the night was moonless perhaps we would be spared any enemy activity. We tramped on in a silence broken only by the odd curse from passers-by bumping into one another.

'Knew I should've worn me white 'at,' Bill joked after one collision.

Having only been completed in 1937, the town hall was a rather conventional yet impressive Art Deco building of four storeys faced with Portland stone.

'Gosh, Phyll,' Mac said, 'I hope the Nazis don't bomb this place. Isn't it grand!'

We climbed the wide stone steps to the main doors, pushed through the blackout curtains and emerged into a brightly lit entrance hall abuzz with conversation and soft laughter. Everywhere my gaze fell I saw smartly dressed people, the women in ball gowns of fine materials and subtle colours, the men in smart black tie or dress uniforms. The air was heady with intoxicating perfumes and colognes. I was glad Mac had put us forward to Matron now.

'Come along, girls,' Sammy said, 'let's go to the powder room and repair the damage the wind has done to our hair.'

'Ready to meet the Mayor?' Bill said as we emerged.

I grinned at Mac as we were swept up the gracefully curved staircase, past huge arched windows to the vast assembly hall. Outside the triple doors of the entrance, a number of dignitaries, including the Mayor himself, were greeting each person in turn. I felt like royalty as we filed in.

My breath caught in my throat. My eyes were dazzled by the beautiful décor and the imposing chandeliers. The walls were bedecked with the flags of the Allied countries, and there were balloons to add to the party look. Smartly dressed waitresses drifted through the crowds, trays of drinks and canapés on their upturned hands. Chairs and tables were placed around the edge of the hall, and there was a twelve-piece orchestra on a stage at the far end. The air was full of beautiful swing music and already a few couples were whirling across the highly polished floor. I couldn't wait to get out there.

'Here we go, girls,' Bill said, handing us all a glass of champagne.

'Crikey,' Eddie gasped, taking a sip, 'this is the real stuff. You'd never know there was a war on!'

'Well, they're hardly going to be serving lemonade, are they?' Mac said.

'Chin, chin!' John said, clinking his glass with ours.

'God bless the Free French!' we toasted.

''Ere, 'ere, we're in trouble now,' John said, nudging Bill.

A familiar diminutive figure in a dashing red Mess-Dress jacket was making his way towards us.

'Isn't that—?' Eddie started to say.

I nodded. 'Yes, the sergeant-major who took us for air-raid drill. Gregory, I think his name was.'

Sergeant-Major Gregory marched up to us and stiffly nodded his head.

'Gents, ladies,' he said rather gruffly.

'Sarnt-Major,' John replied.

'Why, Sergeant-Major, fancy seeing you here! We don't have to throw ourselves down the stairs, do we?' Eddie smirked. 'Not in these dresses?'

Sergeant-Major Gregory pursed his lips and brushed his bristle moustache. 'Er . . . no, miss. Not tonight.' He cleared his throat. 'I was wondering if . . . ' He glanced towards the dance floor.

'Are you asking me for a dance?' Eddie teased, pressing her hand to her chest in mock-surprise. 'Well, I must—'

'Er . . . no, miss,' the sergeant-major interrupted. 'Not you.'

Eddie was stunned into silence as Sergeant-Major Gregory

turned to face Mac head on. Well, chest on, I should say: she rather towered over him.

He held out his hand in invitation. 'Would you care to dance, Nurse MacKenzie?'

'Well I never!' Eddie gasped.

John and Bill were shaking with barely controlled laughter, and I put my hand to my mouth to stifle a smirk. Mac turned her gaze upon me and opened her eyes wide, her face struggling not to break into a huge grin.

'Go on,' I hissed.

'I'd be honoured, Sergeant,' Mac said, taking his hand.

'Sergeant-Major, miss,' Gregory said, leading her off to the dance floor.

'Good ol' Mac,' Bill smirked.

'And I thought he liked me!' Eddie said.

I laughed.

Suddenly the music changed and I recognised the tune. It was 'In the Mood'.

'Wow, that's Joe Loss,' Eddie said.

'Where?'

'The band.' Eddie jerked her chin over to end of the hall. 'It's the Joe Loss Orchestra.'

'Come on, John, you'll do,' I said and grabbed him by the hand. I'd be damned if I was going to let myself miss out on a dance tonight.

'Steady on, Phyll!' he said, as I pulled him towards the dance floor. He knocked back his champagne and dumped his glass on a passing waitress's tray.

Dancing to me was like being on top of the world, and the joy and exhilaration of swishing around in a quickstep made the adrenalin flow through me like an electric current. Oh, it was such a relief to feel free from the constraints of the hospital and the worries of the war. Eddie, Sammy and Bill had joined us, and soon we were all sliding across that dance floor in gay abandon. I was in my element, grinning from ear to ear. Many couples collided with each other, but it didn't matter, such was the exhilaration felt by all, and we just laughed it off with a happy apology.

And so we danced, on and on. John couldn't keep up with me, and he soon bowed out. I don't think dancing was really his thing, and he and Bill were more than happy to go and stand by the bar drinking and goggling at the other girls.

'Any girl but a nurse,' they would joke. 'They're too much trouble!'

But it wasn't long before some serviceman took my hand and spun me around the dance floor.

Joe and his orchestra went through all the classics, including 'the tango, 'Ladies Excuse-me', 'In the Mood' and 'The Lambeth Walk', which was a strange one to dance to.

Mac and the sergeant-major were locked together through most of the numbers, and even though she was a good foot taller and wider than the little NCO, he couldn't half move.

After the interval, Joe and his orchestra started up again, and this time it was more for a sing-along, as they played popular melodies like 'Run, Rabbit Run' and 'We're Going to Hang Out the Washing on the Siegfried Line' to get everyone going.

'Here,' John piped up, pointing towards the orchestra, 'what's Bill doing? Asking for requests?'

'Looks that way,' I said, watching as Bill approached Joe Loss.

They both laughed as if sharing some joke, and Loss waved his baton to attract the attention of a senior military dignitary. The officer walked over and Loss and Bill had a brief conversation with him. Bill bowed slightly and shook the dignitary's hand, patted Loss on the back as if he were an old pal, and jumped off the stage again to weave his way back to us.

'Whatever are you up to, Bill?' I said.

'You'll see,' he grinned, winking at John.

I was about to press him further when the orchestra struck up the 'Colonel Bogey March'.

'Bill! You never!' I said, realising what he'd done.

'However did you do that?' John said.

Bill just shrugged. 'Old Joe was keen, and that General fellow just harrumphed and then laughed and said, "Good for morale."'

And that was it. Two bars in, and the entire hall had broken into a full-gusto rendition of 'Hitler Has Only Got One Ball . . .'

I could barely get the words out as I was in stitches, laughing at Mac, who was singing at the top of her voice whenever the rude words came along. It was as exhilarating as the dancing had been.

The song ended and the ballroom positively exploded with applause.

The Mayor stepped on to the stage and held up his hand for silence.

'Ladies and gentlemen, I would just like to say a heartfelt thank you to Joe Loss and his Orchestra for—'

Applause and whistles drowned him out for a moment.

'Thank you,' the Mayor said. 'But I want to also say how proud I am, how proud Hackney is, how proud London and indeed the whole country is, of all our boys overseas. To those of you in this room, to the soldiers, sailors and airmen, to the nurses and doctors, the policemen, firemen, ARP wardens, to all those in our community, in our society, who are striving, with their lives in many cases, to keep our land free from the tyranny of that silly little man with only one—'

'Ball!' a number of people shouted, saving the Mayor from having to repeat the risqué lyrics.

'Bravo!'

'Hear, hear!'

'God save the King!'

'God bless England!'

The voices were suddenly drowned out by the interruption of the air-raid sirens. An icy feeling descended over my whole body. *Please, not again*, I thought.

But fear is not the same as panic, and every man and woman in that hall remained calm.

'To the shelters, as quickly and as orderly as you can,' shouted the Mayor above the continuing wail of the siren.

'Down to the cellars, if you please. Quickly and calmly does it,' a town official said, waving people down the stairway. 'Down to the cellars, thank you, ladies and gentlemen.'

The musty atmosphere of the cellars is a stark contrast to the grand hall up above, and I note with a snort that there are no chandeliers down here, only basic wall lights to put any illumination into the gloom. Not that there's much to see. It's a vast brick cellar, empty save for a stack of tea chests in the far corner and a few hard benches up against the walls. The waitresses from upstairs had swapped their trays for blankets and were going around handing them out to the now sullen and mostly silent party guests.

'Well, this is a fine way to end a fine evening,' Eddie moaned, looking at the damp stone floor beneath her feet, searching for a relatively clean spot to sit on.

'I wonder if this is where the Man in the Iron Mask lives?' Bill said in a feeble attempt to lighten the mood.

'How long do you think we'll be here?' Eddie said as I sat myself down next to her and Sammy.

'Hours.'

Then there came a distant droning, followed by the thump-thump of the ack-ack guns.

'Here we go a-blooming-gain,' John spat, holding his head in his hands.

'We'll be for it now,' Mac said.

'No, these walls look pretty solid to me,' I said.

'Not the air raid. Matron,' Mac said. 'We're supposed to be back at midnight.'

I glanced at my wristwatch. It was gone eleven already. 'Well, she can hardly blame us for the air raid.'

Mac raised her eyebrows, but didn't comment. She didn't have to.

'So,' I said, 'you and the sergeant-major . . .'

Mac smiled coyly. 'He's really rather sweet.' She leaned forward and lowered her voice. 'His name's Gregory.'

'I know,' I whispered back.

'No,' Mac said, 'his Christian name.'

'What,' I smiled, 'Gregory Gregory?'

'Yes. He's asked me on a date.'

'That's smashing, Mac.'

'Do you think he's too old?'

I patted her arm. 'Do *you* think he's too old?'

She shook her head.

'Well, there you go. If he's right for you, he's right for me.'

'Thanks, Phyll.'

A fitful few hours followed, in which I think a few hangovers kicked in. Every now and again the ground shuddered and rumbled with distant explosions. Dust fell from the ceiling in spurts and one nearby explosion shook the very foundations of the building. A couple of the men tried to get everyone going with a sing-song, but the party spirit had flagged. Even Joe Loss and his orchestra didn't join in, barely making the effort to talk to one another.

*

I gave a sudden start as the all-clear sounded. I stretched my stiff limbs and rubbed my eyes. I must have nodded off: my mouth tasted stale and I had a hollow feeling in my stomach.

I shook Mac awake and she grunted irritably back.

'Come on, Mac, let's get home. I need a cup of tea.'

Mac said her goodbyes to Sergeant-Major Gregory and then we tramped, bleary-eyed, back upstairs, collected our coats and hats, and prepared to shuffle our weary way back to the hospital.

'Sweet Jesus,' Bill said, as we emerged back outside.

All around there was nothing but destruction and devastation, with fires raging and many buildings, if they were standing at all, nothing but blackened shells. The road was now just a carpet of rubble criss-crossed by fire hoses.

It was as bright as day, too, the sky red with flame. The air was thick with smoke and the stench of burning wood, and worse. Sirens clanged in the distance and we could hear shouts from the firemen who were hosing down a particular raging blaze near by.

An ARP warden approached, his face black with soot. 'Where're you off to?' he said.

'The hospital. We're all staff,' Bill said.

'Aye, aye, your lot'll be busy now, I'd wager,' the warden said.

'How bad?' John said.

'Nazi bastards all but flattened the docks. An' the Ol' Kent Road's taken a right beatin'.'

'Crumbs, it's a quarter to four,' I interrupted. 'Perhaps we should have tried to get back when the siren sounded?'

I was really worried about the kind of trouble we faced now. By the time we got back to the hospital, we would be four hours past curfew.

'Don't be daft, girl,' Bill said. 'Look at the place! We'd have copped it.'

He was right, but it didn't make me feel any better as we

picked our way through the debris. The blazing fires cast strange shadows across the street, eerily lighting up the bombed-out buildings which looked like the ragged teeth of a giant corpse. It was so sad. We turned our torches on and concentrated on the road ahead, searching for the white kerbs to lead us back.

'Turn those bloody lights out!' a gruff voice hollered from the gloom.

'Crikey,' Eddie hissed. 'Best play follow-the-leader and hold hands. Who's up front?'

'I am,' I said.

I turned my torch back on, felt Mac put her hand on my shoulder, and set off once more.

It was 4.30 a.m. when we finally reported back to Night Sister's office, cold, hungry, tired, thirsty and completely dishevelled. We must have looked like six street urchins. But far from being relieved that we were all unharmed, Sister threw a fit.

'Report to Matron's office nine a.m. sharp!' she barked.

'What time are you on duty, Phyll?' Mac said.

'Eight,' I groaned.

'Hardly any point going to bed,' Eddie said.

'A few hours is better than no hours,' I said. 'I need my pillow.'

'Matron's all right, isn't she?' Mac asked as we waited outside her office a few hours later.

'Once we explain, she'll understand,' I said.

I couldn't have been more wrong.

'I don't care,' Matron said. 'As soon as the siren sounded, you should have all returned to the hospital.'

'But that's unreasonable, Matron,' I said, getting more and more angry at the injustice. 'We attended the ball on your behalf, and we were caught by an air raid. It would have been foolish to risk our lives trying to get back.'

Matron's face turned a rather disturbing shade of pink and her top lip began to quiver ever so slightly.

'There are men and women risking their lives for far more important things than getting your ball gowns dirty in the dark,' she fumed.

'I—'

'Enough, Nurse Elsworth!' Matron snapped, taking a step towards me. 'You were all back after curfew and there can be no excuses. You will all lose your passes for two weeks. Off you go,' she said with a wave of her hand, 'back to your wards.'

'Matron, we attended that wretched ball on—'

But Mac yanked me back and hustled me out of the office.

'What the hell did you do that for?' I snapped.

'I think we've done enough damage to our records, Phyll,' Mac said. 'You were about to say something you'd regret later.'

'Regret?' I spat. 'I'm not a little schoolgirl, none of us are. How dare she—'

'Hush!' Mac said, pulling me further away from Matron's door. 'That's an end to it.'

I stood still, my chest heaving. Slowly my anger began to subside.

'Blast the woman!' I finally said.

'That's the spirit, Phyll,' Bill chuckled.

'You can shut up,' I snapped again. 'You and John just jump the gate anyhow, pass or no pass.'

Bill shrugged. 'So? Nobody's stopping you doing the same.'

'In these shoes?' I said, and stormed off.

PART FOUR

1941

Daily Mirror
Saturday, April 12, 1941

R.A.F. BATTER PANZERS
"HELL DIVES" ON HUN TANKS

TURKS ORDER MARTIAL LAW
BATTLE STARTS NEAR TOBRUK
YOUR MILK IS CUT TOMORROW

DON'T BLAME THE
SHOPKEEPER
How the Grocer is helping
to win the war

DAILY MIRROR, Saturday, April 12, 1941.

Daily Mirror

APL 12

No. 11,546   ONE PENNY

Registered at the G.P.O. as a Newspaper.

Blitzkey and Soda

R.A.F. BATTER PANZERS

GERMAN Panzer troops suffered severe losses when low-flying British warplanes made terrific onslaught before the Nazis captured Monastir, Yugoslavia. This was officially announced last night.

Many tanks and armoured vehicles were destroyed.

The R.A.F. is hitting hard — and everywhere—in the Balkans. It is inspiring the Greeks and Slavs to fight back even more heroically.

Latest R.A.F. attacks—on the Panzers—was made in bad weather, but the results were good.

British troops in Greece are today engaging German forces on the Greek side of the Monastir Gap. First news of their contact with German forces was given yesterday.

They fought in skirmishes. But the big battles have yet to come.

Last night they had new incentive — a new leader, General Sir Henry Maitland Wilson, the tactician who plotted our victories over Mussolini's desert armies.

FOUND MATCH— 3 SAVED

ONE of four men, stranded in the lifeless, waterless wastes of the Libyan desert, found a match, lit a fire that saved his life and led to the rescue of two of his comrades.

This, one of the most moving dramas of the war, was disclosed by an officer of the Middle East Command he was bomb last night.

The men were Trooper Ronald Moore, D.C.M., of Hailsham, England; Guardsman John Easton, of Edinburgh; Guardsman Alexander Winchester, of Glasgow, and Private Alfred Tighe, of Manchester.

Wounded—Game

Members of the famous mobile "long-range patrol," they were returning from a 700-mile raid into enemy territory when an enemy force aided by planes attacked the patrol.

In a sharp fight the British commander was captured, and, after inflicting considerable damage, the second-in-command withdrew the rest of his men, leaving behind the four men, whom he believed to have been destroyed with their trucks.

They had managed to scatter hills. Moore had a shell splinter in one foot, Easton had a bullet wound in the throat, and Tighe was suffering from a deeper internal injury.

They had no food and only two gallons of water.

This was their choice—"hike" eighty miles to the nearest Italian post and surrender; face almost certain death by attempting to walk 200 miles to freedom. They chose the latter.

Led by Moore they began their incredible march on February 1.

On the third day they found a tin, put of pipes, here dropped off one of the trucks on the journey northward. They ate the whole of it that day.

Tighe became very tired, and on the fifth day eventually persuaded his comrades to leave him behind.

Tighe managed to struggle on, and by nightfall the march had reached a hut by nightfall.

He found one match in the sand.

Continued on Back Page Col. 6

TURKS ORDER MARTIAL LAW

MARTIAL law in the chief districts of Turkish Thrace, as well as Istanbul and Izmit, was proclaimed yesterday.

Everyone not liable to military service is being evacuated from Istanbul, and facilities were to be provided for the inhabitants of a large part of European Turkey.

The Turkish radio said that the evacuation was a precautionary measure "directed against no one."

Von Papen, Nazi Ambassador is said to have assured the Turkish Foreign Minister that Germany had no aggressive intentions against Turkey, and would not, for the time being, put troops on the Turco-Greek frontier.—British United Press. Associated Press. Reuter.

Two of the boys who took part in the great raid over Berlin. The spirit of the R.A.F. is shown in that "sparkling" design—and from reports, the raid was a real "Blitzkey and Soda" visit !

BATTLE STARTS NEAR TOBRUK

NEWS that a battle near Tobruk may be expected was given in a War Office communique last night. It stated:—

Libya: Our troops are in contact with the enemy west of Tobruk.

Eritrea: Our advance southwards on the two main roads has been somewhat slowed up by blocks which are now being cleared. Total prisoners captured from the start at present operations in Eritrea until the capture of Massawa number 41,000, of which 1,000 are Italian officers, 14,000 Italian other ranks and 26,000 colonial troops.

Abyssinia: While our advance into Southern Abyssinia from Italian Somaliland is developing, columns operating from Addis Ababa continue to press the retreating enemy. At Addis Ababa prisoners taken number 5,000, of which 4,000 are Italians.

Armies Line Up in Libya.—Page 5.

YOUR MILK IS CUT TOMORROW

SO that more cheese and condensed milk can be made, the Ministry of Food has made an order restricting milk sales to six-sevenths of the quantities sold in the week beginning March 3 and which comes into force tomorrow.

"HELL DIVES" ON HUN TANKS

BRITISH warplanes, defying sleet, rain and snow, "hell-dived" German Panzer columns attacking Monastir. Their wing-tips appeared at times to scrape the rocky sides of the ravines.

Vivid picture of this and other R.A.F. exploits was given in last night's Middle East communique and news agency messages as General Simovitch, Yugoslav Prime Minister, broadcast a defiant speech from headquarters somewhere in Yugoslavia.

"Our troops are already concentrating on the main battle lines to check the enemy's advance." he said.

"Germany's early successes cannot discourage us. Though present situation is difficult I believe justice of our cause, bravery of our army, the help of our powerful allies and the firm morale of our people will assure us of victory."

German waterland units have pierced the famous Monastir Gap, entering the Florina region of Greece, where they have clashed with Greek troops.

The Middle East communique describing the R.A.F. raids said:

"In bad weather conditions aircraft of the R.A.F. operated throughout yesterday in Northern Greece and Southern Yugoslavia, harassing the Germans by repeated bombing and machine-gun attacks.

"Enemy armed columns between Bitelj (Monastir) and Prilep were bombed and a number of tanks received direct hits, several being destroyed and others overturned.

"Bombs fell close to the road and others burst near the railway line. Railway stores were attacked at Koenke and a petrol dump ten miles south-west of Prilep was set on fire.

"Heavy casualties were caused to enemy troops."

Total communication articles in the Florina area, some thirteen miles north of Monastir have been

Continued on Back Page. Col. 3

We Rescue Italians

IN all parts of Abyssinia where Italians have not concentrated in cities occupied by British and Patriot forces, they are desperately defending themselves against the natives' vengeance.

Two South African armoured cars have just returned to Addis Abeba from a rescue expedition to Ambo, some seventy miles away. Under their escort came 140 panic-stricken Italians, including nine women and six children.

The latter were tucked away in the already crowded armoured cars, which had to run the gauntlet of vengeful natives.

The men had been put into sixteen Italian lorries. When some of the lorries broke down and had to be abandoned the Italians went mad with fear.

Dash by Night

They rushed at the armoured cars and straggled fiercely to force their way inside. The crews had to keep them off at the pistol point.

After shepherding the Italians past aggressive natives and road barricades the South Africans made a night dash to the capital.

In Addis Abeba, the terrified Italians were calmed by a British staff officer, who unconcernedly surveyed them wearing red pyjamas.

Another patrol went to Debra Berhan. There they found 400 of the enemy beleaguered in a hastily-built fort with immense stocks of ammunition.—Reuter.

WAVES OF PLANES ATTACK ATHENS

ATHENS was bombed by successive waves of raiders all last evening, according to the Greek radio.

The All-clear was heard during the broadcast.

Two of the attacking planes were shot down, one by a gun which had been captured from the Germans.

British recently waved Mussolini, through the Vatican, that Rome would be attacked by the R.A.F. if bombs were dropped on Athens.

It has been stated in the House of Commons that there are military targets in the Italian capital which would be legitimate objectives for our bombers.

The man behind the British victories in the Western Desert which carried our troops to Benghazi and beyond, now leads British forces in Greece. Lieutenant-General Sir Henry Maitland Wilson's new appointment was announced last night.

"One of our finest tacticians," was Mr. Churchill's recent tribute to him.

18

As 1940 turns to 1941 the war rages on, with the newspapers and wireless giving daily reports about events in Egypt, the Australians storming into Tobruk, growing American aid, the RAF fighting to protect Malta; but the most worrying thing is the talk of Hitler's renewed plans to invade Britain.

Matters of the heart had heated up too. Eddie was getting quite serious with her Tim, and Mac had been stepping out with Sergeant-Major Gregory on a regular basis. As for me, I felt pulled in two directions. I still felt duty-bound to wait for George, but it had now been nearly ten months since I'd last heard from him, and I was inclined to think that perhaps he was, as Mac suggested, lost to the war. Meanwhile my attention was being claimed by Corporal Alistair Ross.

Eddie must have mentioned my polite enquiry into Alistair's health, because from then on I had received regular letters from him. They were always polite, but laced with a touch of flirtatious humour. Thus far, I had resisted replying, so as not to encourage him further.

Finally I had news that would let me make a decision once and for all. George had been found, alive and well, hiding out in France. He'd been injured in a raid on his airfield during the

British Expeditionary Force retreat to Dunkirk, and a French family had kept him hidden. He was safe from capture by Germans, but it seemed the young *mademoiselle* given the task of nursing him had captured his heart.

I actually laughed out loud when I read George's words describing his feelings for another woman. I was overjoyed that he was safe, but also filled with a sense of release. How foolish I'd been to keep Alistair at arm's length all this time, I thought. I resolved to write to him at once and tell him … Tell him what? That I was available? That was dreadfully forward. Perhaps I should ask Eddie to tell Tim my news instead, knowing full well that he would pass it on to his friend.

The next morning at coffee break, a crowd of nurses was gathered around the noticeboard. There was a buzz of excited conversation and, as I pushed my way forward, Mac saw me and gave me a huge grin. 'Phyll, look!' she said, jerking her head at the board. 'We're off to Claybury again!'

Sure enough, printed there in black and white was a notice from the hospital board. They had decided that, after living and working with the constant air raids for the past seven months, all but a skeleton staff were being sent out of the London area to the countryside for six months' respite, on rotation. There followed a list, chosen at random allegedly, of the first batch to be leaving. And not only were Mac's and Eddie's names down, but so was mine.

'Oh, Mac, how delightful! Do you think we'll be billeted with Mrs Mason again?'

'What, that loony old mannequin?' Mac said. 'I jolly well hope so!'

We practically skipped into the dining room to find Eddie and tell her the news.

'What time do you finish duty, Phyll?' Mac said.

'Four-thirty.'

'Shall we head into town? Go and see a picture?'

I shook my head. 'No. I think I'm going to pay my parents a surprise visit in Sydenham. I'm off duty for two days and, you know, I really haven't seen them in an age.'

'Do you want some company?'

I squeezed her arm. 'Not this time, thanks. I'm going to be a little selfish. Besides, it's not their house, and my aunt and uncle are . . . a little more old-fashioned, shall we say?'

Mac shrugged. 'That's all right.'

'I missed them at Christmas again and, well, it's my birthday tomorrow and I think they'd be delighted to see me.'

Mac put her hand to her mouth in shock. 'Oh, Phyll,' she said, horrified. 'I plumb forgot. About your birthday, I mean. I feel awful.'

'Don't be silly. It's not important.'

'Not important?' she spluttered. '*Every* birthday is important. It's another milestone, another mark of your time on Earth. Which one is it?'

'Twenty-one,' I said softly.

'Your twenty-first!' she exclaimed. 'Oh, now I feel even worse.'

'Don't, please,' I said, draining my coffee. 'I'm late. If I don't see you when my shift ends, I'll see you on Sunday evening.'

Come 6.30 p.m., I was on my way to London Bridge. Already late because I'd fallen asleep after coming off the ward, I hadn't had time to change out of my uniform in my rush to get away. But Hitler and his blasted Luftwaffe had other plans for me and, instead of making the train to Forest Hill, I was redirected to the Elephant and Castle and subsequently caught in the air raid that resulted in my delivering a baby in the tube station shelter.

Dawn was breaking as I emerged on to street level.

'Mind 'ow you go, love,' an ARP warden said to me. 'Took a direct 'it, we did.'

The air was full of smoke from the fires that were still raging all around. ARP crews were digging through the debris, looking for survivors, while firemen were dragging hoses across the cratered road. There was glass, rubble and wood everywhere. One bus was completely crushed, as if a giant had stamped on it, and there was a taxi lying on its side. Two ARP men were cutting away the roof and I could see a bloodied, ragged arm sticking out from the shattered driver's-side window.

'Is there anything I can do?' I said.

One ARP man paused and looked back at me over his shoulder, wiping the sweat from his sooty brow.

'Nah, ducks. Thanks, but 'e's a goner.'

I stepped gingerly across the road towards the temporary bus stop. I lifted the fallen sign back upright again, and was just wondering how likely it was that I'd catch a bus to Forest Hill at all when I was answered by the sight of a no. 12 looming towards me. I held out my hand and the bus juddered to a halt with a screech.

The conductor, looking as dirty and dishevelled as I must have done, grinned down at me from the open platform.

'Where to, love? Paradise?'

I gave him a sickly smile as I climbed on board. 'Last night it could have been,' I said, slumping down on the bench seat. 'But right now all I need is a ride to Forest Hill. If it's still there. You going that far?'

'Goin' to bloody – excuse me French, miss,' he said, doffing his cap – 'to bloomin' Saff Croydon. Unless 'itler's bombed the whole blood – bloomin' route.'

I handed out a penny.

'Put that away, miss,' he said. 'Strictly out of service now. Right, 'old on tight!'

And with a sharp clang of the bell, the bus jerked forward and at last I was homeward-bound.

I was the only passenger and no one else hailed the bus. Despite the odd detour around a wrecked car or a collapsed building, we made good time. I got off at Forest Hill Station, gave the conductor a tired wave of thanks and began to trudge towards Sydenham.

When I finally turned in Burghill Road, it was just gone 7 a.m. It was a beautiful, fresh morning. The air was full of birdsong and although it was hazy, the sun had risen. I found my aunt and uncle's house easily enough, a Victorian bay-fronted semi-detached with a neat front garden enclosed by a box hedge. I knocked, expecting an instant reply. But there was nothing. I took a few steps back and looked up at the curtained windows.

Perhaps . . . ? I had a sudden bad feeling. But no, there was no damage. I glanced back at the road: it looked unscathed. I turned back, knocked twice more and then gave up and slumped down on the doorstep, deflated. I pulled my cloak about me, and huddled my overnight bag to my chest as if it were a cuddly bear.

Had they gone away? What a fool I'd been. I should have written to say I was coming. Was my journey all for nothing? Maybe I should just have stayed at the hospital. I gave a heavy sigh and closed my eyes, trying to stop my mind from asking endless questions. Too late to alter things now, I reasoned.

I must have dozed off, for a gentle shake of my shoulder roused me. Half expecting to see Father, I was momentarily confused by a stranger's face looming down at me.

'Don't be alarmed, dear,' the middle-aged woman said. 'I live across the street. Just been to fetch my Edward's paper. Saw a nurse sat here and thought there was trouble.'

'No, not at all. I'm Phyllis,' I said, pulling myself to my feet. 'Elsworth. Joe and Margaret's niece. I'm Alfred and Violet's daughter.'

'Oh, of course,' the woman said. 'Heard all about you.'

'I came to visit . . .' I shrugged. 'Well, I got rather waylaid actually. But there's no one in. Have they gone away?'

'No,' the woman said. 'They'll still be in bed. The whole street were in the shelters till gone five this morning. I'm only up because I can never sleep after a raid.' She smiled and jerked her head. 'Come back home with me. I'll make you a cuppa, and you can try them in a bit.'

Bless her heart. I really needed that cup of tea. After half an hour or so I thanked her and left, saying that I'd go and buy a newspaper myself as well as some tobacco for Father, and then try them again.

In the event I walked to the nearby park instead. The simple beauty of that place was such a stark contrast to the bomb-damaged streets at Elephant and Castle that I just stood there drinking it all in, gazing in wonder at the green of the trees, some still in blossom, and the fading yellow of the late daffodils. I watched some sparrows picking at the grass, hopping and dancing in the dappled sunlight that streamed down through the gently rustling leaves. My gaze drifted higher. The sky was bright blue now, with just a few wispy clouds drifting by. I closed my eyes and breathed.

And suddenly the emotion of the past twelve hours washed over me, and I wept. How could all this beauty exist with so much death and destruction, so much hatred, all around? I staggered to a bench, and just sat and listened to the birds twitter until I felt ready. It was now past eight-thirty. *They must be up by now*, I thought. Mother was never one to lie in, no matter how tired she was.

I pulled a small mirror out of my bag and did the best I could to tidy up my appearance. My eyes looked puffy and bloodshot, but it would have to do.

Ten minutes later I was back at the front door of my aunt and uncle's house. I knocked and was about to try once more, when the door swung open.

Mother, looking greyer than the last time I'd seen her, dark bags under her eyes, her face drawn, blinked back at me open-mouthed. 'Phyllis ... ?'

I stepped forward and hugged her. 'Hello, Mother,' I said, my voice quivering with emotion.

'I'm ... well, what an unexpected surprise. And on your birth-day.'

I pulled away from her and wiped my eyes. My birthday? Of course, I'd completely forgotten. Today I was twenty-one years old.

Mother took me through to the kitchen, where Father and my aunt and uncle were just sitting down to breakfast. Father jumped up with a huge smile on his face.

'Phyll, dear. Here, sit yourself down.'

He quickly made a space for me and I was handed a cup of tea and a slice of bread and jam.

'You should have told us you were coming,' Mother scolded.

'It was a last-minute thing, Mother. Sorry,' I said.

'Tosh! Sorry,' Father said. 'It's delightful to see you, Phyll. Happy birthday, sweetheart.' He raised his cup in salute.

'How long can you stay?' Mother asked.

'I don't have to be back on duty until Monday morning.'

'Good,' my Aunt Margaret piped up, 'then we insist you stay.'

'I couldn't put you—'

'Nonsense,' Uncle Joe interrupted, 'plenty of room. It's a pleas-ure to see you, girl, a pleasure.'

'Thank you. Thank you all,' I said humbly, biting into my bread and jam.

The weather stayed fine all day, and after I'd washed and changed I sat in the garden with Father.

'You made good time this morning,' he said between puffs on his cigarette.

'I left yesterday night,' I admitted.

'Stupid girl,' he said. 'I thought as much.'

'I got caught at Elephant and Castle Station.'

'Well, probably a bit more comfortable than that Anderson,' he said, nodding towards the shelter at the end of the garden.

It was prettier than our one back in Dovercourt. Uncle Joe had applied plaster and tiles to the front and sides, plus a neat roof garden.

'It looks charming,' I said.

'Hah!' Father scoffed. 'Not inside. Four adults, and now you if we have another raid tonight.'

'I can always head back to the hos—'

'Don't be silly,' Father said, with an apologetic wave of his hand. 'I'm just a little ... shocked, I suppose, and worried about ... about your mother.'

'How is she?' I said. 'She looks ...'

'Older?' Father nodded. 'She's doing bad, girl, really bad. She tries to hide it, but she's a nervous wreck of late. She loves her sister, but she hates it here.'

'It's a beautiful house.'

'I agree,' Father said, 'but it's not hers. She misses her own home, her own things. She's got the shakes, too. Some days are worse than others, and she hardly sleeps now. You being here, it's the best I've seen her in a while. There's a spark in her eyes ...' He paused and went very quiet.

I looked across and realised he was crying. I pulled myself out of my chair and knelt in front of him.

'Oh, Daddy,' I whispered, my heart breaking.

He sniffed, wiped his face and laughed it off. 'You never call me that,' he croaked, clearing his throat.

'I know,' I said softly.

He smiled down at me. 'We're going back, Phyll. To Dovercourt.'

'But it's too dangerous.'

'No more so than London.'

I couldn't argue with that.

'I've put in an official request to get transferred to my old customs post,' he said. 'I've been to a doctor, too. Told him about your mother. He advised I just get her back home.'

'But aren't the Army using our house as digs?'

'Yes. We'll stay at your Aunt Lil's till I can sort the particulars out. Probably just have to offer lodgings,' he shrugged.

I nodded in agreement. The doctor was right, Father was right. No matter what the danger, one's own home can only bring peace. And if that meant that Mother would find calm and solace, which in turn meant Father would too, then I couldn't argue. I smiled, took Father's rolling-machine from him and sat in my chair again.

'I miss the sea,' Father said, watching me attempt to roll a cigarette.

'Me too,' I said. 'Me too.'

19

Two weeks later, Mac, Eddie and I leave the dust and rubble of London and return to rural Woodford for our six months' respite. It is quite a shock to be surrounded by so much tranquil beauty after the devastation of the capital. The bluebells and primroses are starting to come out and the woodlands at Claybury are a picture of an idyllic England, an England I'd quite forgotten still existed. It is as if the war hasn't happened here.

But it was the silence that struck us most forcefully; we found it disturbing. All one could hear was the faint chatter and buzz of insects.

'This will take some getting used to,' I said.

'Are you mad?' Mac said, kicking off her shoes and slumping down on the grass. 'This is just perfect. I love this place. I'd rather be here than Hackney.'

'But what about Sergeant-Major Gregory?' I said.

Mac shrugged. 'He's had his embarkation orders, so he'll be off to war and I probably won't hear from him again.'

'Don't be so defeatist, Mac,' I said. 'That's not like you.'

'I'm not being defeatist,' she sighed, lying back on the grass. Eddie and I lay down either side of her and stared up in silence at the fluffy white clouds drifting across the sea of blue sky high above. 'I'm being a realist,' she said matter-of-factly. Then she passed wind.

Lectures, we were relieved to learn, were temporarily suspended, but that didn't mean we could take it easy. Our hospital final was coming up, so we were all encouraged to bury our heads in our text and medical books every spare moment. Paperwork, essays and tests were sent up from Hackney by courier. How we moaned at the sight of the dispatch rider whenever she came put-putting up the driveway.

Mac, Eddie and I were given rooms in the main complex in the grounds of the asylum this time, but we made a vow to call on Mrs Mason on our days off. In her lovely home once more, we listened to her complain in hushed tones that the three Land Army girls she was now housing were not as nice as us.

'Rather common, my dears,' she sniffed.

She took a real shine to Eddie this time, and they would spend hours together going through her wardrobe. I was slim, but Eddie's figure was similar to Mrs Mason's in her modelling days, so she got to try on everything.

I cannot tell you how wonderful it was to wake up having not heard an air-raid siren all night. Of course, we still read the newspapers and listened to the wireless, but we couldn't help but be relieved to be out of the danger zone.

I had regular letters from Alistair. He and Tim were now part of the newly formed Army Catering Corps, and I would write back and tease him about being nothing more than a chef in khaki. In turn he would reply that he was due to be dropped into Berlin to poison Hitler with one of his dry rice puddings.

Night duty was very quiet to start with. There were only three patients in the ward, all soldiers who had been admitted for minor surgery, and no casualties. It was rather tedious, and the long night hours were spent packing drums with dressings, checking and rechecking surgical instruments, inspecting the theatre adjacent to the ward, but mostly sitting at the ward table reading medical books by lamplight. It was a huge effort to keep one's eyes open when reading about common preventable complications of abdominal surgery at three in the morning. I would rub my tired eyes, glance up at the ward with its ten beds running down each side, and seriously consider pulling a screen around an empty one and curling up to sleep.

Then one night, just after twelve, the telephone rang in the office behind me. I hurried over to answer it before it woke the patients.

'Hello, Nurse Elsworth speaking.'

There was a *pip-pip-pip* then I heard, '*Go ahead, caller.*'

'Hello?' I repeated.

'*Phyll? Is that you?*' a familiar voice said, sounding as if it were talking from the bottom of a bucket.

'Yes . . . ?'

'*It's me!*'

'Who's "me"?' I said, rather irritated.

'*Alistair. Alistair Ross! How are you?*'

Good Lord. I couldn't believe it. I glanced around, worried that Night Sister might be about.

'What is it?' I hissed.

'*Nothing, old girl,*' Alistair's cheery voice said. '*Just thought I'd give you a quick bell.*'

'Well you can't,' I whispered fiercely. 'This is a hospital ward. This telephone is for emergencies!'

'*But this is an emergency.*'

I paused; something dreadful must have happened. Perhaps Eddie's Tim had been hurt?

'What?' I said. 'What's happened?'

There was silence on the other end of the line.

'Hello? Hello? Alistair?'

'*Yes?*'

'What emergency?'

'*I think I'm in love with you.*'

I nearly dropped the receiver.

'*Phyll? Did you hear what I said?*'

'You mustn't call me here,' I spluttered. 'I'm putting the phone down now before Sister catches me.'

But I kept listening to his breathing on the other end.

'*Phyll?*' he said after a minute.

'Yes?'

'*Did you hear what I said?*'

'Yes,' I said. 'Have you been drinking?'

'*No.*'

Silence.

'*And?*' he said.

'Don't talk nonsense. You hardly know me,' I said rather gruffly.

'*But I'd like to.*'

'To what?'

'*Know you.*'

'Don't be so rude!'

Silence.

'Look, I have to get back to my patients,' I said.

'*All right. Good-night, Phyll.*'

'Good-night. And don't call this number again. And don't call me "old girl".' I paused, still not quite wanting to end the call.

'*All right. By—*'

I put down the receiver.

'Loves me! Honestly, he must have been drunk,' I muttered.

But back at the night desk, I found myself flicking through my medical dictionary absent-mindedly, unable to get the strange conversation out of my head.

For the next three nights, at exactly the same time, Alistair called. At first I was exasperated, then mildly irritated, and finally more affable. Sensing the change in my tone, Alistair asked me when I was next off duty.

'Three nights out of seven,' I said, 'so in two days' time.'

'*Then let me take you out to dinner.*'

I hesitated.

'*Go on, Phyll. Just you and me. I promise to behave.*'

'Very well.'

'*Splendid! That's my girl!*'

'I am not your girl!'

He ignored that. '*Great. I'll pick you up at seven.*'

Over the following few months, I got to know that part of the country pretty well. Alistair would come and pick me up and we'd either cycle – or drive, if he'd managed to wangle the use of an ACC motorbike – to the various pubs and restaurants of Enfield, Chigwell and the Epping Forest area. Despite my initial misgivings, he was always a gentleman, and proved to be charming, thoughtful and very romantic. He was obviously very much in love with me. Regularly I would find flowers left for me at reception. And one beautiful sunny afternoon, we rode deep into the woods with a picnic, settled in a glade, and with the sounds and the smells of summer all around us like an intoxicating perfume, Alistair took me in his arms. We knew then that we were meant to be together.

After three nights off, I returned to find a full ward. Suddenly I was back to proper nursing, with barely a moment to study. Twenty wounded soldiers had been admitted following an accident at a munitions works. Going from bed to bed, I gazed down at their faces, some burned and scarred black as charcoal, all so young, as young as me, as young as Alistair. I gave a smile if any were awake, touched a hand in comfort, showing that someone cared. When I'd given out medication and finished treatments, I turned down the lights, screened off the ward table, stretched and settled down to yet more swotting. But it was so hard to concentrate with the fear in my gut, a fear that must affect all women when they look at their men in uniform, that they will, at some point, be going off to war. These soldiers in the ward weren't battle-scarred, but still the worry hit me hard, the worry for Alistair. It was different now from how it had been with George. How my heart ached.

Suddenly I felt two hands clamp around my face. I jumped up, startled, but managed to suppress a cry of alarm. I turned, half expecting it to be Alistair. But it was one of the young soldiers.

'What are you doing out of bed?' I snapped.

'Call of nature, Nurse,' he grinned. 'Sorry, saw you gazing off into space. Couldn't resist sneaking up.'

'Well, get back to bed this instant,' I said, standing with my hands on my hips.

'Yes, Nurse,' he whispered, and scuttled back to his bed.

'Honestly,' I muttered to myself, before sitting back down to my books.

A few hours later, I heard the door to the ward open behind me. I checked my fob watch and noted that it was now 3 a.m., then turned to see the night sister walking towards me.

'Good-evening, Nurse Elsw—' She stopped dead in her tracks, staring at me aghast. 'What in Heaven's name have you done to your face?'

'Sister?' I said, puzzled.

'Go and clean yourself up, girl, while I do my rounds,' she said sniffily.

What's got into her? I thought as I made for the bathroom. I turned on the light and blinking back at me from the wall mirror was my face with two dirty great black handprints planted on it.

'Just you wait, young man,' I muttered as I hurriedly scrubbed my face clean.

Eddie, who was on nights on the next ward, came to meet me in the morning.

'How was your shift?' she said.

'So-so. Didn't get much studying done.'

She smiled knowingly. 'Alistair on the telephone again, was he?'

'No, it wasn't that. Just a patient clowning about.'

'Getting fresh?' Eddie said with a nod. 'Yes, I get those.'

I smiled. 'No, nothing like that either. But I sorted it out with—'

'Gangway!'

Eddie and I jumped aside as the young soldier who'd put his grubby hands across my face rushed by, clutching his backside with one hand and holding his dressing gown closed with the other.

'Don't run, Private Jones!' the day nurse called after him.

'But that's what I've got, Nurse!' he called back over his shoulder as he disappeared into the toilet.

'—a good dose of laxative in his morning cuppa,' I said, finishing my sentence with a smile.

After breakfast I stopped by at the office to see if there was any mail. Sure enough, a letter postmarked HARWICH TOWN was waiting in my pigeonhole. Mother was settled in with Aunt Lil, and Father was confident he'd get a transfer back soon, if not to the quay then perhaps to Ipswich. Negotiations were under way for them to regain possession of their house too, so all in all the news was good.

In spite of this, I couldn't get to sleep and tossed and turned until, cursing, I threw the covers off and decided to get up. It was 3.30 p.m. and, looking out at the beautiful sunny day, I decided to get dressed again and sit outside.

I had a bath first, then collected my books and found a remote spot on the lawn under a cherry tree and settled down to do some studying. If the home sister saw me out of bed she wouldn't be pleased, as I was on duty again that night.

However, a combination of the soft grass under me, the warm early-summer sunshine beating down through the trees, the perfume of the flowers and the hypnotic task of trying to learn long medical terms from my books meant that I was soon fast asleep.

I awoke a few hours later feeling refreshed but ravenously hungry. I checked my watch.

'Crikey!' It was nearly seven. I'd slept for nearly three hours and I was on duty again at eight-thirty.

20

Reporting back, I sense an uneasy atmosphere on the ward, the men being unusually subdued. Nearest the door there are screens around one of the beds, with a lot of activity going on behind them. The ward sister calls me into the office.

'Come in, Nurse Elsworth,' she said. 'Take a seat.'

That was ominous in itself. One always stood for Sister's report.

'Now, we have a new patient,' she said. 'He was admitted two hours ago, a young RAF man, a . . .' she paused and checked her notes in front of her, 'Flying Officer Bates, twenty-two. He's from a nearby air station. He was admitted having jumped off the back of a lorry on to a bayonet. Heaven knows how he managed to do that. But it's very serious: he has a pierced bowel and bladder. He's still in theatre now, but we expect him to be warded within the hour. His condition is critical and you are to special him. Nurse MacKenzie will be taking over ward duties. Is that clear?'

'Yes, Sister.'

How awful for the poor young man, I thought. The fact I'd been tasked with giving him special care meant it was touch and go for him. I was put in mind of Mr Swartzbard. But at least Mac would be with me on the ward tonight for moral support.

I quickly set about checking everything was ready for the patient's arrival. There was a bed cradle in place and hot-water bottles dotted about the mattress. I placed a chair near the head-board, and my books on the floor beside it.

''Ere, Nurse, what's 'appening?' It was the young soldier I'd given a dose to earlier. He was in the next bed.

'Never you mind, Private Jones,' I said, tucking his sheets in. 'A new arrival, that's all.'

'But it seems all serious . . .' He looked really concerned.

I nodded. 'It is. I'm to give him special care when he's transferred from theatre.'

''E a soldier boy?'

I shook my head. 'A pilot.'

'Cor, one of the few, eh?'

Just then the ward doors banged open and the theatre staff wheeled the new patient in.

'Excuse me,' I said to Private Jones, and hurried over to direct them to the bed that had been prepared.

Flight Officer Bates was blond, with chiselled, boyish looks, but his complexion was ghostly pale through loss of blood. There were drips inserted into his arms, and a drain attached to his bladder. I could see that it was blood-stained already. I swiftly removed the hot-water bottles, and with tender care he was lifted on to the warmed bed. He was still unconscious as I gently tucked the bedclothes around him.

The surgeon, a tall middle-aged man with a sweep of grey hair, came to check everything was in order. Sister was at his shoulder and she gave me a reassuring smile.

'Flight Officer Bates will be examined every fifteen minutes, Nurse,' the surgeon said, 'for any change in pulse, drop in blood pressure or rise in temperature.'

'Yes, Doctor,' I said.

'If you notice any signs of restlessness you are to get the duty nurse to notify me immediately on the telephone. Clear?'

'Yes, Doctor.'

'Good. Then I shall leave him in your capable hands.' He gave me a nod and turned to confer with Sister.

'Thank you, Doctor,' I said, feeling rather flattered at being given such a responsibility.

Mac had come into the ward; she gave me a discreet wave. I smiled back, then turned to give my full attention to poor Flight Officer Bates.

I covered the bedside light to protect his face from the glare, then sat down beside him and read through his notes. His internal injuries were appalling. It was going to take a miracle for him to pull through. But he was young and, hopefully, strong. I put my hands on his forehead. His skin felt clammy and his pulse was weak and fibrillating.

Don't let him die, God, I prayed. *Help me fight with him.*

Occasionally he stirred, but not enough to be of any concern. I dipped a cloth in the jug of iced water on the bedside table and touched it to his lips, gently moistening them.

By 3.30 a.m. my back ached, my muscles felt stiff and my eyes were heavy. But I didn't dare relax. Mac, bless her, kept me supplied with sweet tea, but I wouldn't let her relieve me so that I could get something to eat.

'So, how goes it?' Mac whispered.

'He seems stable,' I said, sipping my latest cup of tea.

Suddenly Flight Officer Bates lashed out, knocking his blood stand. I dropped my teacup and grabbed the stand, catching it just in time.

'Call the surgeon, Mac. Now!' I said, gripping the patient by the shoulders as he lay there convulsing.

The surgeon was on the spot almost at once, and I stood by as

he checked that Flight Officer Bates's dressing was intact and the
bladder was still draining.

'I think we'd best administer some morphine, Nurse. Let's
start with five milligrams. If he hasn't improved within the hour,
we'll administer incremental doses of one milligram and take it
from there.'

'Yes, Doctor,' I said, never taking my eyes from Flight Officer
Bates's pale face.

'Nurse?'

I looked up.

'To pull this young man through such a horrific injury is . . .'
he paused, 'well, a challenge. And if he's strong enough and he
does so, then it will be a tremendous compliment to us all.'

I nodded. 'I understand, Doctor.'

'Don't hesitate to contact me if he shows any extreme
change.'

'You can count on me, Doctor.'

Mac came over as he left. 'He's a bit of a matinée idol, isn't
he?'

'What, Dr Payne?'

Mac paused. 'Never! Seriously? That's his name. You're pulling my leg?'

I shook my head, and began to fill a syringe from a morphine
vial. 'I said the same thing. So I checked on the theatre roster. "Dr
A. K. Payne, Surgeon". That's his name.'

Mac was smiling in that mischievous way. 'I've got something
for his Payne.'

'Mac! Cut it out,' I scolded, but with a smile on my lips. Good
old Mac, she could always raise my spirits.

'How is our flyboy?' she said, watching me insert the syringe
into the IV drip.

'Touch and go, Mac, touch and go.'

'Alistair telephoned about half-an-hour ago. I said you were busy. Was that the right thing to do?' Mac said.

'Of course it was,' I said. 'I really wish he'd stop ringing the ward. If Night Sister catches him, or me speaking to him, I'm for it.'

'He said it was important, that he needed to speak to you on an urgent matter.'

'It always is with him, Mac,' I sighed.

'I told him you'd be off duty at eight o'clock. And that you'd telephone him back.'

An hour later, I had such a splitting headache from the constant worry that I finally agreed to take a ten-minute break. The night sister could see how jaded I was and ordered me to go and get some fresh air.

'I will sit with our special case, Nurse Elsworth,' she said, checking her fob watch. 'I don't want to see your face until four-forty-five. Is that clear?'

'Yes, Sister,' I said wearily.

Dawn was breaking as I stepped outside the building. I sat on the front steps, a cigarette and a cup of tea in hand, listening to the birds as they began their dawn chorus.

Come 8 a.m. I was reluctant to go off duty, but I had to let go and accept that other nurses were just as capable as I was. There had been no change in Flight Officer Bates's condition for the rest of the night. He did open his eyes once, but he slipped back into oblivion almost immediately.

Mac walked with me back through the tranquil grounds.

'Sister told me the health authorities have managed to track down the pilot's sister,' she said. 'She's in Ireland.'

'Is she going to be coming over?' I said, glad to know he had someone.

'I don't know. We'll see.' Mac gave me a comforting smile.

The familiar put-put of a motorcycle engine coming up the drive stopped us in our tracks.

'Not more test papers?' Mac groaned.

But as the bike came closer we could see it wasn't a dispatch rider. He pulled up next to us, turned the engine off and removed his goggles.

'Alistair!' I said. 'What are you doing here at this hour?'

Alistair beamed back at us. 'Hello, Mac. How are you? Look, Phyll, are you off duty now?'

'Yes. But what—'

'Oh, I'm in clerical now, I have some papers to deliver to the barracks at South Woodford. Fancy a spin? I've got some breakfast: bread, a bit of cheese and a flask of coffee. ACC perks.'

'I don't know, Alistair,' I said, 'I'm awfully tired . . .'

'Please, Phyll,' Alistair said, looking slightly crestfallen. 'I've something important I need to discuss. Just an hour. I'll have you back in your bed in no time.'

'Oi oi,' teased Mac.

I gave her a withering look, then turned back to Alistair. 'All right, but I want to be back here for no later than ten a.m.'

'That's my girl,' he said, pulling down his goggles. 'Hop on.' He kick-started the motorbike back into life and revved the engine.

I checked that none of the ward sisters were about, then hitched up my skirt and climbed on the bike. No sooner had I put my arms around Alistair's waist, than we shot off back down the hospital drive and out onto the road towards Woodford Green.

It was exhilarating being on the back of that motorbike as the wind whistled past my ears, and pulled at my cloak. I held on tight and pressed my face into Alistair's shoulders, watching the trees rush by in a blur of green.

'Where are we going?' I shouted against the wind.

'A little spot I found,' Alistair called back over his shoulder.

'Don't you have to get to the barracks?'

'Already been, darling! I left an hour early so I could get to you.'

We were heading towards Epping Forest. Soon there were tall trees on either side of the road and I felt the motorbike slow, and we turned into a lay-by. I climbed off the bike, straightened my dress, and Alistair removed his goggles, gloves and helmet. He pulled a haversack from one of the panniers at the side of the bike, grabbed my hand and led me into the thick curtain of the woods. The sun was streaming down through the pine trees and the air felt fresh, full of the scents and sounds of the forest. It was so peaceful, utterly still except for birds calling, the insects buzzing in our faces, and the occasional rustle in the foliage from some unseen wild animal. A woodpecker hammered away high up in the canopy. We walked in silence, our feet swishing through the soft grass and ferns, until we came to a fallen log.

'Let's sit here,' Alistair said, taking off his leather jacket and placing it down as a blanket. We stood there hand in hand, staring into one another's eyes. We kissed passionately, losing ourselves in each other's embrace. Then Alistair gently pulled away and gestured for me to sit on the log. He knelt down before me and took my hand in his.

'Phyll,' he said softly, 'will you marry me?'

It took me utterly by surprise. I found myself speechless as a million thoughts tumbled through my mind. I knew Alistair was passionately in love with me, but was I with him? He was all the things a girl could want – charming, handsome, funny, tender – but we'd only been seeing each other properly for a few months. What about my career? What about my parents? He hadn't even met them yet; and I hadn't met his. What about the war? The war: look at Flight Officer Bates, he was my age and he might be dead this time tomorrow. So many young people were dying every day ... I might not get another opportunity, Alistair might not be here next week, next month, next year. *Stop being such a cautious fool, Phyll*, I said to myself. Life was too precious, too precarious to be cautious.

Alistair got up off his knees, sat next to me on the log and waited for me to speak.

'Everything has happened so quickly,' I said eventually.

'But it feels right, doesn't it, Phyll?' Alistair said, his hand clasped around mine.

'I'm on holiday for two weeks from next Thursday,' I said. 'Do you think you could get a pass and come and meet my parents?'

'Of course!' Alistair beamed. 'Then I can ask your father for your hand.'

'Hold on,' I said rather sharply. 'I haven't said yes yet.'

Alistair's face fell and he stared back at me like a crestfallen cocker spaniel.

'Let me sleep on it, will you?' I said. 'It's all so ... sudden.'

Ever the gentleman, Alistair said no more on the matter. Instead he opened up his haversack, and shared out a breakfast of bread, cheese and fruit and a wonderfully decadent flask of real coffee.

I waved him off at the hospital gates and made my way back to my room in the nurses' quarters. I put on my nightie and stood in front of the mirror, pushing my hair up and pulling faces at myself.

'Mrs Alistair Ross,' I said, curtsying. 'Phyllis Ross.'

I had to admit, I liked the sound of that. I giggled, jumped into bed, a sudden thrill of excitement washing over me. Whatever was the matter with me?

Perhaps I shouldn't have had a second cup of coffee, I thought. *I'll never get to sleep now*.

There was a tap at my door.

'It's only me,' Mac's muffled voice said.

'Come in.'

I sat up in bed as Mac came in. She looked like she'd been crying.

'Whatever's the matter?' I said, putting my hand out.

'Oh Phyll,' she sniffed. 'It's so sad. I'm sorry, I had to tell you. Flight Officer Bates . . . ' She didn't have to finish.

'Such a waste,' I whispered.

Mac nodded. 'He was a fighter. It was just too much for his heart.'

We sat holding hands and thinking of the young airman. But his wouldn't be the only life to be snatched away all too soon while this cursed war raged on. Life was just so short.

'Mac, I know this isn't the time,' I said, 'but I have some news and . . . '

Mac wiped her cheek. 'What?'

'Alistair's asked me to marry him.'

'Oh, Phyll,' Mac blurted out, throwing her arms around me, 'that's wonderful, just wonderful!'

Yes, I thought, it was.

And yes, Alistair, I thought, *I will*.

21

I wrote my parents about Alistair and that I was going to bring him up to visit in a few weeks. But when the day came, the thought of breaking the news of my impending marriage filled me with more dread than an upcoming exam or sitting through an air raid.

Alistair was waiting for me at Liverpool Street Station, and I threw myself into his arms and hugged him tight.

'Steady on, girl, you'll do me an injury.'

'So?' I said. 'I'm a nurse, I'll look after you. I'll look after you until death do us part.'

He prised me away from him and stared back at me, mouth slightly open. 'Phyll? Do you ...?'

'Yes, Alistair. I will. I will be your wife.'

Alistair whooped with joy, grabbed me and spun me round right there on the platform.

'Where's your luggage?' I said as we boarded the train.

'I could only get a twelve-hour pass,' he said. 'I'll have to catch the evening train back. Sorry. But I can get the weekend off in two weeks, and I'll take you to Billingshurst to meet my folks. If you like.'

I was disappointed we didn't have longer together, but at least there was a weekend in Sussex to look forward to.

Once we arrived on the Essex coast, walking from the station to home, we could see how poor little Dovercourt Bay had been taking quite a pounding from the Luftwaffe. Houses were damaged up the Grafton Road, and Cliff Road looked to be almost flattened. A group of men in cloth caps were digging through the debris. What were my parents thinking, coming back to this? But as soon as I turned into Portland Avenue I could see that everything was how it had been the last time I was here.

'Now, Father is a sweetie,' I said as we stood outside my garden gate, and I straightened Alistair's tunic and cap. 'Whereas Mother ... Well, she comes across as a little frosty.'

'Phyll,' Alistair said, 'stop worrying. Come on, I can see the curtains twitching.'

'Yes, I'm just warning you,' I said. 'That's all.'

'It will be fine. After all, we are rather springing this all on them. They haven't even met me yet.'

I gave Alistair the once-over, then, satisfied that he looked presentable, I took hold of his hand and led him through the gate. I knocked on the front door, heart pounding with anticipation.

Father let us in, giving me a warm embrace and shaking Alistair by the hand.

'So I'm guessing that you're the young man who plans to steal our only child away from us, hey?' he said with a wry smile on his lips.

'With your blessing, sir,' Alistair replied.

I felt myself redden, but then Father always could second-guess me. 'Does Mother know?'

Father nodded. 'She's not stupid, lass.' He jerked his chin for me to go in, then turned to Alistair. 'Come on in. Violet's put on a little spread. Bread and dripping and cake and tea.' He lowered his voice. 'We can sneak off for a jar or two later on.'

Mother's reaction was a little cooler, as expected. She was still jittery, and I noted that she was shaking a bit as she carried the teapot from stove to table. But Alistair just jumped up to help her, politely answering her intrusive questions.

She had prepared us a tasty meal of Lord Woolton pie and bread pudding. How she managed on rations I never knew, but I guessed the Army contributed a little: my parents had managed to get possession of their home back on condition that they offer digs to two soldiers.

'How long have you been courting?' Mother asked me as I helped with the washing-up. Father was out in the garden, showing off our Anderson shelter to Alistair. It looked as if he had taken a leaf out of Uncle Jim's book by plastering and decorating it.

'He's done a good job,' I said, nodding outside, ignoring Mother's question.

'At what, dear?'

'Father, with the shelter.'

'Huh,' Mother scoffed. 'He's done a good job getting Henry and Archie to fix up the shelter.'

'Who are Henry and Archie?'

'Our lodgers.'

'Oh,' I said, 'the soldiers.'

'No, sailors,' Mother said. 'The Navy needed rooms first. But they're good clean boys, and very helpful.' She paused. 'So?'

'So?' I said innocently.

'Tisk, child.' Mother scowled back at me. 'Answer my question. About "courting".'

I shrugged. 'A few months. Properly. I actually met him on a double date—'

Mother looked aghast at that.

'Nothing sinister, Mother. His best friend happens to be with Eddie – Edwina. And he, Tim's his name, he and Eddie – Edwina – were going on a date to the Lyons Corner House. Only

Tim had invited Alistair along, and he asked Edwina if she knew of anyone who wouldn't mind making up a foursome.'

'For bridge?' Mother said in all seriousness.

'If you like.'

Honestly, sometimes I wondered just how Mother and Father had ever managed to get together. She seemed so naïve, so ... Victorian at times.

The rest of the afternoon flew by and I sensed Mother gradually warming to Alistair. By the time he had to leave to catch the evening train back to London, she was genuinely sorry to see him go.

As I walked Alistair back to the station, the sky was glowing red and orange in the most glorious of sunsets. I had almost forgotten that the sky could be those colours without there being a building ablaze.

'Your parents seem very nice,' Alistair said, breaking into my thoughts.

'Well, you soon worked your charm on them,' I said, slipping my arm through his.

I gave a heavy sigh as I watched the train disappear from sight. My holiday suddenly seemed more of a chore now. *Two weeks with Mother*, I thought, *yuk!* Then I scolded myself for being ungrateful.

When I got home, two sailors were sitting in the front room, talking with Father. They stood up when I walked in.

'Here she is,' Father said. 'My daughter, Phyll.'

'Pleased to meet you. I'm Archie Brown.'

'And I'm Henry Allbrighton.'

They were both pleasant young men, Archie a little taller than Henry, with fair hair and penetrating blue eyes, while Henry had black hair and sleepy brown eyes. Both men were well groomed and looked smart in their Navy uniforms.

'Hello,' I said, 'Where's Mother?'

'Oh, she popped out to see your Aunt Rose. She's in a bit of a pickle. Bobby' – Father paused to address Henry and Archie – 'that's my nephew, Rose's son, he's in the Merchant Navy. Been out on the Atlantic.'

'A bad place to be,' Henry muttered.

'Nothing's happened, has it?' I gasped, fearing the worst.

'Hope not,' Father said. 'She just hasn't heard from him in a while. Worries each time he goes to sea. Understandable.'

A brief, thoughtful silence fell and we all sat there listening to the ticking of the clock on the mantel.

'Do you play?' Henry asked, nodding to the upright piano pushed up against the wall.

'A bit,' I said.

'Don't let her fool you,' Father said. 'She's a marvel, a marvel.'

'Give us a tune, Phyll,' Archie said. 'Go on.'

I couldn't help but smile. It had been a while since I'd played.

'All right then,' I said, getting to my feet.

'Bravo!'

The evening passed pleasantly, with my playing and Archie and Henry breaking into passable song every now and again.

Mother returned and then she, Father and the two sailors played cards, while I lost myself in the piano keys, my mind full of Alistair.

Mother had made up the box room for me, as Henry and Archie were sharing my original bedroom. As I was undressing there came a soft tap at the door. I pulled my dressing gown about me and opened the door wide enough to poke my head out.

'It's only me,' Archie whispered. 'Say, Phyll, you fancy going to the pictures sometime this week?'

'I don't think that's a good idea . . .'

'Oh, say yes,' Archie pleaded.

'I'm enga—'

'So?' Archie said. 'It's just company. I don't mean it as a date or anything. Bring your mother, if you're worried.'

'Don't be silly.'

'Well, what about it then?'

I looked back at his hopeful expression. Well, I was here for two weeks. Alone.

'All right,' I hissed.

'Top hole!' Archie said rather loudly.

'Hush!'

He put his hand to his mouth. 'Oops, sorry. Great. Good-night.'

The two weeks passed quickly. The weather was hot and sunny and I spent most of my time walking, trying to find a remote spot of beach where I could sneak through the barbed wire to sun-bathe and attempt to study.

In the end I agreed to let Archie and Henry escort me to the pictures twice, and together. Although Archie clearly was attracted to me, I only had thoughts for Alistair. They were wait-ing to be posted and I agreed that they could both write to me, although I had an inkling that as soon as they met a girl – and there were plenty of attractive young women around, particularly the Land Army girls – then I would soon be forgotten.

However, Archie was rather persistent and I eventually relented and let him hold my hand as we walked along the seafront one evening.

'You're as beautiful as the moonlight, Phyll,' he said.

'And you are as corny as a Christmas-cracker joke, Archie.'

He shoved me playfully and I stumbled and slipped.

'Oh, Phyll!' he said, horrified, as he grabbed hold of my waist and helped me to steady myself.

'No harm done,' I said, checking that my stockings hadn't laddered.

'I don't know my own strength!' he said with a grin.

'No, you don't,' I smiled back.

And before I knew it, he had pulled me to him and was kissing me.

For a moment I was lost in his embrace, and then I wriggled away.

'Stop, Archie,' I snapped, slapping his face. 'I've told you, no.'

After that incident he was the perfect gentleman, and the time flew by.

I came down to breakfast on the last Friday to find Mother and Father sat in silence. I raised a questioning eyebrow at Father, who gave me a reassuring wink and nodded to Mother. I sat down between them and poured myself a cup of tea.

Mother gave a short sob, and I noticed how pale she was. I reached out and took her hand in mine.

'Please don't, Mother. I'll be fine.'

She forced a smile. 'I'm just so worried about you returning to London.'

'But after this weekend down in Sussex, I'm back to Woodford for at least another couple of months. Who knows? Perhaps the war will be over by then.'

'Perhaps,' she sniffed, giving my hand a squeeze. 'You're a good girl, Phyllis. And we miss you when you're not here.'

'I'll be perfectly safe, Mother,' I said. 'I am vigilant and careful and Hackney is as likely to be bombed as here. Besides, Alistair says the raids have stopped in the main. The last heavy one was back in May. Even the news is saying they think the worst may be over.'

She nodded all too vigorously and forced a smile. 'I ... I know, dear, I know.'

'What time are you meeting Alistair?' Father said, crunching through a mouthful of toast.

'We're catching the six-thirty from Victoria,' I said.

'I've never been to Sussex,' Father said, slurping his tea.

'Are you deliberately making all that noise?' I scowled.

'So you did read that book I gave you then,' he grinned.

22

Travelling to meet Alistair's parents, I feel totally different from the trip to my family – not apprehensive, just really rather excited. I've never been to Sussex before, and have listened intently to Alistair's stories of growing up in the Weald, with the North and South Downs to either side. He was brought up on a farm by foster-parents, having been given up by his mother when he was just eighteen months old. She emigrated to Australia for a job and, for reasons never explained, she didn't take him with her. Of course, I'm glad she didn't, otherwise I would never have met him. Besides, he adores his foster-parents and I can't wait to meet them.

I had decided to dress up for the journey and was wearing a navy and white polka-dot dress trimmed with white, and a light-weight Burberry mac. Alistair, handsome in his uniform, was waiting for me at the barrier of Platform 12 at Victoria Station in readiness to catch the 6.20 to Pulborough.

We embraced, then grabbing hold of my suitcase, Alistair took my hand and we hurried down the platform, looking for spare seats. But the train was packed; every compartment and carriage appeared to be full of seated and standing troops. Even the lug-gage nets had men lying in them, as if they were hammocks.

'Whatever's going on?' I gasped as we reached the front carriage and had to turn back again.

'Who knows? But "careless talk costs lives",' he grinned.

The guard's whistle blew, so Alistair wrenched open the nearest door and we shouldered our way aboard. A lot of the troops in this carriage were in the 1st Canadian Infantry Division, with distinctive red patches on their sleeves and attractive accents. It was very cramped, but I didn't care.

Thank you, Archie, I thought with a secret smile. *Thank you for your advances, for making me realise just how much I care for, want to be with, love Alistair.*

As the train pulled away from the station, I looked out of the window to see dozens of other troop-packed trains moving off, all heading south. Something major was definitely happening.

'Have you got a newspaper?'

Alistair shook his head. 'No, but Nunky will.'

'Nunky?' I smirked.

'Yes. My uncle. I call my foster-parents "aunt" and "uncle" – well, "Auntie" and "Nunky".'

'I think that's rather sweet.'

I pushed myself up on tiptoes and planted a kiss on Alistair's lips.

There was a cheer and a few cat-calls from the nearest troops.

'Leave off, lads,' Alistair said, 'she's my fiancée.'

Another cheer rose up at that.

Suddenly we could hear the air-raid siren sound, and soon the boom of the ack-ack guns shattered the air overhead. I caught sight of a fleet of Spitfires racing south, and my stomach turned. The train slowed to a halt and we stood there in anticipation, ears pricked at each and every noise from outside. We were so vulnerable, out there in the open, trapped on a packed train.

'Please, God, please,' I muttered into Alistair's chest as he moved me around so I was away from the window.

The carriage was silent now as we stood there listening, praying, hoping. There was a burst of distant gunfire, an explosion and the roar of faraway engines high in the sky.

'What's happening?' I hissed.

'I don't know, my angel,' Alistair replied, his voice calm. 'I think it's a Heinkel raid, but quite a way out. Our boys'll stop them.'

Thankfully he was right. The all-clear sounded and, with a relieved cheer from the Canadians, our train started moving again.

I shuffled back to the window so I could watch the changing scenery, from grimy tenements to suburban semis with pocket-handkerchief-sized gardens to open fields. Cows lazed in meadows, sheep grazed on banks, Land Army girls tilled the fields. I prised open the window and inhaled the scents of the countryside.

As we pulled to a stop at the platform in Horsham, the station was thronged with yet more troops. I kept a tight hold of Alistair's hand as we disembarked and made our way to the platform for the Billingshurst train. It was already in and thankfully empty, so we had not only a seat but an entire Third-Class compartment to ourselves.

Alistair gave me a passionate kiss and we settled down side by side, my head resting on his shoulder. The low sun was streaming in through the window, bathing my face in warmth. I felt so content, so protected in Alistair's arms, as I watched the stunning Sussex scenery flash by.

Billingshurst was a quaint station with two platforms, a raised iron walkway and a timber-clad signal box. Directly opposite the Victorian station house was the Station Inn, a red-brick early-Victorian pub that looked most welcoming. The village itself was dominated by a fine church with a wagon roof and an impressive spire.

'That's beautiful,' I said.

'St Mary's,' Alistair said. 'It dates from the 1100s. Well, parts of it. Come on; we'll have plenty of time for sightseeing tomorrow.'

Auntie and Nunky's cottage stood on its own at the edge of the village. It was thatched and beamed, and lattice windows added to its charm. The garden, even in twilight, was alive with flowering shrubs.

'It's wonderful,' I gasped, totally taken by the beauty of the place. 'Did you really grow up here?'

The front door was flung open and a pair of sparkling brown eyes met mine. The woman was small in stature, and her rounded face was split by a broad smile.

'Well, at last!' she said, embracing Alistair, then pushing him off and doing the same to me.

'Hello, lass. You must be tired and hungry, I'll bet,' she said in her thick Scots accent.

'How do you do, Mrs Ross,' I said.

'Tisk, not Ross, Freeman. Doesn't that lad tell you anything?' She turned and gave Alistair a playful slap. 'Now, you call me "Auntie" – I won't hear another word. Come on, in with the both of you. Nunky's just finishing the milking. He'll be along soon.'

As we passed through the dining room, the smell of freshly baked bread, and something sweeter, hit me and I felt my stomach rumble.

Auntie led the way up a tight, rickety staircase.

'Alistair's in his old room,' she said, 'and Phyll, you're in the guest room, just across the hall here.'

The guest room was in keeping with the rest of the house's

'olde worlde' feel, with low beams, and bare wooden floorboards partially covered by a worn but colourful rug. There was an iron bedstead and the sheets were white and crisp as virgin snow, with a home-made patchwork coverlet over the top. I glanced out of the window, which looked on to the front garden and the sweeping downs beyond, glowing in the golden light of dusk.

'Stunning,' I said aloud.

'It is that, lass,' Auntie said, carrying in a jug of hot water for me. She placed it on the dressing-table, where there was already a towel and a cake of soap next to a porcelain bowl.

'No mod cons here, I'm afraid,' she said. 'But there's a pot under the bed and the privy is out back.'

'Oh, Mrs— Auntie, it's fabulous,' I beamed.

'You're most welcome,' she smiled back. 'Now get yourself settled and come down when you're ready. Dinner will be in half an hour.'

She closed the door after her, and I listened as she clumped back downstairs, humming away softly to herself.

I flung myself on to the bed and stretched. How delightful this all was, and what a contrast to the welcome my parents had given Alistair.

In the dining room, I was greeted first by a bouncy, barking mongrel whose tail was perpetually wagging.

'Down, Judy,' Alistair said.

And then I met his foster-father, a huge bear of a man, who rose from the table to greet me like a leviathan emerging from the depths. His head nearly touched the ceiling

'Phyll, this is Nunky,' Alistair said.

I put my hand out, and he gave a chesty chuckle, tapped it aside and pulled me into a hug, planting a kiss on my cheek at the same time.

'Well, well, you are a doll, aren't you?' he said, holding me at arm's length. His blue eyes sparkled back at me from a ruddy face crowned by a curly mop of grey-blond hair.

'Don't be coarse,' Auntie said with a chuckle.

'Pretty as a buttercup,' Nunky corrected himself, letting go of me. His voice was as rich as butter, and his accent as Sussex as the surrounding hills.

I gave a little curtsy, joining in with the light mood.

'She's a firecracker, too!' Nunky slapped his thigh and laughed. 'Come, sit, sit.'

He pulled a chair out for me and I sat myself down. Judy darted under the table and settled herself between my feet.

My eyes positively bulged from my head as I gazed at the feast laid out before me. I hadn't seen food like it in ages. There was a joint of gammon, new potatoes, thick bread, butter, mustard and fresh salad, as well as bottles of ale and a jug of spring water. There was fresh fruit, too, and a hunk of cheese. The tears welled up in my eyes.

'Whatever is it, lass?' Auntie said.

I shook my head. 'Nothing. Nothing at all. It's just ... so ... '

'Well, good. For a minute there I thought you didn't like ham!'

After the meal we went for a stroll to the nearby pub, Judy running along ahead. We sat in the lounge of the Six Bells and Auntie and Nunky asked me question after question about nursing.

'Fascinating,' Auntie kept saying over and over.

It was like taking an oral exam, but wasn't a chore or a worry. I amazed myself at the depth of knowledge I'd stored up over the past three years, and suddenly realised I wasn't frightened about taking my hospital final. I was actually looking forward to it.

Back home, as Nunky made hot chocolate, with the addition of a dram or two of whisky, I sat watching Auntie prepare the breakfast table. It was done with such meticulous precision and attention to detail that I thought even Sister Dinsdale would be impressed. Finally Auntie put the bread board on the centre of the table and curiously slipped the bread knife underneath.

'Auntie?'

'Yes, lass?'

'Can I ask...? Why did you do that?'

'Do what, lass?'

'Put the knife under the board.'

'Oh, well, if there's a storm in the night, and lightning, we don't want it to strike the knife now, do we?' she said, her face deadly serious.

Then Auntie and Nunky retired to bed, leaving Alistair and me alone to sit by the range, with Judy curled up on the floor in front of us, whimpering and twitching in her sleep.

'Chasing rabbits again,' Alistair said with a smile, giving her ear a rub. 'So, what shall we do tomorrow?' he said, turning to me.

'I don't care. It's all just so peaceful,' I said. 'I could sit here and talk with your foster-parents all weekend.'

'Don't tell them that,' Alistair chuckled. 'They'd be more than happy to oblige. Tell you what, I'll take you on a tour of the village. Maybe have a look at the church.'

'I'd like that,' I yawned.

'Off to bed,' Alistair said. 'Come on.'

He led me upstairs, lighted candle in hand. I opened my door, stepped in, then pulled Alistair in after me.

'Phyll, not here!' he hissed, glancing back at the door.

'Just a kiss,' I teased, pressing my lips to his.

We kissed passionately, then I opened the door again, took the candle from Alistair's grasp, pushed him out into the dark hallway and closed the door on him.

I pinched out the candle, drew back the curtains and lay looking up at the hundreds of stars blanketing the sky. It made such a change not to see searchlights and barrage balloons or the flicker of burning buildings. The war seemed a world away.

'If only I could stay here for ever,' I sighed, and closed my eyes.

'Good-morning, lass. Did you sleep well?'

I opened my eyes to see Auntie hovering over me, a laden breakfast tray in her hands.

'What time is it?' I said sleepily, sitting up.

'It's gone nine,' Auntie said, placing the tray in front of me.

'Oh, I'm sorry, I—'

'Now, enough of that,' Auntie said. 'You're a guest. And guests – well, special guests, hard-working nurse guests – get breakfast in bed. Hope you like eggs. Freshly laid this morning. Take your time and then come down. There's hot water on the dressing-table too.'

I stared down at the tray in front of me and just couldn't believe my eyes. Boiled eggs. When was the last time I'd eaten a fresh egg? Two years ago? Longer? And lovely bread, warm from the oven, with real butter, a cup of tea and, to top it off, a small bowl of ripe wild strawberries. What luxury!

After my feast, I washed and dressed in a primrose silk suit and white shoes. Tripping downstairs, I put my tray down by the sink and was about to ask what the plans were for the day when there came a knock at the door. Auntie came into the kitchen.

'It's a telegram. For you, lass.'

'For me?'

Had something happened to my parents? I tore it open.

'Oh,' I said, reading the words.

'What, Phyll? Not bad news?'

'No, not bad news. Well, sort of. I've been summoned back to Hackney. It seems our respite is over.'

'When?' Alistair said, taking the telegram from me. I put my hand on his arm.

'I'm to report first thing.'

'Blast!' Alistair said. 'The first train's not until seven-twenty-five a.m., and that will be too late for you. You'll have to get one tonight if you're to get back in time. Of all the rotten—'

'Now, now,' Nunky said. 'It's a shame, so it is, but we still have the rest of today to enjoy.'

'That's true,' I said. 'It's a beautiful day. And we're together. Let's make the most of it.'

'I hate this war,' Alistair said moodily, looking down into my eyes.

'We all hate this war,' I said softly.

The morning was spent visiting the parents of Alistair's friends who were serving overseas. In the afternoon Alistair and I walked alone through the woods and across the fields, enjoying the peace and tranquillity of the Sussex countryside.

What a dinner awaited us when we returned home ruddy-cheeked and pleasantly tired! Roast beef from the farm, home-grown potatoes, carrots and cauliflower, followed by an apple pie with real cream.

'I'm glad I'm leaving,' I joked, 'otherwise I'd never fit into my uniform again.'

Nunky, Auntie and Judy walked us to the station to catch the 7.36 back to London.

Alistair was returning with me. 'I'm not letting you travel alone, Phyll.'

'Don't be silly. You've another day of leave.'

He shook his head. 'Without you here, it just won't feel right.'

The train pulled in to the station in a cloud of steam. Nunky hugged me and shoved a box of chocolates into my hand. Auntie had packed a food parcel for us as well, bless her.

'There's some Scotch pancakes and a couple of hard-boiled eggs,' she said. 'Don't eat them all at once.'

The guard blew his whistle and we climbed aboard. Alistair lowered the window and we leaned out.

Auntie blew us a kiss. 'We'll be proud to call you daughter, lass,' she called as the train pulled away.

I turned and gave Alistair a big kiss on the lips.

'They're delightful, you're delightful,' I said, my heart full of joy.

'They certainly are.' Alistair smiled thinly.

'Is everything all right?' I said.

'Nunky asked me when we were planning on getting married, and I couldn't say.'

'Well, we haven't really discussed it, have we?' I said. 'We've been so busy running around all over the place.'

'Precisely. So how about it? A date, I mean. Any thoughts?'

'I haven't even got a ring yet,' I sulked playfully.

'Don't worry about that,' he said, taking my hand. 'Next leave, we'll go to Regent Street, and then after that we'll have a proper engagement dinner.'

I sat upright and studied his face. I'd rather it was sooner than later: one just didn't know what was to happen in this war. Alistair could get posted at any time.

'Well,' I said, 'I have my finals in the new year, so how about just after? I really should concentrate on studying before then. I'm rather behind.'

Alistair nodded, then clicked his fingers. 'How about the four-teenth of February?'

'Valentine's Day? It's a perfect idea,' I said, kissing his cheek.

I couldn't wait to tell Mac and Eddie the news. But the nearer we got to London, the more apprehensive I felt. I could see the city up ahead but the train was beginning to crawl. Then it came to a complete halt. Concerned conversation started up in our compartment.

'What do you think it is?' I said.

Alistair shrugged. 'Congestion, I hope.'

We sat there for what seemed an age until eventually a guard popped his head into our compartment.

'Sorry, folks. A bomb's been dropped along the line for Victoria. We're being diverted to Waterloo.'

The train shunted off again.

'My God, an air raid,' Alistair said, looking up out of the window. 'No, it's all right, they're ours. Going south.'

The train clacked and creaked and eventually slipped into Waterloo Station. Alistair took a firm grip of my hand and we moved through the crowds towards the barrier. Then suddenly a loud crack filled the air.

'Incendiaries!' Alistair said. 'Move!'

We began to run just as the roof of the station shattered above us and splinters of glass started to rain down on the concourse. There was pandemonium, with people running in all directions in the hunt for safety.

'There!' Alistair pointed, and we followed a group of others into the Ladies' Room for shelter.

Firebells were ringing like the clappers now.

'Wasn't this all supposed to be over?' I said, shaking. I'd quite forgotten the terror of being caught in a raid. Had I grown soft in the relative safety of Woodford? *Silly girl*, I scolded myself, *never let your guard down*.

Alistair pulled me close and we sat huddled together, holding our breath, as we listened to the explosions and sirens outside.

Thankfully, it was over as quickly as it had started.

Outside the station, Waterloo was in confusion. There was

bomb damage wherever one looked, but I felt strangely calm. I was home again. This was where I belonged, in London, doing my bit to defy the Fascist pig. *My*, I said to myself, *where did that come from?* But I had to admit, I actually couldn't wait to get back to Hackney and into my uniform.

There were no buses in sight, but we waved down a taxi.

It pulled up beside the kerb and Alistair and I jumped in the back.

'Where to, ducks?' the cabbie said over his shoulder.

'Can you get us to Leicester Square tube? If not, Charing Cross will do,' I said.

'Right-oh!' And he shot off.

Alistair and I were thrown around in the back as the taxi swerved like a dodgem car avoiding craters, rubble and fire crews working at putting out the incendiary damage.

I began to giggle, but I don't think Alistair found the ride all that thrilling.

We screeched to a halt just as we turned to cross the Thames. A policeman was holding up his hand. I could see a bus lying on its side across Waterloo Bridge. The taxi did a quick U-turn and sped down towards Westminster Bridge.

'We'll 'ave to go past Parliament and along Whitehall, folks,' the cabbie shouted back to us.

'Can't we just take off from here?' Alistair said dryly.

I giggled even more at that.

The taxi wove through Trafalgar Square, past the proud lions at the foot of Nelson's column, and on up the Charing Cross Road. It pulled up sharply opposite Leicester Square Station.

Alistair paid the driver and we trotted over to the Underground entrance. I dropped my bag and we clung to one another, kissing as we were jostled by people hurrying in and out of the station.

Two red caps standing nearby eyed us suspiciously, but I just ignored them.

'You'll be all right getting your bus?' Alistair said, brushing a lock of hair from my forehead.

I nodded. 'Of course. The stop's just up there.'

'Good. I love you.'

'I love you.'

'We'll get engaged properly soon,' he said. 'I'll write when I know what my duties are.'

We kissed again, and I watched as Alistair first showed his pass to the two MPs, then with a final wave, he disappeared down the steps to the station. I turned and made the short walk up to Shaftesbury Avenue, where I hoped there would be a bus to get me back to the Hospital.

23

The devastation around Homerton High Street is more depressing than ever, but despite having suffered still further incendiary bombs (judging by the scorch marks up and down its walls) Hackney Hospital itself appears to be miraculously undamaged.

Once inside, all that had changed was that I was back on day duty and therefore my room was on the third floor. The hospital final was looming, and I had fallen far behind in my studies.

The first thing that happened on our return from Claybury was a summons before Matron.

'Nurse Elsworth,' Matron said, glaring back at me from behind her desk, 'you have been disappointing me of late. Your lecture notes are behind and you have been requesting and taking far too much leave. And, to top it all, I hear you are now engaged. Is this true?'

'Yes, Matron,' I said humbly, angry that I still felt like a naughty schoolgirl having to take what I deemed an unreasonable dressing-down. I was an extremely hard-working, conscientious and dedicated nurse. Did she not know what I'd been through with Flight Officer Bates?

'Having said that,' Matron continued, 'I still have faith in you and know you will make a fine nurse some day. *If* you knuckle down.'

'Yes, Matron.'

'How old are you now? Twenty?'

'Twenty-one last April, Matron.'

'Don't you think you're a little young to be getting married?'

I took a deep breath before I answered. Then I looked her directly in the eye. 'No, Matron. No, I don't.'

'I also note that you have once again put your name down as pianist for the hospital revue,' she said with a small shake of her head. 'I know that I personally recommended you a few years back, but how do you think you are going to cope?'

'I will fit it in around my lectures and studies, Matron,' I said firmly.

She studied me thoughtfully for a moment. 'I hope you are right. Very well, off you go. You're on . . .' she paused as she flicked through the duty roster on her desk, 'Women's Surgical. Dismissed. And remember,' she called just as I was stepping through the doorway, 'work before pleasure.'

I left her office fit to explode. How infuriating she – all the seniors – could be! But part of me knew that she was right. What with my parents returning to Dovercourt and my increasingly close relationship with Alistair, I had rather lost focus on my career.

'Right,' I muttered as I made my way to the Women's Surgical Ward, 'I'll show the lot of you!'

So, rehearsals aside, I did nothing but work and study for the weeks that followed, turning down invites to the pub and the pictures. I made only rare appearances in the lounge, where, despite listening to the wireless for news, I was always encouraged to play a tune on the piano to lift spirits.

'Is everything all right, Phyll?' Mac asked, sitting down with me at tea one afternoon.

242 PHYLL MACDONALD-ROSS with I. D. ROBERTS

'Of course, I just need to catch up,' I said. 'Don't worry. I'll be back in the party spirit soon. So, how's your Sergeant-Major?'

'He sends me letters, which is something. I think he's in Africa, but you can never be sure. What about Alistair?'

'Oh, you know him,' I smiled, 'he writes every other day, which I don't know how he fits in. He's away for a while on some technical course in Wiltshire.'

'Swindon, apparently,' Mac said. 'At least that's where Eddie says Tim is. They're both in the same unit still aren't they? Tim and Alistair?'

I nodded. 'As thick as thieves.'

Mac left me to finish my tea, and my thoughts turned to Alistair. I realised I hadn't been as prolific in replying to his letters. I was finding it difficult to find the time, what with lectures to write up. I'd also heard from my parents again, and thankfully Mother appeared to be getting back to her old self. I think she was actually looking forward to me getting married.

Then, towards the end of October, I had a letter from Alistair saying he had a forty-eight-hour pass. He wanted me to ask if I could get the Friday off to meet him so that we could go and collect the engagement ring we'd chosen and to make sure it fitted.

Having made no requests for time off since I'd returned to Hackney, I went down to Matron's office to ask for a half-day off.

'No, Nurse Elsworth,' she said, without even looking up from the papers she was reading. 'You have the coming weekend off already, and if your fiancé is here, then I doubt you'll be doing any studying, will you? Other than anatomy, I dare say.'

I was utterly flabbergasted. Did she really just say that? Or was it my imagination? How rude, how forward, how ... presumptuous! I took a deep breath, forced a 'Thank you, Matron' through gritted teeth, and turned on my heel.

I am not a violent person, but I think I could have punched the first smiling face I saw if I hadn't dodged into the toilet. I sat in the cubicle and had what I can only describe as a mild tantrum. Thankfully there was no one else in there. Feeling rather ashamed at my loss of control, I tidied myself up in the mirror above the sink and returned to my duties.

During my afternoon break, the maid came up to me.

'Nurse Elsworth,' she said, 'there's a visitor for you at the gate lodge.'

'Thank you, Gladys,' I said, pushing my chair back.

I trotted across the forecourt to see a familiar figure standing under the cloaked light at the porter's door.

'Alistair!' I said, jumping into his arms.

'How are you?' he said, planting kisses all over my face.

'Angry that I can't see you today.'

'Not to worry. Here, give me your left hand.'

I held it out and, practical as ever, Alistair produced a piece of string and made a measurement of my ring finger.

'You think of everything,' I said watching him work.

'I do my best,' he smiled.

'Where are you staying tonight?'

'The barracks in Finchley.'

'That's good,' I said, glancing at my fob watch. 'I'll have to get back now. So, listen, my pass starts tomorrow at ten a.m. I'll catch the bus and mee–'

'Meet me under Eros in Piccadilly Circus at midday.'

'You romantic, you,' I smiled, and rising on my toes, kissed him on the lips.

Alistair gave me a wave, turned and headed off to catch a bus.

'Nice lad, that.' It was Joe, the porter.

'He's not bad, Joe,' I said with a smile.

The rest of my day flew by and after the routine drill of pulling the beds away from the walls in the ward in preparation for any air raids during the night, I went to the dining room with Mac and Eddie. Later we went through some old exam papers, taking it in turns to ask one another the questions.

The following morning, 23 October 1941, was a beautiful autumn day. There was a slight frost dusting the trees and the fallen leaves sparkled in the bright sunshine. I felt elated.

I fashioned my longish hair in a roll-and-tuck style, then put on my brown two-piece in jersey wool, with brown lace-up shoes and matching handbag. I studied myself in the mirror, checked the seams were straight in my tights and that my slip wasn't showing, then put on my tilted Derby bowler hat and hurried out of the nurses' home. I couldn't wait to see Alistair. Today was our day and, with a glance up at the clear blue sky, I prayed that the Germans would keep away.

Piccadilly was busy with off-duty troops, ARP clean-up squads and people trying to live as normal a life as they could among the devastation. Eros was hidden away beneath a protection of sandbags and advertising hoardings, and looked more like an Egyptian pyramid than a statue, but it didn't take long for me to spot Alistair waiting near by. He looked really dapper in his uniform, with a smart peaked cap and, I suddenly noticed, three stripes on his arm.

'You've been promoted!' I said.

'Just this week,' he said, snapping a fine salute. 'Sergeant Alistair Ross at your service, miss. Would you care to accompany me to the finest restaurant Lyons Corner House has to offer?'

I gave him a salute in return. 'On the double, Sergeant, sir,' I grinned.

He offered me his arm, and dodging the traffic, we skipped across to the Lyons building.

It was to the Viennese restaurant we went and, as was usual, a queue had already formed. But we didn't care, we were just so happy to be together. Eventually a waiter came up to us and led us to a table for two, near to the orchestra. Alistair ordered champagne and we toasted one another.

'How can you afford this?' I asked.

'Please, Phyll, just enjoy it,' he smiled.

He leaned back in his chair and indicated for the waiter to approach. He whispered something to him and pressed a note into his hand.

The waiter bowed his head, glanced at me with a smile on his lips, and moved over to the band leader.

'What are you up to?' I said.

Alistair leaned forward. 'I love you, Phyllis Elsworth. And I would be honoured if you'd be my wife.'

'I've already said yes, silly.'

'Just put your hand under the table.'

I frowned, but did as I was told, and felt him slip a ring on to my finger. I pulled my hand back and stared at the ring. It was beautiful. As I looked up, tears blurring my vision, the orchestra started playing Jimmy Dorsey's 'Yours'.

A small round of applause broke out amongst the diners at the tables nearest to us.

'Oh, Alistair,' I said, and he leaned forward and kissed me across the table.

After our meal, we took a romantic stroll around Hyde Park, and stopped for tea at a small café. But time seemed to be against us and before long we were parting company again.

'I wish we were getting married tomorrow,' I said, holding him tight as we waited at my bus stop.

'Do you want to? Sooner, I mean?'

I shook my head. 'No, Valentine's Day is perfect. Besides, there's lots to organise before then. Here's my bus.'

Alistair removed his cap and, taking me in his arms, kissed me long and hard.

'Alistair,' I said, breathlessly gazing into his eyes.

'I love you, Phyll.'

'I love you, too.'

He guided me up onto the bus, and I made my way quickly up the stairs to my favourite seat at the very back. I turned and waved to him from the rear window, and sat like that until Alistair had disappeared from sight.

PART FIVE

1942

Daily Express
Monday, February 16, 1942

"This is a moment when the British nation can
show its quality and draw from the heart of
misfortune the vital impulse of victory."

ANOTHER DUNKIRK BEFORE
SINGAPORE SURRENDER

Japs say most British
troops got safely away

ESCAPING TRANSPORTS BOMBED

Daily Express

No. 13,018   Monday, February 16, 1942   One Penny

"This is a moment when the British nation can show its quality and draw from the heart of misfortune the vital impulse of victory"

ANOTHER DUNKIRK BEFORE SINGAPORE SURRENDER

BURMA: BIG NEW ATTACK

Japs say most British troops got safely away

ESCAPING TRANSPORTS BOMBED

TOKYO early today followed up an official announcement that Singapore had surrendered unconditionally with reports that most of the British and Australian forces left the island on Friday night.

These messages said that 20 or more ships, none smaller than 1,000 tons, and a 10,000-ton cruiser were seen at anchor late on Friday. On Saturday morning they had all gone.

"Obviously," said the Japanese, "the British went to Sumatra."

First official statements in Britain that Singapore had fallen was made by Mr. Churchill last night.

A German broadcast claimed that Sir Shenton Thomas, the Singapore Governor, "had by plane with a number of officials to Batavia or Calcutta."

Tokyo's regular daily communiqué made no direct reference to an evacuation, but, referring to operations between Wednesday and Saturday, claimed that heavy attacks were made on British convoys south of Singapore.

A dagger at heart of the Indies

Express Naval Reporter
BERNARD HALL

SURRENDER at Singapore is the Japanese in the west the Very Area suffered in this way. It is more than any dozen of capital ships.

For over weeks, the offensive car has been divided in the lines. Now its use to have passed to the enemy, next par'l gateway to the East Just a dagger at the Indies, turning the enemy's gateway to Singapore.

160 BOMBS AT ONE SHIP

It listed, as ships afloat, a light cruiser, an auxiliary cruiser, a submarine, two gunboats, a mine-layer, a ship of special type, and eight transports—one of 10,000 tons, one 6,000 tons, four 5,000 tons, and two 2,000 tons.

Ships said to have been damaged were a Dutch cruiser, a British destroyer, two special type ships, 18 transports, and a torpedo boat.

From Batavia the Express special correspondent said that one of the last evacuation ships from Singapore was bombed by 32 'planes in 48 separate attacks between 8 a.m. and 1 p.m. The vessel was 90 miles from the island

Another was attacked for four hours before entering the Banka Strait (between Sumatra and Banka Island), where the raids were even fiercer. In fifteen runs over the ship by seventy flights of warplanes, about 160 bombs were dropped. Few were near.

A Reuter message from Batavia reported the arrival in Java of "a party of the Australian Imperial Press from Singapore"—whether wounded or not is not stated.

ONE-MAN SUB. MISSES

This despatch added that a small warship, one of the many "little ships" which have been daily dodging death between Singapore and the Indies, reported port with only one piece of mail left to the bunkers. It, too, was bombed in the Banka Strait.

The Australian captain said it measured out of the concentrated attack of 37 machines, and was then attacked by a one-man Japanese submarine, whose torpedo passed within five yards. It grazed a sandbank, went on, and hit it by a second vessel but missed bombing while.

INTO THE WAR
A Japanese island, with the 150,000,000 naval base, surrendered at 1 p.m. Singapore time (12.30 p.m. B.S.T.), Japanese Imperial headquarters announced.

The surrendered of the semi-official Domei News Agency added that the "cease fire" was sounded along the entire front at ten o'clock. He reported that at maximum of 7,000 armed British soldiers will be left in the city to maintain order until the Japanese complete occupation.

WHITE FLAG

"The British," he says, "used for peace at 2.30 p.m. when they found themselves surrounded in Singapore City and in the central section of the island, helpless to defend themselves against bombs and shells.

"The British and Japanese Commanders-in-Chief, Lieutenant-General Percival and Lieutenant-General Yamashita, met in the Ford water plant at the foot of Bukit Timah Hill (six miles north of the city) and signed the surrender documents.

"A peace mission of four British officers, headed by Major C. H. D. Wild, of the British staff, approached Japanese Army headquarters bearing a white flag of truce."

They were handed Japan's terms. They left headquarters at 4.20 p.m. after arranging a meeting for 7 p.m. between the leaders of the victorious and vanquished armies for the formal British surrender.

"With General Percival at the signing were Major—

→ BACK PAGE, COL. THREE

Bigger problem

Ends and larger members more alike the in war and inside of the the in Japanese. With the British maw Far East of the Last Pacific, More forces, and greater a great problem of the Indies, not so the Saturday to such them.

To above on the Allies go far from where they're big while than whom now see to that purpose. Indies and the West Pacific, bombing of the Americans in Java. There is now a battleship at Pearl—

Chiang Kai-shek awarded G.C.B.

KING, by conveying and Emperor and Chiang Kai-shek the Grand Cross of the Order of the Bath, the most distinguished honorary by the Order of the G.C.B.

WHOSOEVER IS GUILTY . . .

This is Churchill's appeal to all men and women of the British Empire, taken from his broadcast

The same qualities which brought us through the awful jeopardy of the summer of 1940, and carried us through the long autumn and winter of bombardment when we fought alone, until comfort and then later strength and might arrived from the new order, though it comes not as fast as we might desire, these same qualities and will certainly be found in us to our complete deliverance and, under God's guiding hand, to final victory.

But it is the duty of all who take part in these high matters to make sure, as far as they can, that tragic mistakes like those that caused the fall of France, and the catastrophe, of Dunkirk, shall not happen again. Evil things are being done in the name of Government in those of whom are expected victory and then when failure occurs, and then when other leaders are put in charge who have been found guilty of mismanagement. We must search ourselves in a spirit of hard times and of sober wisdom and of just proportions before we put our own self right and our most forward stage.

The whole future of mankind may depend upon our action and upon our conduct. So far we have not failed. We shall not fail now. Let us move forward steadfastly together into the storm and through the storm.

SINGAPORE REFUGEE SHIP HIT FOUR TIMES—GETS THROUGH

Children face 5-hr. bombing

Express Special Correspondent

BATAVIA, Sunday.

THREE HUNDRED European women and children who left Singapore under Japanese mortar fire, dive-bombing and shelling, have arrived safe in port after an experience which a tough merchant skipper described as "hell."

THE EIGHTEEN BRAVE MEN

WHO were the men in the six feverish planes — the condemned planes that flew into the Channel Battle and did not return?

Of that crew, only five came back. They took delivery in the crash. Today, in tribute, the Daily Express prints the names of the eighteen men who failed to return:—

FIRST PLANE: Lieut.-Commander Eugene Esmonde, D.S.O., Lieutenant E. Kingsmill, Sub-Lieutenant C. M. Clinton—all missing.

SECOND PLANE: Sub-Lieutenant B. W. Rose, Sub-Lieutenant Edgar Lee, Leading Airman A. L. Johnson—

THIRD PLANE: Lieutenant-Commander R. C. Thompson, Sub-Lieutenant C. R. Wood, Leading Airman E. Tapping—all missing.

FOURTH PLANE: Sub-Lieutenant P. Bligh, Sub-Lieutenant W. H. Beynon, Leading Airman W. J. Smith—all missing.

FIFTH PLANE: Sub-Lieutenant C. R. Kingsmill and Lieutenant R. Fraser, Airman—all missing.

SIXTH PLANE: Sub-Lieutenant C. M. Bennett, Sub-Lieutenant L. Williams, Leading Airman

Nurses under fire

The ship was hit four times, once by a torpedo, others by bombs. Australian nurses sheltering in the hold volunteered to climb to the deck and help to dress and bind the wounded.

The skipper said to the crew: "Better — "refugees, I was" "Every time we were hit we felt a sickening thud and quivered for a moment or two. It took nearly nine minutes and sometimes a quarter of an hour then, and more nine shells burst over us in another fierce attack. Another shell hit us in the magazine and set it on fire. But the captain of a warship coming alongside us poured water on the flames and put them out.

This is one of three accounts when the British reached Java.

The port is reported on Page Four.

JAPS CLAIM OIL CITY IN SUMATRA

Express War Reporter

BATAVIA, Sunday.

DUTCHMEN today carried out the greatest scorched earth devastation of the Pacific war by wrecking their oil installations in the Palembang zone as the Japanese began a big-scale invasion of Southern Sumatra from the sea.

Tokyo tonight claims that the oilfield city of Palembang, 50 miles inland, in oil-rich southern Sumatra, with its surrounding refineries producing one-third of the Dutch Indies oil, has fallen into the stronghold east of southern Sumatra.)

No details of the Sumatra landings are known in Batavia, but it is assumed that they come from Pontianak, in West Borneo, where troop and other concentrations have been observed for several days.

Richest prize

March of the Jap blitz in S. Pacific was as great prize was the fall of the islands in Southern Sumatra, richest prize of the entire offensive of the South-West Pacific.

So "scattered" they all would clear in front the Palembang oil with their main prize. They made a sacrifice equal to the destruction of oil plants in Burma.

Mopped up

The Dutch were ready for years; it is understood that all but five of the main wells remained in repair two short years. But the remainder are useless.

Oil engineers foresaw that it apparently it an air battle was first with mass parachute over Palembang with the forced to leave the country.

No enemy prepared for warship parties not do the destruction. For months there were demolition squads to wreck

→ BACK PAGE, COL. EIGHT

---

4 A.M. LATEST

AMERICANS PRAISE CHURCHILL SPEECH

WASHINGTON, Sunday.—Americans to-night praised Mr. Churchill's steadfast and courageous speech. Senators and Congressmen called here it the most determined of the war.

Mr. Stimson, War chairman, said: "I have not read or heard the speech, but from news flash I think it admirable."

The White House dominant staff sent to the Prime a message a man from the Americans saying: "We are with you. We are behind you. The fall behind you and get well soon and will say that nation fight to death."—Reuter.

MOVED OUT

Hundreds of thousand minute pamphlet bombs fell on Japanese in Malaya at the moment of the yesterday's landing in the coastline, bringing new leaflet and smartly dropping.

All Jap planes scoured areas. The bold man aid thick the fog and the Jap planes appeared more than one in Commonwealth two for all Service forces in the ocean.

A Select force of Britannia was bombing in raid over Tulsa waters this morning.

HITLER CALLS BRAUCHITSCH

Back to old job?

STOCKHOLM, Sunday.—It was reported from Berlin last night that Hitler had reappointed Field-Marshal von Brauchitsch, former German Commander-in-Chief, who was dismissed last December.

Field-Marshal von Brauchitsch, the officer who had not been in good health for many weeks, had retired on a Commander-in-Chief.—Exchange News Service.

Dublin guns fire

Dublin anti-aircraft guns fired at an unidentified plane yesterday.

RAIDER DOWN
Night bomb victims

A raider was shot down over Britain last night. Bombs fell in a village in Aberdeenshire. Several people were injured.

Bombs were also dropped in east Scotland and north-east England. Dutch raiders attacked Dieppe yesterday.

Cutler lone of 20 from U.S.) sunk

Petain sees North African leaders

Marshal Petain yesterday received Admiral Darlan, Minister for the Fighting Services, and several North African leaders, including General Weygand.

U.S. launches new battleship today

WASHINGTON, Sunday.—The 35,000-ton United States battleship Indiana will be launched tomorrow at Newport News, Virginia.

Fine and cold

British: Fair, calm, cloudy, cold.

GENERAL PERCIVAL
Signed at 7 p.m. Rushition General three hours hour

map captions:
MALAYA
SINGAPORE
SUMATRA
OCCUPIED BY JAPS
JAPANESE PARATROOPS WIPES OUT
Palembang
BORNEO
PONTIANAK
DUTCH BURNING OIL WELLS AS THEY LEFT
AFTER TOWN AND AIRPORT OF TRANSPORTS
LARGE-SCALE LANDINGS FROM SEA
JAVA
Soerabaya

24

December 1941 and into January 1942 not only sees the Americans join the war after they are attacked at Pearl Harbor, but my mother descending on London, and all around my Hospital Finals, too. I haven't heard from Alistair in a while, but Mother has written to say she is coming to the city to help me shop for my wedding trousseau.

It was a Thursday, two weeks before Christmas. Matron condescendingly gave me the day off, and so I headed off to Liverpool Street to meet Mother off the 8.55 from Dovercourt.

It was a bitterly cold day and light flurries of snow had been falling but, thankfully, not settling. Yet. Clothing coupons were not plentiful, and we were well into the 'make do and mend' way of living now. But I had not been extravagant with my allowance of late, and living in uniform for most of the week was actually a godsend. So I had been poring over fashion magazines with Mac and Eddie, looking for ideas.

'What a shame we're not at Claybury any more,' Mac said. 'I bet Mrs Mason would help you out.'

'Golly, yes, Phyll,' Eddie chipped in, 'perhaps we should write to her and ask.'

'Don't!' I said. 'I couldn't possibly.'

Mac and Eddie exchanged a knowing glance, but said no more on the matter.

'Please don't,' I repeated. 'It's embarrassing. And I have enough money saved. Really, I do.'

'All right, Phyll,' Eddie said. 'But if you're stuck for anything you must ask. You only get married once.'

'Unless y–' Mac started to say, but Eddie elbowed her in the side. 'Hey? What was that for? I was only going to s—'

'Don't!' Eddie and I said as one, and laughed.

'What about a wedding dress?' Eddie said.

'Ah, that's sorted,' I said. 'Alistair's friend, Henry – remember? He got married in June and Matron wouldn't give me the time off to go—'

'I remember, the cow,' Mac said.

'—well his wife's the same size as me and has already said I can borrow her dress. I tried it on when I visited Alistair's folks in Sussex. It's beautiful, in ivory satin embossed with fleurs-de-lis. And it has one of those Tudor-style collars. Very chic, with a slightly scooped neckline.'

'Perfect,' Eddie said. 'After all, why buy one when you only need a wedding dress the once?'

'Unless–'

'Mac!' Eddie and I shouted again.

So, by eleven o'clock, I was armed with a list, ready and waiting at the platform barrier for Mother's train to arrive. I hadn't seen my parents since the two-week break in late summer when I'd introduced Alistair to them, so I was actually rather looking forward to her arrival.

The station was swarming with personnel from all three forces, with a heavy presence of Military Police keeping a beady eye on each and every one of them.

Black smoke puffed into the station as the locomotive chuffed

and chugged to Platform 10. With a mighty hiss of steam it came
to a standstill and the doors flew open. And then I spotted the all-
too-familiar brown corduroy cloche hat, a relic from the early
1930s and still going strong. How it made me cringe.

'Now, Phyll, be nice,' I muttered to myself and waved.

Mother saw me and raised her hand.

'Hello, Phyllis dear,' she said, giving me a kiss as we met at the
barrier. 'My, you do look glamorous.'

'Hello, Mother. How was the journey?'

'Draughty. I shall catch my death, I wouldn't wonder.'

'Well, let's pop across the road to Dirty Dick's and have—'

'Dirty Dick's!' Mother said, aghast. 'I am not frequenting an
establishment with a name like that, young lady! This may be
London, but I have my principles.'

I didn't bother to argue, just took her arm and headed for the
station café for tea and cake.

'Father sends his love, and ten pounds, too.'

'Oh, Mother, he shouldn't have. I've sav—'

'Hush, hush. We have a lot of things to purchase that you're
going to need. So,' she said, picking up the menu, 'where shall we
start?'

'Oxford Street,' I said.

The journey on the Central Line was quick, but it made conversation impossible. The crush of people shoving their way on
and elbowing their way off was relentless: even though war was
raging, Christmas shopping was in full swing. This wasn't the
perfect time to be collecting my trousseau, but in two weeks I'd
be busy with the Christmas concert, then the new year would be
taken up with exams. No, it was now or never. I gave Mother a
smile over the heads of three rather shrill WAAFs, glamorous in
their blue-grey service uniforms with RAF insignia, and just
hoped the day would go well.

At Oxford Circus sleeping-bags and blankets were stacked neatly against the platform walls. Even though the air raids were less common now, with so much devastation up above, the Underground was still home for hundreds whose only safe refuge was the station. We took the escalator up to ground level and were met by a biting wind that stung our cheeks. We walked briskly, arm in arm, down Oxford Street towards Selfridges.

John Lewis & Co. had been completely destroyed during the bombing in September 1940 and was still just a shell, but miraculously part of its East House was now trading again. The other major stores, Selfridges, Bourne & Hollingsworth and Peter Robinson, had also been damaged, but they too were open for business as usual. The war was not going to get in the way of the British shopper, that was certain. There was also Swan & Edgar for us to try at Piccadilly Circus.

Thankfully, whatever the state of their façades, the insides of the department stores were wonderfully warm and inviting.

Lingerie was first on my list, but the choice was rather poor. White satin knickers were the fashion, and thankfully my coupons allowed for one pair, as well as a satin slip. While I was umming and ahhing, Mother spotted a dream of a nightdress in coffee satin trimmed with deep-set lace and a matching negligée. That, she told me, was her and Father's present to me.

Just before two o'clock we decided to get a spot of lunch. The store's menu wasn't very inspiring, but our toad-in-the-hole was passable, the rice pudding warming and the tea refreshing.

'So, how's life at home?' I said, picking through the Yorkshire pudding in search of a piece of sausage.

'Quieter,' Mother said. 'There's very infrequent air raids now. But there are still a lot of soldiers about. Sailors too.'

'How are Henry and Archie?'

'They're nice clean boys.'

'And Father?'

'Tired. It's a bit of a trek for him, toing and froing to Ipswich each day. And then there's his Special-Constable duties at night at the docks,' Mother said with a sigh. 'We hardly see one another.'

'Well, now the Americans have joined the war, let's hope it'll all be over soon.'

'I pray you're right, my dear.'

Selecting a hat proved to be a trial. There wasn't a great selection, but in the end I found a burgundy felt bowler with a shallow square crown and a narrow rolled brim. It was held in place with a pearl hatpin and worn at a tilt towards the back of the head. I thought it most becoming, Mother just sniffed.

The coat was less troublesome and I decided on a double-breasted one, in burgundy again, with a Peter Pan collar edged in black velvet, and a half-belt at the back.

Shoes, handbag and gloves were the last items I needed. However, we were both feeling a little jaded by now and we had little more than an hour before we had to head off for Liverpool Street.

'Let's just pick some shoes, Mother,' I said. 'I can get a handbag and gloves after Christmas on my day off.'

It didn't take long for me to find a lovely pair of brown lace-ups with a Cuban heel, and fortunately the size I needed was the last pair in stock. So, laden with our parcels, Mother and I headed back out to Oxford Street.

'We'll catch a bus, it's more relaxing than the tube.' I said. 'We've time enough for a last cup of tea at the station.'

We hovered in the entrance hall of the Department store, then I spotted a no. 38, and we hurried outside. It was bitterly cold and there was snow in the air.

'Are you happy with the purchases, Phyllis?' Mother said, as we sat ourselves down on the top deck.

'I think we've done really well, in spite of the clothing coupons,' I said. 'Thanks for all your help, Mother. And thank Father for the money.'

'Don't be silly, dear,' she smiled. 'We want your day to be perfect. Now, talking of the day, I've had a word with your Aunt Rose and she'll be making the cake. And I've been up to see Father Hole at St Nicholas' and so we need to arrange the reading of the banns, and—'

'Mother,' I interrupted, 'Alistair and I have decided to be married here in London, in St Martin-in-the-Fields.'

The colour rose in her cheeks and the corner of her left eye started twitching.

'Listen, Mother,' I said, 'try and be reasonable, to understand. Time is short. Alistair's foster-parents are quite elderly. They live on the other side of the city, down in Sussex. We thought it would be fair on everyone, under the circumstances, to hold the ceremony in the middle, in London. That would give both our families limited travel.'

'But,' Mother spluttered, 'you must be married from your home.'

'Oh, Mother, please,' I gasped in exasperation. 'This is 1942, not 1842. All my friends are here, as well as Alistair's. And London is my home.'

'Next stop Liverpool Street,' shouted the conductor from downstairs.

Mother huffily gathered up her packages and got unsteadily to her feet as the bus swerved towards the kerb.

'Goodness knows,' she said, glaring down at me, 'your Father won't like this one bit. Our only daughter ...' She shook her head. 'We had such plans!'

'Please, Mother,' I said, getting to my feet.

'No. You stay,' she snapped.

She hesitated, pecked my cheek rather coolly and moved to the stairs.

'Mother,' I called after her, 'When I get back to the hospital, I'll write and explain.'

But whether she heard me or not I didn't know. I watched her walk stiffly into the station entrance without so much as a backward glance. I cursed under my breath as the conductor pressed the bell to tell the driver to move on.

25

I have to put my anger and frustration with Mother aside quickly: there is too much to be getting on with at the hospital – the Christmas concert, my studies, then the exams themselves. When I got back to the Nurses' Home, I sat and wrote a detailed letter to Mother and Father explaining Alistair's and my decision about getting married in London. It greatly angered me that I had to, but I wanted my parents to be on my side. It was supposed to be the happiest day of my life, and I wanted nothing to spoil it.

I'm delighted to say the exams went well, and Mac, Eddie and I were all confident that we had passed, and moved into the fourth year of our training with great hope and enthusiasm. I was back on Women's Surgical working with Maggie O'Reilly again, and on Wednesday, 28 January I had a split shift, off for the afternoon then back on duty from 4.30 to 8.30 p.m.

The early evening was quiet. Staff asked me to check and record the intake and output charts, so I had my head buried in adding up the tedious figures when I became aware that the office phone was ringing.

The main ward door opened and Rosie, the ward-maid, hurried over to me.

"Ere, Nurse Elsworth, Matron wants you in 'er office!'

What have I done now? was the first thing that flashed into my head.

I put down the charts I was working through, wrapped my cloak around myself and hurried through the maze of corridors to Matron's office. My mind was tumbling with scenarios, for being summoned by Matron was never a good sign. Perhaps there had been a mistake with my exam papers and I'd have to resit my hospital finals. My mouth had gone dry by the time I reached Matron's door, and my heart was beating like a broken clock. I removed my cloak, straightened my apron and checked my hair was properly tucked under my cap. Then I knocked and waited.

'Come!'

I opened the door and was relieved to see that it wasn't Matron after all but her deputy, Miss Mills.

'Don't look so worried, Nurse Elsworth,' she said with a friendly smile. 'Your fiancé is on the telephone. Take the call on the extension in my office through there.'

What! I thought, absolutely horrified. *How could he?*

'Thank you, Miss Mills,' I said and hurried into the next room. The receiver was off the hook, lying on the desk, staring back at me accusingly. *Just you wait, Alistair Ross*, I fumed.

'Yes?' I said, tersely.

'*It's Alistair, I—*'

'How dare you ring me?' I hissed. 'I'm on—'

'*Shut up, Phyll, and listen.*'

I was stunned into silence. Alistair had never used that tone with me before. An icy chill ran over my skin.

'*Phyll? Are you there?*'

'Y-yes, Alistair. What is it? What's happened?'

'*Listen, darling, I've been given forty-eight hours' embarkation leave, as from now, and I want to marry you before I go.*'

I felt suddenly faint, and plonked myself down in the desk chair. My God, they were sending Alistair off to war. Please, no. Where? Where would he be going?

'Oh, Alistair,' I sobbed.

'*Phyll, listen to me. Hush.*' Alistair's voice sounded hollow on the other end of the line. '*I'm coming over in two hours. It's – what? Five-past six now. I'm yet to collect my kit. Can you get immediate leave?*'

'Oh, Alistair, I ...' Tears filled my eyes and my voice was choked with emotion. 'Yes, yes, of course. I'll talk to Deputy Matron now. She'll understand.'

'*Good. Hurry. Get yourself packed and ready for when I arrive. We don't have much time. Chin up.*'

'I—'

But the line was dead.

I replaced the receiver and sat staring back at the telephone in stunned silence. Wiping my face, I returned to Matron's office.

'Is everything—'

I burst into uncontrollable tears, and Miss Mills pulled herself out of her seat and came and put her arms around me.

'There, there, Nurse Elsworth. Phyllis, isn't it?' she said. 'Tell me, what's happened?'

'I'm sorry, Matron,' I blubbed. 'It's nothing serious ... It's not a death, it's—' I broke down again, unable to get the words out.

'Just tell me in your own time. That was your fiancé on the telephone, is that right?'

I nodded. 'Yes. He's just been given forty-eight hours' notice of embarkation. He wants to marry me before he leaves.'

'I see,' Miss Mills said. 'Then you must marry him, child.'

'But, Matron,' I said, sniffing, 'I'm on duty ... I have no leave ... I have no money ... Our salary isn't payable until the end of—'

'Hush, hush, girl,' Miss Mills said. 'As of now, you may have four days' compassionate leave. That will give you until Sunday evening. All right? Now, I have two pounds ten shillings that I can loan you.'

'Oh, Matron.' I broke down again.

'Now, now, you really must pull yourself together. Go and pack, and I will have your pass waiting for you at the porter's lodge.'

Miss Mills moved into her own office, unlocked the drawer in her desk, and came back in with a cash box. She opened it up and took out the money.

'Here you are. Run along now back to the ward. Tell Staff what's happened. I'll go and get relief sent to you and when she arrives you must get going. Fifteen minutes, tops. All right?' She smiled down at me.

I put the money in my apron pocket, wiped my tears and smiled back.

'Thank you so very much, Matron.'

'Good luck, Phyllis,' she said, picking up the telephone at her elbow.

I hurried back to the ward and burst into tears as soon as I saw Maggie's concerned face.

'Phyll, whatever's up?'

'Oh, Maggie. It's all going so horribly wrong.'

I told her what had happened.

'Come and sit in the office,' she said. 'Rosie, get her a cuppa, would you?'

''Course I will, poor mite,' Rosie said, and she disappeared off to the kitchen.

'Look,' Maggie said, 'I'll nip back to my room. I've got three pounds I can loan you.'

I started to protest, but she insisted.

'If you don't take it, I'll be forever offended.'

I nodded and smiled my thanks.

''Ere you go, ducks,' Rosie said, coming back in with a cup of tea in her hand. 'You drink up, and 'ere's an aspirin, too. Yer 'ead must be bangin', what with the worry.'

Maggie was gone but five minutes, and when she returned the relief nurse was with her.

'You can repay it when you can,' she said, handing me the money.

We hugged each other. I gave Rosie's hand a squeeze, then I hurried off the ward and back to my room to pack.

Just as I was pulling open the door to the nurses' home, Mac was coming out.

'Phyll!' she said, smiling. Then her face dropped.

'Oh, Mac,' I said, bursting into tears once more.

'Come on,' she said, taking my arm. 'I was off to the cinema, but I'll not go now. Tell me.'

By the time we'd reached the third floor, I'd put Mac in the picture. My hand was trembling as I unlocked my room, but once inside, Mac took over.

'Right,' she said, throwing off her coat and hat. 'You go soak in the bath while I start packing. What time is Alistair getting here?'

'He said two hours.'

Mac checked her watch. 'It's just gone seven now. We can have supper at half-past.'

'No, Mac. I couldn't,' I said.

'Go and bathe!' Mac snapped.

'But, Mac,' I said, looking about my room totally lost. 'I haven't bought stockings or gloves or a handbag. What am I to do?'

'Nothing,' she said. 'Leave it to me. Here.' She picked up my towel and soap and pushed me out of the door. 'Hurry up.'

When I reappeared ten minutes later, much calmer, Mac was sitting at my dressing-table with two cups of tea in front of her.

'Better?' she said.

I nodded. 'Yes. Sorry. I'm being rather pathetic, aren't I?'

'Nonsense. Just shocked and flustered.' Mac said, handing me a cup of tea. 'Get that down you, and then get dressed.'

I started to pull off my bathrobe and then froze. There on the bed, next to a half-packed suitcase, were a pair of new silk stockings, a pair of lace gloves and a brown leather handbag.

'Where on Earth ... ?' I said, turning to Mac. 'You're a wonder, girl.'

'I have friends in low places,' Mac winked, tapping her nose. 'Here.' She held out her hand. 'Another three pounds. So now you have eight pounds ten, more than enough for some sort of honeymoon.'

My eyes filled with tears again. I grabbed Mac and hugged her tight.

The dining room was abuzz with excitement as word of my last-minute departure spread like wildfire. Sammy and Eddie were there as I walked in wearing the new clothes that were supposed to have been for my honeymoon.

The nurses all fussed and cooed over my outfit, while the maids kept trying to ply me with food. But I just had no appetite. All I could think of was Alistair.

'Where will you go?' Eddie asked.

'I've no idea,' I said. Where *did* one go for a last-minute wedding?

'Do the ACC have a military chaplain?' Sammy said.

I had no idea.

The girls all waved me off, Sammy and Eddie crying like babies as they had to get back to their wards. Mac walked with me to the visitors' room, the room where I had waited with Mother back in

November 1938 on my first day at Hackney. Now I was pacing the floor again, nervously awaiting Alistair's arrival, stopping and glancing in the mirror every few minutes.

'Do I look OK, Mac?'

'You look radiant,' she said. 'Although your eyes are as red as your lipstick.'

'Mac!'

She smirked.

I glanced at my wristwatch. It was now 8.15 p.m. Where could he be?

The door opened and there he stood, my Alistair arrayed in full battle order, kitbag in hand, rifle over his shoulder, hard hat on his head. He dropped them to the floor, and I flew into his arms.

'Oh, Alistair, my Alistair.'

'Hello, darling,' he said, kissing me tenderly. He let go, turned to Mac and gave her a huge hug. 'And dearest Mac. Thank you.'

She chuckled and pulled away. 'You promised not to in front of Phyll!'

'Right, are you ready?' Alistair said.

'But where are we going?'

'To Dovercourt, of course,' he said, picking up his kitbag and rifle. 'We've got time to catch the last train. I checked.'

'Really?' I said.

'Of course. Can't marry you last-minute without your father giving you away, can we? And besides, your mother would never forgive me if we married without her on the scene,' he added with a sly smile.

I picked up my suitcase and turned to Mac.

'Thanks, Mac, thanks for everything.'

'Don't be daft.'

'I so wanted you and Eddie with me as bridesmaids.'

'We can play dress up when you get back,' she said, and pulled me to her.

We held one another for a moment.

'Phyll?' Alistair said softly.

I let Mac go, kissed her cheek, then hurried after Alistair.

26

It has been snowing heavily in the last few hours. The cowled headlights of passing taxis and cars glisten on the flakes as they begin to fall again. The air is icy cold in my nostrils as we slip and crunch our way out of the hospital gates. I collect my pass on the way, and we slither towards the bus stop. It was now 8.25 p.m.

'Do you know where you're posted?' I whispered to Alistair as we stamped our feet to keep warm.

He shook his head. 'Somewhere hot, I hope,' he grinned.

It wasn't long before a bus arrived. The journey took fifteen minutes, and upon arrival at Liverpool Street it was hustle and bustle as usual. There were lots of troops about all laden with kit-bags, hard helmets and rifles like Alistair's. It looked as if the entire British Army was going off to war. There were a lot of ordinary citizens about too, many laden with blankets, hot-water bottles and food parcels in readiness for a night in the Underground station. One woman was pushing a pram with a gramophone player inside, a toddler tottering along beside her.

We paused at the bookstall. 'You wait here with our bags and I'll get the tickets,' Alistair said, slinging his rifle over his shoulder and pushing his way through the throng towards the booking office.

My ears were filled with shouts and whistles and the sound of doors slamming and of trains shunting forward in great gasps of steam. But still there was no sign of Alistair.

'Hurry, Alistair, please hurry,' I muttered. I glanced up at the clock and checked my watch. Both said 8.43 p.m.

As I looked back towards the ticket hall, I saw Alistair bolting towards me.

'Come on, girl, grab the bags. Platform ten.'

We ran, me doing my best not to turn an ankle in my new shoes. But the barrier to Platform 10 was closed and I could see the final carriage of our train disappearing out of sight at the far end.

A ticket inspector appeared at the gate.

'Excuse me,' Alistair gasped. 'Was ... was that ...'

'The eight-forty-five to Harwich Town?' the ticket inspector said. 'Yes.'

'And the next one? To Dovercourt Bay?'

The inspector shook his head. 'Sorry, son, that was the last. Next one to the Essex coast is the mail train.' He shrugged apologetically and began to walk off.

'When's that?' Alistair said.

'Four-thirty-three a.m.,' the inspector called over his shoulder.

'Bugger and blast it!' Alistair fumed, throwing down his kitbag.

'Please, Alistair,' I said, putting my hand on his arm. 'Please don't get angry.'

It was all I could do no to burst out crying in frustration. Everything seemed to be against us.

'I'm sorry, Phyll.' He smiled thinly back at me, pulling his helmet off and passing a hand through his hair. 'But after all the hassle, all the rushing and the favours ... for this to happen.' He glanced back at the now-empty platform. 'Do you know,' he sighed, 'I don't mind missing trains by, say, ten minutes, five minutes even, but by one bloody minute! There were so many troops in the ticket hall, it took an age to get served.'

'What shall we do?' I said. 'We could go to Cambridge. But there may not be a connecting train until first thing anyway.'

'No, best to wait here,' Alistair said. 'At least we know there's one at four-thirty. How long's the journey again?'

'Two-and-a-half hours,' I said. 'But I imagine the mail train will be longer. More stops.'

'All right then. So we won't be in tonight, we'll be in tomorrow morning instead, at seven-thirty or thereabouts.'

'If only I could telephone, let them know we're on our way,' I said.

'Can't we?'

I shook my head. 'There was a telephone at the shop a few streets away, but it got flattened in a raid months back. Besides, even if it were still there, no one would be around to answer.'

'Should we get a hotel room?'

I shook my head. 'By the time we find somewhere, it will be time to leave. And what if we overslept?'

'You're right,' Alistair said. 'We'll just have to huddle up, keep warm. Let's get a cup of tea and a sandwich. I'm starving.'

The station restaurant, however, was closed. It was nearly nine o'clock now.

'How about a pre-marriage drink at Dirty Dick's then?' I said. 'At least it'll be warm in there. Then, come closing time, we can snuggle up in the waiting room for a few hours.'

'Good idea, darling. Come on.'

He took my hand in his, and we made our way out of the station and across Bishopsgate to the sanctity of one of London's most famous pubs.

Inside, it was smoky, noisy and packed with servicemen. But

we didn't care: we were together, and that was all that mattered for the time being. We found a corner and Alistair went off and returned with a pint of mild for himself and a pink gin for me.

We had to leave the pub when it closed at 10 p.m., and trudged back through the compacted snow to the station.

What a beginning to our wedding, I thought as we entered the waiting room. It was a gloomy, soulless place, with hard benches, a bare wooden floor and fly-blown propaganda posters pasted to the walls. A single light bulb hung down from the ceiling, spilling its sickly yellow glow over the waiting passengers. There was a fug of cigarette smoke, mixed with a musty smell of damp wool and gun oil, and it was bitterly cold, the fire being little more than cinders. Every seat and most of the floor space was taken up by troops, dozing, playing cards or reading news-papers – or, much to my embarrassment, well-thumbed copies of *Lilliput*.

'Oi oi,' one of the soldiers said as Alistair and I closed the door behind us, 'the Windmill has sent us a dancer.' There followed a few whistles and cheers, and I felt my face redden. To my horror, I was the only female in there.

Alistair glared at the soldier. 'I'd kindly ask you not to talk about my fiancée that way, pal.'

But this did little more than feed the soldiers' taunting, and they whooped and hissed and booed.

Alistair put his arm around me and guided me towards the fire.

'Quieten down, lads,' a strong voice barked out from the far corner.

I glanced over to see a soldier sat, arms across his chest, his helmet down over his eyes. He was a sergeant, like Alistair, but seemed to exert some authority over the troops in the waiting room. The voices quickly quietened down to a low murmur.

'You two,' the sergeant said, pushing his helmet up and fixing Alistair and myself with a squint, 'take these seats. Perkins. Up!' He thumped the young corporal sat next to him, and both men got up.

Alistair took a firm grip of my free hand and led me over there. 'Thank you,' he said.

The sergeant nodded. He was a rugged, tall man, clean-shaven, with fierce brown eyes staring back from either side of a large bulbous nose. 'You miss the last train?'

'Yes. I've only got forty-eight hours' embarkation leave,' Alistair said. 'We're supposed to be getting married.'

'Hear that, lads?' the sergeant said, raising his voice. 'These poor blighters are getting married . . .'

A cheer rose up.

' . . . so you show the couple some respect. Clear?'

'Yes, Sergeant,' came the uniform reply.

The sergeant tipped his helmet at me. 'Miss,' he said, then moved away.

We sat down on the hard bench, and Alistair put his arm around me.

I pulled away. 'No, Alistair. Not with these soldiers here,' I hissed.

'Blast them,' he said. 'They're half asleep anyway. Stop being such a prude. You're going to be my wife, and I want to comfort you. Please.'

I couldn't help but smile, and I lifted his arm and put it back around my shoulders. He was right, I should stop being so silly. I was as tired, cold and irritable as he was. We had to stick together. It was going to be a long night.

I glanced up at the clock high above the fireplace. It wasn't even 10.30. We still had an uncomfortable six hours to go.

'I'm so sorry about all this, darling,' Alistair said softly. 'It shouldn't be like this. I do love you, and I wanted it to be just right.'

I shifted in my seat so I could look back into his eyes. My heart wrenched. Bless him, he looked so pained. I pushed my head against his chest and sighed.

Sleep came in short doses, and despite Alistair wrapping his greatcoat around me, I just couldn't get warm. At one point, around 2 a.m., a dilatory porter appeared with a block of wood, throwing it on the dying embers in the fireplace, killing any spark of visible comfort entirely. A few of the soldiers cursed him, and then set about doing their best with a book of matches and some scrunched-up newspaper.

At 4 a.m. the call of nature woke me and, with stiff limbs and bleary eyes, I took up my handbag and picked my way over the snoring troops to the Ladies Room.

A ghastly sight awaited me in the mirror. My face looked drawn, my eyes bloodshot, my hair a mess. I felt myself on the verge of tears again.

Just you stop this, Phyllis Elsworth, I mentally snapped at my reflection. *Think yourself lucky you're getting married at all! Now, work some magic.* I opened up my bag and set about trying to repair some of the damage.

I emerged ten minutes later, to find Alistair waiting for me with our bags.

'Wow,' he beamed, 'you certainly scrub up well.'

'Cheeky,' I said.

'We'll have to do this more often.'

'Not bloody likely,' I said.

'Language, Phyll,' Alistair said mockingly. 'Come on, our train's in, so at least we can sit on slightly more comfortable seats now.'

Goods and mail were being loaded on to the baggage car, and

Alistair and I climbed into an open carriage, which we found we had all to ourselves. It too was cold. I shivered.

'Let's find a compartment, it'll be a little warmer,' Alistair said.

We managed to find a compartment further down, and so sat huddled up next to the frosted window. I scraped enough away with my nails to peer out on to the platform. As I listened to the muffled thuds of the mail sacks being loaded, my thoughts turned to Mother and Father. Here I was, once again, about to turn up unannounced on their doorstep. What a mess this all was. Perhaps we should delay getting married? But no, Alistair's heart was set on it and, after all the trauma and fuss I'd caused, how could I return to Hackney without a ring on my finger?

The guard blew his whistle, the train shuddered and jolted forward and with a toot and a hiss of steam, we were finally on our way. It wasn't long before I felt Alistair's head slump on my shoulder, and I put my arm around him this time, stroking his fine hair. What a beautiful man he was, I thought.

About an hour after we'd left Liverpool Street, I prised my arm gently from around Alistair and went out into the corridor to stretch my legs. The train was swaying quite vigorously and I felt like a drunk as I made my way to the toilet, the dim blue bulbs the only illumination.

On my return, I stopped and pulled down the window. A blast of icy air laced with coalsmoke hit me in the face. But it was refreshing and, despite the pitch blackness outside, I fancied I could just see the sea on the horizon, shimmering in the starlight. There was certainly a hint of salt in the air. I closed the window again and returned to our compartment.

Alistair was awake now, sat smoking a cigarette. He offered it to me.

'Sorry, darling,' he said, 'I didn't mean to nod off. Where are we?'

'Close. I can smell the sea. I'd say around half-an-hour now.' I took the cigarette and had a few puffs before handing it back.

Alistair got to his feet, stretched like a cat, then grabbed me in a bear hug.

The train suddenly lurched and we were thrown back down onto the seats.

'Why, Mr Ross,' I said coyly, 'how forward of you?'

It was gone 7.30 a.m. when the train pulled in at Dovercourt Bay. We were the only two passengers to disembark, but there were a few sacks of mail to be unloaded as well as bundles of the day's newspapers. Alistair pulled a copy from one bundle, a *Daily Express*.

'More doom and gloom to remember our wedding day by,' he said, scanning the front page. '"Thursday, twenty-ninth of January 1942. Japs blitz Malaya troops." Singapore's in trouble . . .'

'Don't, Alistair.'

I felt a chill run through my veins. What if that was where he was being sent? The Far East?

'Ho, ho! How about that instead?' Alistair said, tapping the advert printed on the bottom corner.

'Keep smiling. Guinness is Good for you' it said.

Alistair scoffed, and folded and tucked the paper away in his overcoat pocket. Using each other as balance, with my suitcase in my right hand and Alistair's kitbag over his left shoulder, we picked our way cautiously towards home. There was an icy, cutting wind whipping in from the North Sea and the tinkle of a passing milk float was the only sound other than the crunch of our feet in the snow. We trudged on, until, at last, we turned into Portland Avenue just as dawn was breaking on the horizon. I glanced at my watch. It was 7.55 a.m.

Home was dark, the curtains drawn. I lifted the gate latch and we walked up to the front door.

'Well,' I said, 'here goes.' I knocked tentatively.

'They're not going to hear that, are they?' Alistair said, leaning forward and banging the letterbox a few times.

A moment passed and we heard footsteps approaching. The bolt was drawn and the door opened spilling yellow light out on to the path.

'Phyll!? Alistair!?' Wh—' Father said, a piece of half-eaten toast in his hand.

I rushed past him and up the stairs. I burst into my parents' room and flung myself into my dumbfounded mother's arms. I was sobbing uncontrollably.

'There, there, child,' Mother said softly, rocking me. 'What's happened? Why are you here?'

Between sobs I relayed to her the events of the past twelve hours. She didn't say a word until I'd finished.

'Very well. You make yourself a bit more presentable and I'll go and make a fresh pot of tea,' she said, putting a headscarf over her curlers. 'I'll rustle up some breakfast and then it's action stations. Phyllis, my child, we have a wedding to organise.'

27

After a hearty breakfast Father and Alistair hurry off to see
Fr Hole, the minister of St Nicholas' Church, as a priority.

'It shouldn't be a problem,' Father said, pulling on his coat.
'Provided he can get a telephone call through to London. St
Martin-in-the-Fields, you say?'

I nodded.

'It'll only be a matter of checking their register to confirm your
banns have been called.' He slapped on his hat. 'Right, off we go,
Alistair. You girls get yourselves spruced up.'

'What about work?' I said.

Father gave me a wink. 'It's not every day a man's daughter
turns up on the doorstep saying she's getting wed. They'll understand. They'll have to understand.'

In little over the seven inches allowed during wartime, I had
a recuperating bath and then dressed with meticulous care. I put
on the soft satin underwear I had bought in Oxford Street and
stopped to admire myself in the mirror. Would Alistair approve?
I smiled: yes, I thought he would. I carefully pulled on the silk
stockings Mac had conjured up for me, then my new slip, and
finally my dress. It was a pale-strawberry jersey wool, baby-soft
to the touch and flattering to my figure. I took my time doing my

hair and make-up, then put on my new burgundy hat and coat. Slipping off my engagement ring, I strung it through my gold chain and clasped that around my neck.

Alistair popped his head around the door. He was clean-shaven, his hair neatly slicked back, and he was smart in his brushed uniform, boots and buttons freshly polished.

'You look beautiful,' he said, coming in and holding me in his arms.

I pressed my face against the rough serge of his tunic.

'Any regrets?'

Looking up into his hazel eyes, bright with love, I knew, in spite of the disappointment of not having our friends and Nunky and Auntie with us, and not standing in a white wedding dress about to head off to St Martin-in-the-Fields, that we were doing the right thing.

I shook my head. 'Only that this damned war is taking you away from me.'

We kissed long and passionately.

'Enough,' I gasped. 'Now I shall have to redo my lipstick.'

'And I,' Alistair said, checking himself in the mirror and rubbing his mouth, 'shall have to remove mine.'

Mother and Father were waiting for us downstairs, both smart in their Sunday best. I was pleased to see that Mother had a new hat on, too, a much more flattering and modern mushroom style.

'"It is my daughter's wedding day,"' Father said, holding his hand out for me as I descended the last few steps, '"Ten thousand pounds I'll give away. On second thoughts, I think it's best to keep it in the old oak chest."'

Mother gave a sob and put her handkerchief to her mouth. But I could see she was happy.

I kissed Father's cheek. 'You are silly,' I whispered.

We stepped out into a light snow flurry and piled into the waiting taxi. In less than ten minutes, it turned into Church Street and I could see the majestic tower of St Nicholas' towering above the houses.

'Christopher Jones, the captain of *The Mayflower*, was married here in 1593,' Father said to Alistair. 'He too had to leave his wife to make a journey, when he carried the Pilgrim Fathers to America.'

'I don't think I'm going to America, though, sir,' Alistair said, peering out at the church.

Mother and Alistair went into the church, and I waited with Father until Alistair had taken his place at the altar. I could see the huge painting of Moses giving the law staring down at him, and the light streaming in through the three east windows. It was a large church with enough seating for 1,500, and I suddenly felt very small as Father took my arm in his and gave it a reassuring squeeze.

Apart from Alistair, Mother and the minister, the only other witnesses were my aunts, Lil and Rose, standing behind Mother on the left. Poor Alistair had no one. *No, that's not true*, I told myself. *Alistair has me, he will always have me.*

At a nod from Fr Hole, a genial, bespectacled man with receding hair and a slight stoop, Father led me down the aisle.

There was no music, no flowers, no best man, no bridesmaids, no friends, just the sound of my heart beating in my chest, the swish of my dress and the click of my heels on the polished wooden floor. We approached the altar steps and I glanced at Rose and Lil. Their faces were grinning back at me with pride. My eyes met Mother's and she smiled warmly.

Father let me go and I went to stand next to Alistair. He gave me a cheeky wink, then we both faced the vicar. He peered back at us over the top of his glasses, and the ceremony began.

'. . . I now pronounce you man and wife.'

And Alistair was kissing me.

The responses had been made, there was a pretty gold ring chased with tiny roses on the third finger of my left hand, but I felt as if it had been a dream. Walking to the vestry, my arm clutching Alistair's for support, my legs felt like jelly. With trembling hands I signed the marriage certificate. Fr Hole extended his hand in congratulations, and Alistair put out his own to take the certificate from him.

Fr Hole smiled. 'No, my son, this is the property of your wife. Here, Mrs Ross.'

I relaxed, and grinned like an excited schoolgirl as I took the certificate and kept a tight grip of it. *Mrs Ross*, I thought, *how . . . grown-up!*

After kisses, hugs and tears from Mother, my aunts and Father, Alistair and I walked down the aisle together and out into the afternoon sun. It was no longer snowing, but the pavement was icy underfoot and then a sudden flurry hit us as Rose and Lil threw paper confetti with a cheer. We somehow all squeezed into the waiting taxi together, and were driven back home for our wedding reception.

Crushed in the back seat, I slipped my hand into Alistair's and he kissed my head. In a few hours we would be away for our honeymoon, to Nunky and Auntie's down in Sussex. And the following morning I would have to send Alistair, my darling new husband, off to war. It was all I could do not to scream in frustration.

Back at Portland Avenue, Mother, bless her, had done her best with rations – and pulling in a few favours, no doubt – and put together a small buffet for us. There were Spam rolls, a few currant buns thinly spread with what was probably the butter ration for the week, and a solitary bottle of sherry. The BBC Home Service was on in the background, with George Scott-Wood and his band playing a merry tune. Then, disappointingly, the music ended and the schools programme started. Mother turned it off.

If only we had a gramophone to liven things up a little, I thought.

The conversation was limited, polite at best. I was still rather irritated with Lil and Rose for having had such little faith in my nursing career, remembering their muttered 'I'll give her six months' as I left Dovercourt for the first time back in November 1938. I was just daring them to say the same about my marriage now.

'Charge your glasses, ladies and gents,' Father said, as he stood up in front of us all. 'Let me start by saying that I'm delighted to see so many of you here today . . .'

There was a brief chuckle of laughter, then Father raised his hand to quieten everyone down again.

'As I look at Phyll, I can't help but reflect on the girl she was and the woman she has become. She was "Daddy's girl", though she never calls me that,' Father lowered his voice momentarily here, 'far too common,' he grinned, 'on the day she was born and, well, has always been a princess to me. She has brought joy to her mother and me – well, more irritation to her mother—'

He dodged a swipe from Mother here as we all chuckled again.

'—and whilst not every day has been perfect, the love I feel for her, the pride in her nursing career, her choices, her . . . just her,' he sniffed, 'has always been constant. And today she has joined hands with a charming young man. Today, in a world where there is so much darkness and hate and destruction, Phyll and Alistair have completed each other, bringing sunshine and hope to us all.

'So,' he paused and raised his glass, 'before I break down, please join me in wishing Phyll and Alistair all the happiness possible and a long and joyful life together as husband and wife.'

'Phyll and Alistair,' Mother, Lil and Rose said.

As the room erupted in applause, I threw myself in Father's arms, feeling the warm tears flow down my cheeks.

'I love you, *Daddy*,' I grinned.

There hadn't been time for Rose to finish making the wedding cake, but somehow Mother produced an iced sponge cake for Alistair and me to cut.

'Thank you, Mother,' I said, kissing her cheek. I had to smile to myself. She'd got her way after all, me having to wed at home.

There was just time for a final cup of tea, and then a toot of a car horn told us that the taxi had arrived again, this time to take us to the station.

In we all crammed for the short journey. Rose and Lil pushed their way out of the taxi first and produced even more confetti to throw over us as Alistair and I passed through the station building onto the platform. The train was quick to arrive and, with final hugs and kisses and promises of letters to be sent home as soon as I was back at Hackney, Alistair and I climbed aboard. Thankfully it was almost empty, and we had a Third-Class compartment to ourselves. We loaded our luggage on the racks, then lowered the window.

Lil pushed herself forward as Father dropped down out of sight.

'Damned laces,' I heard him mutter.

Lil kissed my cheek and stuffed an envelope in my hand.

'What's this, Lil?'

'From me and Rose,' she said. 'We owe you an apology.'

'For what?'

'Not believing in you, in your career.'

'Oh, Lil, don't be—'

'Ah ah,' she said, holding up her hand. 'You proved us wrong. And that's a little something to help you newlyweds on your way. He's a lovely man, your Alistair is.' She smiled and I kissed her cheek.

'Thank you, Rose,' I said, waving to my other aunt, who was standing arm in arm with Mother.

Father suddenly popped up. 'That's better.'

'Mind the doors, please!' The guard shouted, then blew his whistle.

Alistair pushed his head out beside mine.

Lil threw one last handful of confetti in our faces, and then the train pulled away.

'Good luck!' Father shouted as they all waved us off.

'Bless them,' Alistair said with a sigh, pushing up the window again. He sat back in the seat and pulled me down with him. 'That was a lovely speech your father made.'

I began to brush my coat and Alistair's tunic with my hand. There was confetti everywhere.

'It was, wasn't it? Husband,' I smiled, taking his hand in mine.

'Wife,' Alistair grinned back. Then he planted a kiss on my lips.

The train made good time and, although we made a few stops, nobody got into our compartment. One man did open the door at Manningtree, only for his wife to pull him away again.

'No, Wilfred, not that one,' she said, closing the door and smiling apologetically back at me.

'What was that about?' I said.

Alistair shrugged. 'Women's intuition?'

As we pulled into Liverpool Street, I was about to open the door when a porter beat me to it. He bowed with a flourish as we stepped down, confetti blowing out with us.

'Congratulations,' he said.

'How did he know ...?'

The other alighting passengers were smiling, nodding and tipping their hats at us as they hurried by.

'What is going—? Oh,' I said, and giggled. 'Father!'

I pointed to the outside of our compartment. Alistair gave a snort of laughter. Chalked on the train's side were the words JUST MARRIED. He hadn't been doing his laces up at all.

28

The journey to Billingshurst is long and tedious, as it is pitch-black outside the windows. It is gone eight o'clock by the time we reach Auntie and Nunky's cottage, but they are over-joyed to see us.

'Damn that bloody Hitler for spoiling yer plans,' Nunky said. 'But, by God, we'll give you a wonderful honeymoon if we can.'

In complete contrast to the fare at Dovercourt, Nunky and Auntie had laid on a real feast for us. They pulled our coats off us, took our bags and bustled us inside. The fire was raging and Judy gave us a bark of welcome as Alistair ruffled her ears. A wonderful aroma of woodsmoke and freshly baked apple pie filled my nostrils as my eyes drank in the bread, cheese, cold chicken and ham, mashed potatoes and bottle of wine. My stomach grumbled noisily in anticipation.

'I think that's a sign to tuck in!' Auntie chuckled.

'I've been saving this for a special occasion, but I suppose tonight will do! A toast,' Nunky said, pouring us all a glass of red wine.

'To our darling son, who may not be blood,' he said, 'but who is more than that in our hearts. And to our new daughter-in-law, the vision, the nurse, the sweetheart. Cheers!'

'You old softy,' Auntie said, reaching up and giving Nunky a kiss on the cheek.

As we ate and drank, Alistair and I told them about our day, and then suddenly it was midnight.

'We'll to bed,' Auntie said. 'You've our room tonight, Alistair, Phyll.'

I felt myself redden. 'We couldn't possibly,' I blurted out.

'It's made up and ready for you,' Auntie said, 'and that's the end of it.' She held her hand out to mine. 'I'll take you up, leave the men to clear the dishes.'

Auntie lit two candles, handed me one and led me up the stairs. She opened the door to her bedroom and, her eyes sparkling with knowing, bade me good-night.

Their room was sparsely furnished, but the linen on the double-bed was fresh and there was a posy of dried flowers tied with ribbon placed in the middle of the pillows. My suitcase and Alistair's kitbag were on the floor beside the dressing table, upon which was a bowl and a jug of warm water.

'Bless your heart, Auntie,' I smiled, and placing the candle down on the bedside table, I began to undress.

I washed, and then pulled the sheets back and lifted out the stone hot water bottle. The sheets were wonderfully warm against my skin, and I curled up and waited, my heart thumping in my throat.

Footsteps came up the stairs and I heard a muffled 'Night lad.' Then the door opened and gently closed again.

I breathed softly, my skin tingling all over with nervous anticipation, as I listened to the sounds of Alistair undressing. I felt him draw back the bedclothes and gently get into the bed. I turned and slid into his arms.

*

Late to rise the next morning, we awoke to the intoxicating smell of frying bacon. Downstairs we found a grand wedding breakfast had been prepared for us.

'Is that truly bacon?!' Alistair said, his eyes on stalks and his nose right in the pan. 'Wherever did you—'

'Ask no questions,' Nunky said, holding up his hand.

It had been snowing again during the night and the view out of the kitchen window was of a winter wonderland. The sky was bright blue and the sun dazzling as it reflected off the white landscape.

'To the bride and groom,' Nunky said, raising his teacup.

'To the bride and groom,' Auntie seconded him.

But time was against us, and a quiet mood descended; even Judy was unusually still.

The wireless was on and Victor Harding was singing 'The Sergeant's Song'.

'They're playing our tune, Sergeant Ross,' I said, forcing a smile.

'*Rollicum-rorum, tol-lol-lorum,*' Alistair sang lustily.

We all joined in with the song, yet with each passing minute my heart felt heavier and heavier. Then Big Ben struck 1 p.m. prior to the news on the wireless, and it was time for us to say farewell.

Auntie placed a parcel of food in Alistair's kitbag, then, wrapping our coats around us, we all trudged up to the railway station together.

As the train pulled up to the platform, we could see that it was packed with troops. I had no idea where Alistair was going: the train was heading to Horsham, but from there it could be taking him anywhere. My stomach tightened with dread as I watched Alistair say goodbye to Nunky and Auntie, who was sobbing as she hugged him tight.

'God go with you, my lovely lad,' she sniffed.

'Take care of yourself, son,' Nunky said, gently pulling Auntie away and putting a huge, reassuring arm around her. 'And don't worry about Phyll. We'll see she's all right.'

'Thanks, Nunky. Thanks to you both. For everything.'

Alistair turned to me, and Nunky guided Auntie a few steps back to give us some privacy.

I held Alistair's hands in mine, his fingers twisting the new gold band on my left hand.

'My darling little wife, my Phyll,' he said softly. 'All too soon we have to part. I'm so sorry, sweetheart. But when this damned war is over we shall have a real honeymoon, in Devon, like we planned.'

I looked up into his eyes, unable to find the words. The guard blew the whistle. 'I—'

Alistair pulled me to him and, to a chorus of cat-calls and whoops from the soldiers on the train, we kissed. I just wanted time to stand still, for us to be waking up in bed again, for the bells to be ringing out telling us the war was over.

'Goodbye, my love.'

Alistair climbed aboard and the guard slammed the door shut after him. He dropped the window open and leaned out. We kissed once more and the train began to pull away.

'I'll write as soon as I can,' he called, waving.

I stood there, tears flowing down my cheeks, until Nunky put his arm around me. I stared up at his kindly face, his ruddy cheeks red with the cold.

'Here,' he said, handing me a handkerchief.

Auntie put her arm in mine and gave me a reassuring squeeze. Bless her, she looked like she needed the handkerchief more than I.

'Will you be offended if I leave tomorrow?' I said. 'But I don't think I'll be much fun on my own, and you've been so kind and wonderful, I don't want to spoil things. I'm sorry if I've let you down . . .'

'Don't be so daft, we quite understand. But are you sure, lass?'

'Quite sure. I think I'll be better off throwing myself back into work than moping around thinking about Alistair. Keep my mind active, you see?'

'Of course. Now, stop worrying. We'll have a lovely meal together, listen to the Light Programme and play some cards. Then after a good sleep and a good breakfast we'll walk you to the station first thing.'

'Thank you, Auntie. Thank you both so very, very much.'

Auntie gave my arm a pat. 'Anything for our daughter,' she grinned.

'Good,' Nunky said. 'So what say you to toasting your marriage at the Six Bells?'

'Yes,' I sniffed, 'let's. I think I could use a stiff drink.'

29

I try to keep my spirits up for Nunky and Auntie, but I find it so hard to pull my thoughts away from Alistair and where he is being sent. I know he is only in the ACC, but he is still a soldier, he has still been issued with a rifle, and he is still off to war. Despite their generosity and kindness, I am glad to leave Billingshurst. I need to occupy myself, and can't wait to get my uniform back on and report for duty on the wards.

Checking in at the porter's lodge, I pondered whether I should go straight to Matron's office to report back, or up to my room to unpack and tidy up. Deciding Matron could wait – after all, I was back more than twenty-four hours early – I made my way to the nurses' home.

I went up to the third floor and opened the door of my room. It was in a bit of a state, not surprising really considering the shocked rush I was in – what? – just a few days ago. I sat on the bed for a moment and my eyes fell on the ring on my finger. I toyed with it as my mind drifted. Where was Alistair now? On a train? On the high seas? In an aeroplane? When, if at all, would I see him again?

'Please, God, take care of him,' I prayed under my breath. 'Take care of him and the thousands of other men with him.'

I spent the next half-hour unpacking and straightening out my room then, after putting on my uniform, I made my way downstairs to check the noticeboard. PHYLLIS ELSWORTH, D4 NIGHTS. Well, that was something, I thought. It was the Children's Ward and should be fairly easy. I'd have plenty of time to study for my state final in the autumn.

I didn't need to be in uniform at the moment after all, as I wasn't going to be on duty until 8.30. *Best go and report to Matron and get it over with*, I thought.

To my amazement, Matron commended me for returning early. 'Better than kicking your heels,' she said. 'I am very sorry that your husband had to leave you so soon. But look on the bright side, Nurse ... what is your name now? I must alter your contract and the duty roster.'

'It's Ross, Matron,' I said.

'Nurse Ross,' she nodded.

I felt a tingling of excitement as she said my new name. Never again would I be Elsworth, I thought. That would take some getting used to.

' ... your finals?' Matron had said something else, but I only caught the tail end of it.

'I beg your pardon, Matron?'

'You SRN finals? When are they?' She moved over to the filing cabinet and started to flick through the top drawer. 'I shall have to move you from A–E to P–T, shan't I? Ah, here you are: Elsworth, P.' She pulled my file out and returned to her desk.

'Of course, your contract has actually been broken now that you have married, not that I ever had any misgivings that you would retract it,' she said, smiling up at me. 'Your ward reports have always been excellent.'

'Thank you, Matron,' I said, feeling a warm glow of pride.

'Let's see ...' Matron said as she opened up my file. 'You joined

PTS in November 1938 ... You passed your hospital final with flying colours ... So your SRN state final will be this coming October.' She looked up at me once more and frowned. 'Have you not had your square cap?'

'Sorry, Matron,' I said. 'I don't understand.'

'Tisk, Nurse. Did you not look at the noticeboard upon your return?'

'Yes, but only the duty roster.'

'And you didn't read that correctly, either. All duties start tomorrow, not today,' she said, glancing at my uniform. Shaking her head in that rather patronising manner she had, Matron tutted again. 'Never mind, Nurse. But I suggest you go back and look.'

She picked up a pen, put a neat line through my old surname on my file and started to write in my new name. Then she glanced up.

'That's all, Nurse Els ... Ross. Off you go.'

I returned to the hallway outside of the dining room and gave the noticeboard a proper read.

'Oh, my Lord ... ' I said.

There it was. The hospital final results. I'd plumb forgotten, what with the whirlwind I'd been through these past few weeks. I'd passed, we'd all passed, save one poor soul. I gave a squeal of delight and put my hand to my mouth, looking to my left and right. Nobody was around. What fantastic news! Next stop the last exam, to become a State Registered Nurse.

'Oh, Alistair,' I said aloud, 'I wish you were here so I could tell you.'

That was it. No more moping. My fellow nurses and I had tonight to ourselves, so we would celebrate passing our exams and me getting married. I was so thrilled that I decided to run up the stairs to my room rather than take the lift. I couldn't wait for teatime.

I was the first back to the dining room, where I sat at our usual table with a pot of tea and a currant bun in front of me, waiting for my friends.

'There's the bride!' Mac called, and hurried over with Eddie and Sammy at her heels.

'Oh, Phyll,' she said as we embraced. 'It's so good to see you. How did it go? Were your parents all right? How handsome did Alistair look? What food did you have? What was the w—'

'Take a breath, Mac dear!' I laughed.

We huddled together and I told them all about it.

'Spam sandwiches?' Eddie said. 'How utterly ghastly.'

'I'm rather partial to a bit of spam,' Sammy said.

'Among other things,' Mac smirked.

How I missed my friends.

'Are you all free tonight?' I said. 'We have to celebrate passing our exams.'

'And your wedding,' Eddie said.

'Yes. Night duty starts tomorrow, so we're all off from 8.30 p.m. this evening.'

'Good,' I said, 'I'll go out and rustle up some bottles and some snacks of some sort. I've got a little money left over. Then it's to the lounge. Nine o'clock?'

'Good-oh,' Eddie said.

'So, why aren't you all in square caps?' I said.

'Oh, we actually get them tomorrow. Some mix-up,' Mac said.

Eddie nodded. 'In the morning. Report to the sewing room.'

'We'd better be careful about having sore heads to put them on then, eh?' I smiled.

'One more hurdle to go,' Sammy said, 'and then we're all fully qualified nurses! Can you believe it?'

*

In the lounge we rolled back the carpet and, with a few bottles of ale, some gins-and-bitters and the measly snacks I'd managed to rustle up, we held our celebrations. I played tune after tune as the girls from our intake paired up and danced away. Plenty of staff, senior nurses and younger trainees came to join the celebrations and partake of some free booze. Even Sister Dinsdale popped her head in at one point.

'Nurse Elsworth,' she said.

'It's Ross now, Sister,' I said, keeping as straight a face as possible. I could see Mac and Eddie out of the corner of my eye, sticking out their tongues and waggling their fingers from their noses.

'Yes, of course,' Sister Dinsdale said. 'Ross. I must remember that. But I'd just like to say congratulations on your marriage and on passing your final. Well done.'

I was rather taken aback. The Dragon, offering praise?

'I ... well, thank you, Sister. Would you care for a drink?'

Sister Dinsdale gave a thin smile. 'Thank you, no. I'm on duty. Just popped my head in. Have a good time.' She turned to address the whole room.

'All of you who passed your finals: congratulations. Enjoy yourselves but do keep the noise down. And not after ten-thirty.'

There were a few muttered 'Thank you, Sister's, and then Dolly Dinsdale left us to our revelry.

'My, my, personal congratulations from the Dragon,' Mac said, coming up to me rather unsteadily, two glasses in her hand. 'Here.'

'Oh, she's all right really,' I said.

Mac snorted in derision. 'Play "Tiger Rag" for us, Phyll, will you?'

'My pleasure, madam,' I said with a bow.

'Thanks awfully, Mrs Ross.' Mac curtsied, but kept on going, falling heavily on her backside. She burst into laughter, which set me off too as I tried to help her to her feet again.

Then the air-raid sounded.

'Not now!' I said. 'Not tonight.'

30

Two weeks pass without a word from Alistair. Worrying about him, coping with a twelve-hour ward routine, attending lectures and studying hard for the SRN final, I feel like I am going to collapse with nerves. I trawl the daily newspapers and listen to the news, hoping and praying that Alistair isn't in the Far East, what with the dreadful reports about the Japanese closing in on Singapore. But then what if he is in North Africa, facing Rommel's tanks? *I have to stop this*, I tell myself.

I was leaving the ward building, my cloak wrapped tightly around me against the cold morning breeze, when Mac came trotting along behind me, her feet squelching noisily in the slush.

'Happy Valentine's Day, Phyll.'

I stopped short. *Oh my Lord*, I thought, *Valentine's Day*.

'What?' Mac said with a frown.

'Today was the day Alistair and I originally set for getting married. Remember? We should all be getting ready to go off to St Martin-in-the-Fields.'

'Don't, Phyll,' Mac said, putting her arm through mine. 'Let's get breakfast. Say, do you fancy a romantic film this afternoon?'

'Good idea. I think we deserve a break.'

As we entered the dining area, there was a small crowd

gathered around the noticeboard. A few were crying or shaking their heads.

Eddie spotted us and came quickly over. Her face was drained of colour.

'Have you heard?' she said, tears running down her cheeks.

'No, what?'

'Maggie O'Reilly. She's dead.'

'Rubbish!' I blurted out.

Eddie shook her head. 'No, she was killed last night. During a raid.'

'Oh, please no,' I said, pushing towards the noticeboard.

There it was in black and white, cold and unfeeling, a notice of her passing, as if it were nothing more than a notice of a fire drill or a jumble sale.

'Who put this up?' I said, furious at such insensitivity.

'Home Sister, I presume,' Eddie said.

'She's such a cold bitch,' Mac hissed.

'Do they know what happened?' I said.

'One of the maids is dating a policeman,' Eddie sniffed, 'and she said there was a quick raid over Liverpool Street. Maggie was on her way home for a long weekend. Her body was discovered blown against a wall. Her hospital badge on her coat was the only way she could be identified.'

Maggie, beautiful, friendly, kind-hearted Maggie O'Reilly. She'd been so good to me on my first ward duty, taking me under her wing when I was nervous and clumsy, and then the perfect nurse when I had scarlet fever, and so generous when I had to rush off to marry Alistair. I started to cry; Mac and Eddie closed in and we held each other for a moment.

'I couldn't eat breakfast now,' I sniffed, wiping my face. 'Shall we go for a walk around Victoria Park? I need to get out of here for a bit.'

Mac nodded. 'Yes, I think that'll do the trick. We can have a cuppa at the café.'

'I'll come with you,' Eddie sniffed. 'Let me just fetch my cloak.'

'Have you got a cigarette?' I said, feeling suddenly very shaky. 'I've run out.'

Mac pulled out a packet of Three Threes.

'Nurse Elsworth, Nurse Elsworth!'

I glanced over my shoulder to see Miss Lee striding towards us.

'God, now what?' Mac said.

'She's can't even get my name right,' I said under my breath.

'Bother,' Miss Lee said as she reached us, 'I mean Nurse Ross. I cannot get used to name changes.'

'No, Sister,' I said.

'Nurse Ross, you are to report to Matron.'

I glanced at Mac.

'Now, Nurse,' Miss Lee snapped. 'It's not an RSVP.'

'Yes, Sister,' I said. 'Wait for me, Mac,' I called as I hurried off.

I had a sudden feeling of dread wash over me as I paused, fist raised, at Matron's door. 'Please, no more bad news,' I muttered, then knocked.

'Enter.'

'Ah, Nurse Ross. Come in,' Matron said. 'Sit down.'

That was a bad sign already.

Matron fixed me with her gaze. 'Keep calm, there's nothing to worry about. I have some bad news, but it's not tragic.'

Just tell me! I shouted in my head, about to explode with worry.

'Your husband ... Sergeant Alistair Ross ... ?'

I nodded. My stomach was turning in on itself. I felt sick and dizzy.

' ... has been admitted to Woking Hospital,' Matron said. 'I received a telephone call from them a short while ago. I suggest you have the night off and get down to visit him.'

I nodded again, feeling my whole body tense. 'Do . . . ' I cleared my throat. 'Do you know what happened, Matron?'

'Only that he was admitted first thing.'

'I see,' I whispered.

'Let me know the situation as soon as you can,' she said with a thin smile. 'One must expect these . . . unexpected circumstances in wartime.'

'Yes, Matron,' I said shakily, getting to my feet.

Matron scrawled her signature on a pass and handed it to me.

'Oh, Alistair,' I moaned, as I hurried back to my room to change and fetch my money.

I didn't have time to look for Mac or Eddie, so I scrawled a note and popped it under Mac's door on my way out.

As I stood at the bus stop I suddenly realised that I hadn't the faintest idea of how to get to Woking. I knew it was south of London, in Surrey, but should I go to Victoria or Waterloo? Or would it be London Bridge?

I hopped on the bus and sat on the long bench seat downstairs.

'Where to, miss?' the female conductor said.

'Woking!' I smiled with a shrug. 'I don't suppose you've any idea how I get there?'

'Course I does,' she said. 'Change at Liverpool Street. Catch the 6A to Waterloo. Trains to Woking run from there.'

I gave her my money and she handed me a ticket.

'Thank you.'

'Glad to 'elp,' she smiled. 'Fares, please,' she called, walking down the length of the bus.

Thankfully there was a train to Woking from Waterloo every half-an-hour and I managed to catch the 9.54, which would get me in at 10.25 a.m.

Outside Woking Station I stood looking about, wondering just where the hospital was. There were no buses or taxis to be seen, in fact very little sign of life at all. Two old ladies approached, carrying shopping. Well, at least there were shops around somewhere.

'Excuse me,' I said. 'Can you direct me to the hospital?'

'Brookwood, dear?' one of the women said.

I shrugged. 'I'm not sure. I was told Woking Hospital. My husband was admitted last night.'

'Soldier, is he?'

I nodded.

'That'll be Brookwood then. It's the asylum in between the Basingstoke Canal and Knaphill Village,' the woman said. 'It's an emergency war hospital now.'

'Is it far?'

'Four miles, that way,' the woman said pointing down the road. 'But you'd be better getting back on the train,' the woman said. 'Brookwood's the next stop. There's another train along in five minutes, and then it's just a mile's walk.'

How frustrating, I thought. *Why call a place Woking Hospital if it's not in Woking at all?*

The guard amended my ticket for me and ten minutes later I was alighting at Brookwood, where a railway worker pointed me in the right direction.

The hospital put me in mind of Claybury Asylum almost immediately: a Victorian building, more like a stately home, built over four floors in a rich brick red, all overlooked by a beautifully designed clock tower, surrounded by wooded countryside. It was very peaceful. I crunched up the driveway, lined with Victorian streetlamps, and made my way to the reception area.

Inside, a nurse asked if she could help me.

'Yes. I had an urgent call. My husband was admitted this morning. Sergeant Ross, Alistair Ross.'

'Have a seat,' the nurse said. 'I'll go and enquire for you.'

She disappeared and I sat my weary self down on the nearest chair, pulling off my hat and closing my eyes for a minute.

'Nurse Ross.'

I opened my eyes, momentarily confused at the unfamiliar surroundings. Where had Hackney Hospital gone?

'Nurse Ross,' said the nurse, 'your husband is in Albert Ward. It's not visiting until two this afternoon, but as you're a nurse, Sister says you can stay for a while.'

I got to my feet. 'Oh, thank you so much. Can I see him now?'

'Of course. I'll take you,' she said, leading the way. 'Did you find us all right?'

'By way of Woking Station, eventually,' I said.

'Yes, that happens a lot. This way.'

The ward was long and smelled strongly of carbolic. Each bed was occupied and a sea of faces turned as the nurse and I entered. There were a few whistles and many grins.

'That's a dry sponge-bath for you, Corporal Riches,' the nurse said to one of the young men.

'Promises, promises,' he called after us.

'Typical servicemen.' The nurse smiled wryly at me.

'I usually spike their tea with laxative if they get too fresh,' I said.

The nurse chuckled. 'There he is, sixth bed from the end. Cup of tea?'

'Yes, and thank you, Nurse . . . ?'

'Nurse Allison. Judith.'

'I'm Phyll.'

Alistair's eyes were closed, his face flushed, his fair hair ruffled and damp. I pulled a chair to his bedside and, taking his hand in mine, leaned forward and kissed him lightly on the lips.

His eyelids flickered open and he blinked back at me.

'Phyll?' His face was full of bewilderment, then delight.

'Happy Valentine's Day, darling,' I said, kissing him again.

'But how did . . . ?'

'Shhh,' I said. 'Matron called me to her office this morning. Told me to leave to be with you straight away.'

'Oh, sweetheart . . . I feel rotten . . .'

'What happened? Are you injured?'

'No,' he said, shaking his head and breaking into a coughing fit.

I picked up the glass of water from the bedside cabinet and lifted it to his lips.

'Thanks,' he winced. 'No, not injured. Bloody pleurisy.'

'Pleurisy!' I couldn't believe it.

Alistair nodded. 'I didn't even get out of the country. We travelled to some place at a holding battalion, waiting for the draft to move on. But it was so overcrowded we had to sleep on the floor. We were all soaked to the skin and I must have got chilled.'

'I'll say,' I said, feeling the anger swell inside me. 'It's a wonder the lot of you aren't in here! Damned stupid ba—'

'Don't sweetheart. It's just—' He fell silent, emotion overwhelming him.

'Can I get you anything? From the shops?' I said, stroking his hand.

'Mrs Ross?'

I looked up to see the ward sister.

'May I speak with you in my office?'

'Of course.' I turned back to Alistair. 'I won't be long.'

He nodded and closed his eyes again.

I followed the ward sister to her office, where she invited me to take a seat next to her.

'I understand you've only been married two weeks, Mrs Ross,' she said with a shake of her head. 'Most unfortunate for you. But I can assure you your husband will be fine. He's been diagnosed with pleurisy and ... Well, you're a nurse yourself, so I don't have to tell you the treatment.'

'Yes, Sister. I understand,' I said.

'He will be hospitalised for about three weeks. But the M&B* we're giving him will make him feel quite ill for a few days.' She paused for a moment. 'You do realise that he's missed the draft. Which has dreadfully upset him.'

I hadn't even thought about that. But yes, he wouldn't be going off to war just yet.

'May I use your telephone, Sister?' I said. 'I promised Matron at Hackney that I would let her know the situation. I'm on nights currently so will stay over this evening somewhere nearby and return to London tomorrow afternoon.'

'Of course. When you've finished, I'll direct you to a very good bed-and-breakfast.' She got to her feet and left me alone to use the telephone.

'Thank you, God,' I said softly. 'Thank you for sparing Alistair.'

I telephoned Hackney, then as I put the receiver down, I hesitated. What about Auntie and Nunky? I really should let them know. I picked the receiver up once more.

'Telegram, please,' I said. It would put the wind up them, receiving a telegram – they were dreaded things, always purveyors of tragic news – but what choice did I have? I wanted them to know immediately. A letter would take too long.

I returned to Alistair's bedside; although conversation was at a minimum, with him drifting in and out of sleep, I knew it was a comfort to him to know I was there. Official visiting time came

* Sulphapyridine, an anti-bacterial drug

and went, and by the time the orderly arrived with the evening meal I was struggling to keep my eyes open.

Alistair smiled up at me weakly. 'You go get some sleep, angel. Come see me for breakfast.'

I was hesitant to leave his side.

'Don't fret, love,' the injured serviceman in the next bed said. He had a bandaged head and face. 'He'll be OK. I'll keep an eye on him – my only eye,' he grinned.

The bed-and-breakfast was comfortable and only five minutes' walk from the hospital. I slept for nearly ten hours solid, and after a hot bath I returned to Alistair's side.

I spent the morning helping to nurse him, but mostly just watching him sleep. At 2 p.m. a couple of familiar faces were amongst the visitors. Nunky and Auntie came hurrying over.

'Thanks for that telegram, lass,' Nunky said. 'A bit of a shock seeing the postman with it in his hand. But I'm glad you let us know that quick. How is he?'

I explained Alistair's condition to them both in as simple terms as I could, but, like me, they were just relieved he was alive.

'He's very down about missing the draft,' I whispered to Nunky.

He nodded. 'I can understand. Alistair always wants to do his best, to stand by others. But he'll come round. God has chosen him for other things, and once he accepts that, he'll be lighter of heart.'

After waving them off at the end of visiting, I went to speak with the sister.

'He'll have to rest and continue on a special diet,' she said. 'But he's responding well and I expect he'll be able to return to his unit by mid-March.'

'Thank you for everything,' I said.

'We do our duty, Nurse Ross, as you do yours, I'm sure,' she smiled.

Alistair was sitting up in bed now, and had a touch of colour to his cheeks.

'How do you feel?'

'Like a coward,' he said.

'Now stop that, you hear?' I snapped. 'You are not. How can you blame yourself for incompetent Army procedure? If you don't buck up, accept your fate and get on with getting better, then I shall write to your commanding officer and give him a piece of my mind.'

'Heavens,' Alistair gasped, eyes wide in abject terror, 'don't do that, Phyll. Please.'

'Behave then,' I said.

He blinked back at me and nodded his head meekly. 'Sorry.'

'Good. Now, I have to return to London, but I'll come and see you in a few days. So just behave.' I kissed him sharply and moved away.

Alistair reached out and pulled me back. 'Mrs Ross?'

'Yes?'

'You're adorable when you're angry.' He smiled sheepishly.

'I'll write as often as I can, darling,' I said, 'and telephone each day to check on your progress. Just tell Nurse Allison to let me know if you want me to bring anything.'

'Thanks, darling,' he said.

I retreated in haste before the tears started to flow again. My emotions were so topsy-turvy: fear, anger, love, despair, shock. But I was also so happy, happy that Alistair was in safe hands, and that I knew, finally, where he was.

31

The worst part about waiting for Alistair to recover is not knowing where he will be posted. I am hoping he'll be back at his barracks in Finchley, but with the war now raging on several fronts, so many men are needed overseas. I can't shake the bad feeling that, as soon as he is fit again, Alistair will be gone.

I went to visit him at Brookwood as often as I could and, although we had no privacy, it was good to spend time getting to know my husband, talking of our plans for the future, particularly my career, and my upcoming SRN exam. I would often sit at Alistair's bedside while he tested me on all manner of subjects.

'I'll be able to take the damned exam myself,' he joked, 'my head's so full of medical terms and procedures nowadays.'

One afternoon, I could tell by the look on his face that he had some news. It was mid-March, the birds were singing, the daffodils were in bloom; spring had arrived, and with it Alistair's commanding officer.

'He'd read the MO's report and was glad I'd made a full recovery,' Alistair said with a heavy sigh. 'I can finally get out of bed tomorrow properly and leave.'

Here it comes, I thought. 'And?'

'And leave for my new posting.'

'What? Immediately?' I couldn't believe it.

'Yes, sweetheart,' Alistair said with a sad smile. 'I've been off duty for nearly a month. They're short-staffed, and I have my posting.'

'Where to? Abroad?' My heart was thumping in my chest.

'I suppose one could say it was abroad.'

'Stop being so bloody cryptic and tell me!' I hissed.

'Scotland.'

I didn't quite know what to make of that. On the one hand he was still going to be in this country and not being sent overseas to a war zone, but on the other ... Scotland. It was a long way away.

'It's rotten luck, isn't it? No sooner do I get to see you than I'm whisked away.'

'But you'll have leave?'

'Yes, but it'll take me all of that to get down to London and back again. I wouldn't even have time to stop for a cup of tea. The posting's an administrative one at Combined Operations HQ on the west coast. "Ayrshire's" all I can tell you.'

'I see.'

'The nearest mainline station is Glasgow. The journey takes at least twelve hours from there. I could try to—'

I was shaking my head. 'That's impossible. You'd be exhausted. And what if there were any delays? An air raid? No, we'll just have to get plenty of paper in and spend our salaries on stamps.'

Even though I was trying to make light of it, I was feeling dreadfully depressed.

Alistair travelled to London the following morning, in order to catch the 8.30 to Glasgow. Matron, much to my surprise, sent a relief nurse to cover the final few hours of my night shift so I was able to get to Euston to meet him. We had half an hour, which we spent holding hands in the station café, not saying much, just gazing into one another's eyes.

'I thank God that He saved you from the draft, Alistair,' I said. 'I'm sorry – I know how much it meant to you – but I do. But I am so fed up with always saying goodbye. If I never see another station again I'll be happy.'

'Perhaps I won't be posted for long,' he said. 'I'll try and get long leave for your birthday next month, but I'm not hopeful. It will more than likely be in the summer.'

The call to board the 8.30 to Glasgow came over the Tannoy, and I walked with Alistair to the barrier.

'Let's say goodbye here,' he said, pulling me close. 'Don't wave me off.'

We kissed for what seemed like an age, and then he was gone. I watched him disappear amongst the other passengers, then turned and made my way to the bus stop outside. I didn't cry, I'd had enough of that. It was time to be strong. *I'm lucky to have a husband safe and in this country*, I told myself. Poor Eddie and Mac, they had no idea where their boyfriends were. It was about time I appreciated just how lucky I was.

It was coming up the third anniversary of Chamberlain's announcement of hostilities, and there was still no sign of the end. The USA had surrendered the Philippines to the Japanese, and Britain had abandoned Burma to them too. Germany invaded Egypt, and soon began a summer offensive towards Stalingrad. The world was well and truly engulfed in conflict.

The nation was briefly cheered when Princess Elizabeth signed up for active duty, and the newspapers were filled with photographs and stories of her being put to work changing a tyre.

The air raids continued, but only intermittently now, with maybe as little as two or three aircraft flying in under the radar.

One clear, balmy evening, I was sitting quietly packing dressing drums, my mind far away with Alistair, when the sudden whine of the air-raid siren set my pulse racing. In an instant all the nurses were rushing about, placing babies and small children on mattresses under their cots for protection. Seconds later, the ack-ack guns started to beat out their familiar rhythm.

The children were terrified, crying and bawling, and we did our best to calm them as the drone of the bombers filled our ears. I held my breath, listening for the dreaded whistle of a falling bomb. I was cuddling a very tiny child, who whimpered quietly in my arms, when a nearby explosion shook the building. There was a pattering of heavy debris falling, then a tremendous crash and a smash of falling glass. A hail of incendiary bombs began to rain through the balcony roof. I passed the child I was holding to the maid and rushed towards the stirrup pump. The ward doors crashed open and two of the night porters came running in, grabbing hold of more stirrup pumps. One of them kicked open the balcony doors, and the three of us pounced on the flames, putting out the ominous-looking firebombs before they got out of control.

With a hiss of steam and the stench of scorched metal and oil fumes, the danger was over. I wiped my brow and stared off at the docks in the distance. There was a blaze roaring away, and already I could hear the sirens of the fire crews on their way. Casualty would be busy soon, I thought.

'Good job, Nurse,' one of the porters said, rolling up a hose.

'Thank Mac's Sergeant-Major for that,' I said.

'Eh?'

'His training. First time I've had to use it!'

I crunched back into the ward. The children were wailing, but there was no damage, thank God, just a lot of smoke and broken glass. The all-clear sounded.

'Best get this lot cleaned up before Matron does her rounds,' I joked to the ward sister as I made my way over to the sluice to fetch a broom.

Things were back to normal within the hour and, having helped to settle the whimpering children, I returned to the dressings room. This kind of evening was so normal now. Rubble and burnt-out buildings, living on rations, being fed daily reports of death and destruction, of victory and defeat. Would it ever end?

Eddie, Mac and I studied hard and earned our light relief, which was always a visit to the pictures, not the news theatres. And I wrote to and had letters from Alistair. If there was one thing about my husband, I thought, it was that he loved to put pen to paper. Life was good in Scotland and he was full of praise for both the people and the stunning beauty of the countryside. He was unable to get leave for my twenty-second birthday in April, but promised he'd come down in July or August so we could go to the seaside.

Spring turned to summer and, although I still hadn't seen Alistair, I had more than enough to occupy my life, and buried my head in study when off duty. I had come to the decision that, when my contract was up in November – provided I passed my SRN, that was – I would specialise in midwifery. This would mean another six months' training, but I greatly enjoyed working with children, and more so with expectant mothers and newborn babies.

However, by the autumn I was becoming more and more withdrawn. I was reluctant to party, to play the piano or to join in when off duty. I missed Alistair desperately. It was something that Mac and Eddie, bless them, were well aware of but, try as they might, they just couldn't drag me out of my depression.

The SRN final exam arrived and, although nervous, I

answered every question as well as I could and left the rest to fate. After all, I was well and truly out of control of the rest of my life, so why should I worry about this?

My friends and I all passed. That was it: I was now a State Registered Nurse. I sat down to write the news to Mother and Father, to Nunky and Auntie and, of course, to Alistair.

Two days later a heartfelt reply came from Ayrshire.

I love you with all my heart and I miss you. I'm so over the moon about your SRN results. Congratulations. I am very, very proud of you. But now that you have finished your training, what's to stop you from joining me in Scotland? I can look for a flat. It would be wonderful for us to be together, to finally live as man and wife. I would not be half out of my mind worrying about you in a bomb-torn city that never sleeps. Please think on what I ask of you. I miss you and I want to be with you. I want you at my side. For always.

I folded the letter away and sat staring off into space, thinking about what Alistair was asking me.

A knock aroused me from my thoughts. A blonde, uncapped head popped around my door. It was Eddie.

'Hello, Phyll. Can I come in?'

'Of course!'

She sat cross-legged on the floor and, taking out a pack of Craven "A", offered me one. 'Any news? About Alistair?'

'No. He's still up there in Scotland,' I said putting my cigarette to her match.

'I thought it was just, you know, training or what-not. Felt sure he'd be sent back to London by now.'

I sighed a cloud of tobacco smoke. 'Seems it's pretty permanent.'

'Golly, you really have had a whirlwind marriage. Anyway, what are you up to this evening? Fancy a drinkie at the pub? Drown one's sorrows?'

'No, I'm on tonight. What about you?'

'Two days off, then back on days in Theatre.'

'Let's do it tomorrow then.'

'Good-oh. Ah, come to mention it,' she said, sitting up straight, 'clean forgot. We've all got to be X-rayed and weighed from tomorrow morning.'

'Whatever for?'

'Well,' she said, lowering her voice dramatically, 'two nurses are off sick, Scottie and Billings. Loss of weight, apparently. An X-ray showed that they had spots on their lungs. They've been shipped off to the Isle of Wight for three months. So the whole staff have to be checked over in case of an epidemic.'

'Poor girls.'

'Tosh. Three weeks on the Isle of Wight, at the end of summer? It's a fix!'

'Don't be silly, Eddie,' I smiled. 'How can they fake the X-rays?'

She frowned. 'True. But it's very fishy.'

I returned for my final night on the Children's Ward and the following morning, with gifts of fruit and sweets from some of the kids bulging my pockets, I called in at Supplies to get my soap ration and stuffed that in my pocket too.

I was just making my way back to the nurses' home when I remembered what Eddie had told me about having to get weighed.

Joining the queue of others assembled outside Miss Lee's office, I waited my turn, fighting to stay awake as one by one we were weighed and then X-rayed.

'Ross, P... ,' Miss Lee said to her assistant, who was writing down the figures.

I stood on the scales stifling a yawn.

'... eight stone, two pounds.'

'Are you sure, Miss Lee?'

'Of course I am, Nurse Brackett. Why?' Miss Lee said irritably.

'Well, it says here that Nurse Ross at her last medical ... er ... six months ago ... was seven stone four.'

Miss Lee frowned at me, then back at the scales. 'No, it clearly says eight stone two. Curious.'

'It could be ...' Nurse Brackett giggled.

'Whatever is so amusing, Nurse?'

'Nothing, Miss Lee,' she said. 'Sorry.'

But I could see she was still smiling. I rubbed my eyes 'May I go now, Miss Lee?'

'What? Oh, yes. Get down, Nurse Ross. Then get undressed and gowned for the X-ray. Won't keep you long.'

'Thank you, Miss Lee,' I said with a watery smile, stepping off the scales.

'Next!' she called.

As I left the room I caught part of a hushed exchange between Nurse Brackett and Miss Lee just before the door closed behind me.

'Oh, now I understand,' Miss Lee was saying. 'I never thought, but yes, I—'

It was good to be out with Mac and Eddie. We went to see Cary Grant in *The Talk of the Town*.

'You know, Mac,' Eddie whispered from the seat next to me, 'Cary doesn't look a bit like your Sergeant-Major. I'd have thought you'd like someone smaller. John Mills say. Or one of the Three Stooges. More your preferred height.'

'Shut up!' Mac said, but with an amused tone.

'Shhh!' came an irritated voice from the row behind us.

'Do you know what, girls?' I whispered, 'I do believe a

rumour's going to spread about me very soon. I'm going to be
"The Talk of the Hospital".'

'Whatever do you mean?' Mac said softly.

'The weighing.'

'The weighing?'

'Yes, I was nearly a stone heavier than six months ago.'

'So? It's all that cake you get sent.'

'What do you mean "So"?'

'Golly, Phyll,' Eddie gasped, turning in her seat. 'You're
not . . . ?'

'Not what?' Mac hissed.

I shook my head. 'No, I'm not. I completely forgot to empty
my pockets, that's all, before I got on the scales. Only remembered
as I was undressing for the X-ray. Had my soap ration and some
fruit and sweeties from the kids.'

Eddie put her hand to her mouth and sniggered. 'Why didn't
you say something?'

I shrugged. 'Thought I'd play a little bit of mischief for a
while.'

'Mischief at what?' Mac hissed again.

'That she's pregnant!' Eddie said.

'Pregnant?' Mac said. 'Are you?'

'No!' Eddie and I said in unison.

'Look,' the man behind us growled, 'will you kindly be quiet?'

'Oh, blow it out of your pipe, Grandpa!' Eddie snapped.

'Eddie!' I exclaimed, and we all three shrank down in our seats
giggling.

The film came to an end and the house lights went up.

'Do you want to sit through it again?' Mac said hopefully.
How she adored Cary Grant.

'No, let's go and have a drink at Lyons. I've got something I
want to tell you.'

'You *are* pregnant,' Mac gasped.

'Mac, I am not. Please, I've hardly seen Alistair.' I lowered my voice glancing about. 'Chance would be a fine thing.'

We linked arms and headed out of the cinema and into the bustle of Piccadilly Circus. The Lyons Corner House was, as always, busy, but a waiter found us a table soon enough.

I gave a heavy sigh as we sat down. 'Perhaps coming here wasn't such a great idea,' I said.

'Why?' Eddie said.

'She and Alistair got formally engaged here,' Mac said.

'Oh, yes.' Eddie said. 'Shall we leave? Try a pub?'

I shook my head. 'No it's fine. Let's have a nice cool lager. My treat.'

When our beers arrived I raised my glass.

'To you, my two wonderful friends. And to the best four years of my life.'

'Hurrah!' Eddie said, and we clinked glasses.

'You're not pregnant, are you?' Mac said, giving me a sideways glance. 'You can trust us. We'll keep it a secret.'

I smiled. 'I promise you both, I'm not pregnant.'

'But there's something on your mind, isn't there?' Eddie said.

'Yes, there is. I'm leaving.'

There was a shocked silence for a moment.

'No, Phyll . . . ' Mac said.

'Yes, Mac. I've made up my mind. I'm handing in my resignation for the start of November.'

'But, Phyll, why? You've trained so hard,' Eddie said. 'What about midwifery?'

I shook my head. 'Not now. Not yet anyway. I've thought long and hard and I intend to join Alistair in Scotland. He's already talking about looking for a flat. I shall miss you both so very much, but I must grasp what happiness Alistair and I can have together.'

'But it's so far away,' Mac said.

'And so damned cold and wet,' Eddie added.

I smiled at them both. 'It's what I want, to be with my husband. You can understand that, can't you?'

They nodded, but they both looked so crestfallen.

I put my hands out and took theirs in mine. 'Look, we were all going to be heading our separate ways at some point next year, if not sooner. I'm just going a little earlier, that's all.'

'But all that work, Phyll,' Mac said. 'What will your parents say?'

'They'll understand. And they know better than anyone that once my mind's made up, that's it. Besides, I'm not giving up nursing. I still want to be a midwife. I'll look for a private nursing post up in Scotland, and if I'm lucky there'll be a midwifery training school in one of the hospitals up there.'

Mac and Eddie sat silently staring into their drinks. *Oh dear*, I thought, *and we were having such a good time*.

'Please be happy for me,' I said. 'You can come and visit. Get away from London.'

Mac sniffed and smiled in agreement.

'We'll support you,' Eddie said, 'whatever you decide. You know that, Phyll.'

'Yes, I know that. And another thing,' I said with a sly grin, 'this rumour that's about to start, don't deny it. If their one-track minds want to think I'm pregnant, especially when they find out I'm leaving, then so be it.'

32

I awake refreshed and full of joy. My decision has been made and I know it is the right one. Looking critically at myself in the mirror, I observe a smart, crisp appearance. My apron is starched so stiff that it whispers as I move, and my cap, equally well starched, sits erect on my head. Matron will have no cause to complain. I move to my desk, sign the letter I composed last night, fold it, seal it in an envelope and put it in my pocket.

'Well, Phyllis Ross,' I said to myself, 'here goes nothing.'

As it was, Matron was unavailable until ten o'clock. With the wind rather taken out of my sails, I wandered back to the dining room. Mac waved me over to her and huddled close, taking my hand.

'Please, please tell me you've slept on it and changed your mind.'

I smiled back at her. 'No, Mac, I'm sticking to my decision. I'm seeing Matron at ten.'

'But you could stay and take midwifery *here* for two years.'

'Please, Mac,' I said, toying with my teacup.

'All right,' she said. 'I'm sorry.'

'Don't be. Just support me.'

'Always,' she said, with a tear in her eye.

*

As I hung my cloak up in the laundry room of Men's Medical, I was greeted with a cheery 'Good-morning, Staff' from Male Charge Nurse Callorum.

'Hello, Pete,' I whispered. 'How's things?'

'Good, good,' he said, nodding his round head. He was built like a rugby player, but he had a gentle nature and a wicked sense of humour. 'We've got a little trainee joining us,' he said. 'She's a bit dippy, but keen as mustard.'

'We were all there once,' I said.

The first hour passed relatively easily as the junior nurse and I attended a fireman who'd been admitted after suffering an insulin shock and a diabetic coma. Even in wartime people still suffered from 'normal' illnesses.

The junior and I eased Mr Healey into his dressing gown, then lifted him from the bed and into an easy chair.

'Get some clean sheets, Nurse,' I said. 'We may as well strip the bed, turn the mattress and wipe down the rubber sheet. Bring the trainee nurse back with you.'

As the junior went off, I stripped the bed. Just as I was in the process of turning the mattress a sharp rebuke came from Male Nurse Callorum at the end of the ward.

'Staff,' he said, rushing over, 'whatever are you doing lugging the mattress?'

I stared back at him open-mouthed as he took it from my grip.

'Shouldn't you be at Matron's office?' he said.

'I . . .' Looking at my fob watch I noted it was a 9.45 a.m. 'Not until ten o'clock,' I said.

'Well, go and get a coffee,' he said. 'You don't want to be late. I can finish this.'

Slightly bewildered, I left him to it, collected my cloak, and headed off to Matron's office. I wanted to see her before I returned to the dining room. It was five-to when I knocked on her office door.

'Enter!'

Looking up from the paperwork in front of her, Matron's steely gaze met mine.

'Yes, Staff? What is your business with me?'

'Good-morning, Matron,' I said, my voice calm and steady. 'I wish to tender my resignation.' I held out the envelope.

Ignoring my outstretched hand, she sat back in her chair.

'Why this sudden wish to end your career, Staff?'

'It isn't because I'm not happy, Matron, with nursing,' I said. 'I love my work. But my husband has been posted to Scotland and it appears to be pretty permanent. My training is over and I wish to join him.'

'What about your midwifery?' Matron said. 'Don't think I haven't been keeping an eye on my nurses and their abilities. You are one of the most promising we have here at Hackney.'

'Thank you, Matron,' I said, with a flush of embarrassed pride. 'But I have given that careful thought. I can take it up at any time. Perhaps even in Scotland.'

'Don't you think you're being a little hasty, Staff?' Matron said, softening her tone a little. 'You've only just finished your finals.'

'Matron, with all due respect, I have thought the matter over very carefully. I am not a rash person. I do sincerely wish to take my midwifery training, but the need to join my husband is paramount. One has to live one day at a time just now.' I stood perfectly still, looking back down at Matron, my face fixed and relaxed.

She lowered her eyes for a moment. Then she gave a heavy sigh.

'It seems that your mind is made up. In that case, with regret, I accept your resignation.'

She held out her hand and I gave her the envelope.

'I will see you again before you leave. That will be all.'

Matron returned to her paperwork and didn't look up again. I hesitated, then left.

Standing outside, I felt a sense of relief wash over me. The first hurdle was done. I glanced at my fob watch. I had time to have a coffee with Mac, as promised, then it was back to the ward. I was off at 4.30 p.m., so I'd write Alistair and my parents then and try and catch the last post.

Alistair would be beside himself with joy at my news, my parents less so. Not only was I leaving nursing, but I was moving to Scotland. Mother would be in a state, saying moving to the moon would be closer. Father ... well, he'd be sad, but he'd also understand, he always did.

Mac was nowhere to be seen in the dining hall, and I was just finishing off my coffee when Miss Lee approached, a sickly grin across her face. I started to get to my feet.

'No, no, Staff,' she said hastily, 'sit down. I just wanted to congratulate you. Hope all goes well.'

Before I could ask what she was talking about, she had turned on her heel and left. Perhaps Matron had told her the news of my resignation already? Yes, that must be it. But to congratulate me?

'Funny woman,' I muttered.

I caught the gaze of a couple of my intake, and they raised their coffee cups.

'Congratulations, Phyll!' one said.

'Hope it's a boy!' another said.

Oh. Now I understood everyone's behaviour. The pregnancy rumour had obviously spread like wildfire. *What a foolish thing for me to do*, I thought. *I'd best put a stop to it right away.*

'Listen—' I started to say.

'Well, I 'ope it's a girl,' one of the kitchen staff said as she began wiping down my table.

I didn't have time for this now, so I gave her a withering smile, drained my coffee cup and hurried back to my ward.

I told Male Nurse Callorum the news of my impending departure.

'Well, I'll be sad to see you go, Phyll. You're a damned good nurse,' he said. 'Still, it's for the best. You'll be with Alistair in a quieter part of the country. War-torn London is no place to bring a child into the world.'

Ah, I thought. *That's what the business with the mattress was about.* This rumour really was beginning to get out of hand. I didn't want people to start thinking I couldn't do my job.

I was trying to think what to say when the telephone rang in the office. I glanced over and saw the young trainee nurse pick up the receiver.

'Well?' I asked as she approached. 'Any message, Nurse?'

'Yes, Staff. They're sending a patient from Casualty.'

'So?' I said. 'What is it?'

'His . . . his name is Arthur Shaw, aged seventy-four,' she stuttered, blushing.

'Was that all?' I said.

'Yes, Staff.'

'But that's ridiculous! We must know more than that for preparation.'

I huffed over to the office. What on Earth was the silly girl talking about? I picked up the receiver and dialled Casualty.

The trainee was watching Pete set up the dressings trolley when I returned.

'Get your ears checked, girl,' I snapped. 'Arthur Shaw aged seventy-four, indeed. It's an abscess of the jaw!'

The girl looked back at me, horrified. It was all I could do to keep a straight, stern face, as I could see Pete start to shake with amusement.

'If you don't understand a message,' I said, 'ask them to repeat it. There's no disgrace in that. But there is no excuse for such a stupid mistake.'

Tears welled up in the girl's eyes as I stared back at her.

'Nurse?' The patient nearest to us put his hand up in that embarrassed way that only means one thing.

'Go and fetch a bottle for Mr Smith, Nurse, would you?'

'Yes, Staff,' she said, and scuttled off.

'And don't forget the cover,' I called after her.

I turned and my eyes met Pete's.

'Arthur Shaw aged seventy-four!' he smirked, and we both burst out laughing.

33

The excitement of joining Alistair is building up. I feel so happy and nothing can upset me. The busiest of days on the wards, sudden emergencies, even the continual gloom of the outside world at war, it all just flows over me. News that I have resigned spreads rapidly, but not as rapidly as the presumed reason for my leaving. No matter how I try to deny it, no one will believe me. Part of me rather enjoys being the centre of so much gossip, but it is rather bothersome that I have to be wary of lifting if anyone is around, because of the fuss it causes.

To my pleasant surprise Mother and Father were understanding and totally supportive of my decision to move to Scotland. And the fact that I was leaving at the very end of my four-year contract pleased Father.

You have done what you set out to do, he wrote.

You have stuck at it through thick and thin. Four years' hard work and we are proud that our daughter is a fully qualified State Registered Nurse. Of course, we shall miss you, but Scotland is as safe as safe can be and I know it won't be for ever. This war will end, peace will return, and we will all be

together once more. Either that or your Mother and I could
come and live in Scotland, too!

I had to laugh at that last bit. Father was such a tease. I'd miss
them both terribly. But he was right, the war would end and life,
God willing, would return to normal.

As for Alistair, his letters were full of passion, excitement and
plans for when I finally arrived. His commanding officer had
been most kind in helping him find a delightful bed-sitting room
near Troon on the Firth of Clyde coast.

The landlady is a widow, but a dear soul, and although
reluctant to take in Army personnel, I soon worked my charm
on her, he wrote. I can't wait for you to see our room, it's at
the top of her very large house and overlooks the Isle of Arran.

What a contrast it would be to the nurses' home and the rubble
of Homerton High Street.

My last day of duty, Friday 30 October 1942, came around so
quickly that I didn't quite believe it when Eddie, so easily brought
to tears, hugged me tightly as we left the dining room together.

'This place just won't be the same without you, Phyll,' she
sobbed into my shoulder.

'Come on, Eddie,' I said, squeezing her. 'I'll see you again.
Besides, you need to stop this crying or you'll set me off, and we'll
both look dreadful for my farewell party. And we can't have that,
can we?'

She sniffed and shook her head. 'No, that would be absolutely
ghastly!'

We both grinned, and I put my arm in hers as we make our
way to the nurses' home together.

'Did you know Sister Dinsdale has organised it with Matron

that all our intake, the gals of '38, are off duty tonight?' Eddie said.

'Really?' I was genuinely touched by that.

'Who'd have believed the Dragon would be so kind?' Eddie said.

'She's hard but fair,' I said. 'Come on, even Matron has her good points. They all do.'

'That's easy for you to say,' Eddie said. 'You're leaving tomorrow.'

I'd had my suitcases brought out of storage a week earlier and had slowly been packing away my things in my spare moments. Most of my books I'd sold to incoming students, although I kept hold of the *materia medica* for reference, for who knew what post I might end up with in Scotland?

After I'd bathed and changed, I took my uniform down to the laundry. By the time I got back to my room, Mac and Eddie were waiting for me outside.

'We'd thought you'd left,' Mac said with a huge grin.

'Don't be daft,' I said, opening up my door and showing them in.

'Here, gifts,' I said, handing Mac my collection of attractive cake and biscuit tins and Eddie my china breakfast set.

'We can't,' Mac said.

'No, you'll need these yourself, Phyll,' Eddie said.

I held up my hands. 'Too late. No arguments.'

'What about all your bags?'

'The porter's collecting them later,' I said. 'They're going on ahead on the sleeper. Alistair will collect them in the morning. I hope.'

'I'm going to see if Matron will let Eddie and me escort you to Euston tomorrow,' Mac said.

'Don't, Mac. Please.'

'Why ever not? We can't let you leave without waving you off.'

'No, please. It'll be harder that way. Let's say our goodbyes tonight.'

'You're so damned independent, Phyll,' Mac shrugged.

'So they keep telling me,' I grinned. 'Come on, time we were heading down to the lounge.'

The entire intake from November 1938 were there, drinks in hand. 'Chattanooga Choo Choo' was playing on the gramophone, and even Sister Dinsdale managed a smile as the girls raised a toast to me.

'This is a little something for you,' Winters said, handing me a large flat box tied with a huge blue bow. 'From all of us.'

I didn't know what to say, looking round at their smiling faces.

'Thank you,' I choked eventually.

I undid the bow and lifted the lid. There was a card on top of a fold of tissue paper.

To dear Phyll, with every good wish for the future. And may it be a boy! With love from the intake of 1938

I unfolded the tissue paper to reveal a beautiful cot blanket in baby blue. I stood there holding it for a moment, feeling terrible that this rumour had gone on so long. What could I say? But as I lifted my gaze to each and every one of them, all I saw was friendship and caring. So I accepted the gift and reasoned that I might not be pregnant now, but I planned to be one day, and I would keep the blanket and treasure it always.

'Thank you all. I'll miss you so very, very much.'

A round of applause broke out, and then I was surrounded and patted and kissed and hugged.

'Good luck, Phyll.'

'Cheers, Phyll.'

'We love you, Phyll.'

As I hugged Mac, I whispered in her ear, 'No one will believe me. About my not being pregnant. I feel awful.'

'It's of no matter, Phyll,' she said. 'Just enjoy it. Their affection is real, and that's all that matters.'

I nodded and wiped away my tears. 'You're right, Mac, as usual.'

'Come on, play for us!'

A cheer rose up as Mac dragged me over to the piano and sat me down in front of it.

'So, what shall I play?' I sniffed, fingers poised over the keys.

'Well, as you're off to Scotland,' Mac said, 'how's about "There'll Always Be An England"?'

I awoke on the morning of Saturday, 31 October 1942 clear-headed. Every time I had tried to have a drink the previous evening, it was snatched from my grasp and replaced by a Schweppes or a tea. 'Serves you right,' Eddie sniggered to me at one point, before draining her glass of gin and tottering off for a refill. I grinned. There would be a few sore heads and short tempers on the wards this morning.

I glanced at my alarm clock: 7.15. I threw off the bedclothes and shivered. The temperature had really dropped in the past few days. All my friends were on duty by now so I breakfasted alone. I wasn't sad though. It had been my decision to leave quietly. With a final goodbye to the maids and kitchen staff, I headed off to Matron's office.

'I hear you had a good send-off last night,' she said. 'Sorry I couldn't make it myself. Here's your book of service.'

'Thank you, Matron.'

'Well, Staff . . . er . . . *Mrs* Ross, I wish you good luck.' She rose from the desk and shook my hand limply.

'Goodbye, Matron.'

'Safe journey,' she said and sat back down and continued with her paperwork.

Back in my room, I checked through my freshly laundered uniform one last time before boxing it up ready to take back to the sewing room. Three dresses, twelve aprons, six caps and one cloak. I'd miss the cloak, especially at Christmas time when the whole nursing staff wore them inside out with the red lining showing. Such a festive sight. I checked my watch. It was 9.10 a.m. I had an hour-and-a-half to get to Euston. I headed for the sewing room, and didn't see a soul on the way there.

The seamstress was busy helping one of the ward sisters with a dress, and my mind went straight back to that first day when I had come here with the other late arrivals to find Sister Dinsdale in the very same pose.

The sewing assistant checked off my uniform and I signed the book. As I turned to leave, I heard the sister ask, 'Isn't that the Staff off to Scotland?'.

'In the family way, I believe,' the seamstress said.

I closed the door with a roll of my eyes.

The maid had already stripped my bed by the time I got back to my room, so all that was left for me to do was to change into my travelling clothes and head off. I decided to wear a navy blue woollen dress in case the temperature was even lower in Scotland. It was very becoming, I thought, with its pale blue satin collar. I put on my last pair of stockings, checked the seam was straight, then slipped on a pair of navy blue lace-up shoes with a three-quarter heel. I pulled on my double-breasted dark tweed coat, and carefully placed a velvet beret on my head. Applying a touch-up to my lipstick, I gave myself the once-over in the mirror. Satisfied, I closed my suitcase, picked up my handbag and surveyed my now-bare room. I locked the door and made my way down to the home sister's office.

I handed her the keys, signed the book for the very last time, and left the nurses' home behind me.

Crossing the forecourt, part of me wanted to see Mac and Eddie running out to bid me farewell. But they didn't, and I was glad: it would have broken my heart.

The last signature I gave was to dear old Joe, the porter, who was always there, through thick and thin, keeping a fatherly eye on us all.

'I have a little something for you, madam,' he said, handing me a package. 'Open it on the train.'

'Thank you, Joe,' I said planting a kiss of lipstick on his cheek. 'I'll miss you.'

'You keep safe. Have a good journey.'

With a smile on my lips and a tear in my eye, I turned out of the gate lodge for the last time and on to Homerton High Street. A bus was lumbering towards me and as I waved it down I glanced back at the majestic old building of Hackney Hospital, my home for the past four years.

How I'd changed. From that naïve, eager young girl into an experienced nurse and a married woman. *Regrets? Not one*, I thought. And despite how many people say, 'Who'd be a nurse?', all I knew was that I would, over and over again.

'Hold tight,' the conductor called as I climbed up to the top deck and sat down in my favourite seat at the very back.

I was off, ready for the start of my latest journey, the journey to join my husband and to begin the next chapter of my nursing life.

Acknowledgements

Nan's story has come a long way and without these people, it would never have become a published novel. So, to you all, I'd like to express my heartfelt thanks:

ROBERT DINSDALE
HANNAH BOURSNELL
RHIANNON SMITH and the team at Little, Brown (Sphere)
DI ROBERTS
JULIA LAFFERTY and NICK PERRY of THE HACKNEY
    SOCIETY
THE HEALTHCARE IN HACKNEY PROJECT
DAVID WHITTLE of THE HARWICH SOCIETY
THE HISTORICAL NOVEL SOCIETY
PATSY SHARP

and, of course, my grandfather, ALISTAIR MACDONALD-ROSS, for badgering Nan to put her nursing memoirs down on paper in the first place.